BIG MINE RUN

Recollections of the Coal Region

by
Harry M. Bobonich, Ph.D.

authorHOUSE™

1663 LIBERTY DRIVE, SUITE 200
BLOOMINGTON, INDIANA 47403
(800) 839-8640
WWW.AUTHORHOUSE.COM

First published by AuthorHouse 09/02/05

ISBN: 1-4208-6536-6 (sc)

Printed in the United States of America
Bloomington, Indiana

This book is printed on acid-free paper.

BIG MINE RUN

Recollections of the Coal Region

by

Harry M. Bobonich, Ph. D.

For my wife, Gloria
and my mom, Pauline.

Contents

Acknowledgements

Most notably, I would like to thank my family, A special thank you to my wife, Gloria, who has been the inspiration for writing this book.

I'm especially grateful to Chris and his wife Karen for their on-going encouragement and support. I am indebted to Chris not only for suggesting that I write about the coal region, but he was always available to comment on a story and to do some editing. I have also received valuable help from Karen, especially for the many suggestions she made to add this and that.

I also appreciate the continued support I have received from Greg and his wife Arlene.

I also want to thank Hattie, my sister, who has been helpful in recalling some past events in our lives.

I'm especially indebted to Nick Kalathas, a superb photographer, who has placed all the photographs into the text. He worked diligently on the photos and made many helpful suggestions. I also appreciate the encouraging comments he made to me while writing the book. Nick's outstanding web site is www.NaturesMoments.com.

I want to express my appreciation to Christine Goldbeck, a first-rate photojournalist and coal region researcher for her support and encouragement. I am grateful to Christine for editing several articles, which are included in the book. She is editor of the excellent web site www.MineCountry.com, and has also posted the articles on the MineCountry web site.

I also want to express my sincere thanks to Diane Rooney, also a first-rate photojournalist and coal region researcher. She has graciously furnished me with a number of excellent photographs, which I have included in the book. I also want to thank her for her helpful comments and insights that she has provided from time to time.

I would like to express my sincere gratitude to the following dedicated people in the library at Shippensburg University. I especially want to thank Diane Kalathas and Teresa Strayer for their assistance in processing my requests and for obtaining books, articles, and microfilm from the Interlibrary Loan Department.

I have received valuable help from Gay Jones, librarian, for her goggling expertise, scanning photographs and also for her comments. I also want to thank Mary Mowery, library technician, for her assistance and suggestions.

I would also like to thank the following Shippensburg University library staff: Chantana Charoenpanitkul, Dr. Douglas Cook, Karen Daniel, Dr. Signe Kelker, Melanie Reed and Dr. Madelyn Valunas.

Rick Kerr, Lt. Colonel U. S. Army (retired) was always available to solve a printer or computer problem I had. I am truly indebted to him for his kindness and support.

The many coffee breaks I had with Dr. William Smith while writing this book served me well. His persistent questioning nature was helpful in reminding me to look at some issues in more detail.

My sincere thanks to Diane Spokus, a doctoral student in Gerontology at the Pennsylvania Sate University, for her support. She also provided me with helpful information including articles and photographs.

My conversations with "Hard Coal Joe" Baldino about our experiences when we were kids together in Big Mine Run was helpful. Joe, who is a "coal region buff" has sent me several photographs and provided other information for the book. I thank him for his support.

I want to thank the following people and organizations for permission to use their photographs: John Anis, Joe Baldino, Leonard Cooper, John J. Dziak, Robert Evans, Vincent J. Genovese, Bill and Stephen N. Lukasik, Dottie Miller, Diane Rooney, Diane Spokus, Attorney Harry Strouse of Strouse and Strouse, Watch Tower Bible and Tract Society of Pennsylvania, and Robert P. Wolensky.

My appreciation to Lucas Kalathas for several drawings he did for the book.

I also want to thank the following people who have helped in one way or another: Shirley Baird, Dwayne Burt, Colee, Larry Cottle, Beth Dole, JoAnn Grandi, Stephanie Misner and Pat Shay.

Introduction

Childhood is a short season.

Helen Hayes

Backward, turn backward, O time in your flight,

Make me a child again, just for tonight.

Elizabeth Akers Allen

At one time or another, we all look back to our childhood days. I suppose we usually tend to recall pleasant, fun-loving times. But then, many of us probably also have memories of silly or dumb things we did as children. You know, "the way we were."

One day after reading Eric McKeever's Tales of the Mine Country, I was pleasantly surprised to learn that I also experienced many of the same things that Eric wrote about so wonderfully. So I decided to write some short stories about people and events as I remembered them growing up in Big Mine Run during the 1930s. I did not rely much on others for information, because I wanted this brief oral history to be just what my recollections were during those formative years. Although I do from time to time draw on others' stories and especially photographs.

The other stories, which I have included in the book, vary greatly in time and place of occurrence. They are selected stories of courageous people, noteworthy events and terrible disasters. They are moments of the past that are a part of the history of the hard coal region of Pennsylvania.

Chapter I

A SNAPSHOT OF BIG MINE RUN

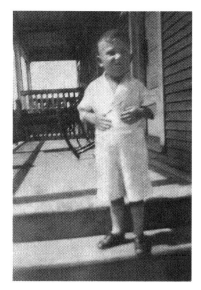

Harry age nine months.   Harry age four.

Big Mine Run is a small village, or as we called it a "patch," situated mid-way between the two towns of Ashland and Girardville (we said jarred-vill). The name of the patch came from the Bast Colliery (we said call-ree) that was built over a major coal deposit there, hence the name Big Mine Run.

The lower part of Big Mine Run (about 35 homes) is located adjacent to Big Mine Run road running east and west. Here's a listing of the families as I remembered them starting from the west end of Big Min Run: Gallagher, Cannon, Verbish, Hatter, Yost, Yuhas, Nocton, Sterling, Tarpy, Hoban, Wilson, Burke, Sweeney, Sweeney (later Bielarski), Medrick, Dolan,

Baldino, Bresnock, Kimmel, Turako, Haluskie, Mikurak, Studlis, Conyham, Conway, Haluskie, Bender, Navitsky, Grabowski, Cleary, Hendricks, Dumboski, Adamavage, Bresnock, McGwire, McCormick, Weber, Cannon, and Pahira.

The upper part of Big Mine Run (situated halfway up a hill) is called Woodland Heights and is made up of nine two-family dwellings. Our family moved from Ashland to 16 Woodland Heights in 1920, and I was born four years later in 1924. Here is a listing of the families that lived in Woodland Heights during the years that I lived there. Starting with the first double dwelling which was numbered one and two through seventeen and eighteen Woodland Heights: Young/Horvath; Petrusky/Buhl; Petrusky/Latsko; Bielarski/Chuplis; Kroh/Mickel; Balunis/ Wolfgang; Kilkuskie/Pechansky; Colahan/Bobonich (Bonish); Navitsky/Cunningham (later Neary).

The Philadelphia and Reading Coal and Iron Company owned all the newly constructed houses in Woodland Heights. The first floor of our home had a kitchen, dining room and a living room. The basement was quite large and the floor and walls were concrete. On the second floor we had two bedrooms and a cubbyhole. The third floor (attic or garret) consisted of a large room with two slanted walls. In addition, our house had a fairly large yard. The homes were quite nice. The rent was also reasonable, which was in contrast to the rent charged by the owners of company houses in earlier times.

When I was just a kid, my mother said that Mrs. Sally Cunningham, one of our neighbors, found me behind a large tree at the back of her yard, and that she gave that tiny baby to my Mother. I recall saying to my mother, "That one mom" pointing to a certain tree, "No, that one over there," she said. As a small child I often wondered about that tree.

We had a large, black, nickel-trimmed coal stove in the kitchen; it was the warmest room in the house. Our kitchen stove was kept burning almost continuously, not only to keep our home warm but also for cooking purposes and to have hot water when needed. We had a bucket full of coal with a small shovel on top setting on the floor next to the stove. It was my job to see that the bucket was always full of coal. When it was empty, I would pick it up, go down into the basement and fill it up with coal and carry it up to the kitchen.

During the cold weather, I took a bath in a large round wooden tub in the kitchen. When the water in the tub cooled down, I would tell my mom that I needed more hot water. As she reached toward the coal stove to get the hot water kettle, I would get up and move to the edge of the tub but still stand inside. Then my mom would pour hot water from the kettle directly into the tub. When I felt the hot water around my ankles (sometimes it got very hot) I would say, "that's enough, mom." Then I would sit down and finish my bath. When I was through bathing, I would reach over and take off the nice warm towel that was draped over the open oven door of the coal stove and dry myself off.

I also used our coal stove in the kitchen to make toast. I took a lid-lifter to remove the round lid from the top of the stove. Then I took a long-handled fork and stuck it into the edge of a piece of homemade bread or bought sliced bread and held it over the red-hot coals to toast one side. Then I turned the bread over and toasted the other side. I had to be careful because the coals were very hot. Sometimes the slice of bread would fall off the fork and land on the hot coals; the bread would burst into flames and burn to a crisp in a few seconds. We always had a lot of homemade jelly, which we spread on our toast; however, we rarely put butter on our toast because it was too expensive,

We also had a smaller, round; nickel-flanged coal stove in the dining room that helped keep our house warm during the winter. Those two stoves provided the only heat we had. During the cold weather, we closed off the parlor (living room) with a large curtain to keep the other rooms warm. While I had central heating for most of my adult life, I must confess that it is a poor substitute for the nice old warm kitchen stove and the cozy dining room heater of my childhood.

I recall that for a while we also had a kerosene lamp to provide light, and I remember reading next to the light at night. We did not have running hot water; if you wanted a bath you had to heat water on the coal stove. During the summer, I took a bath in a large wooden tub in the basement.

We didn't have a bathroom; we had an outhouse. It was a two-seater, with one large oval seat for adults and a small oval seat for kids. Not to be too graphic, but each outhouse had a magazine or a Sears and Roebuck catalog in it.

While we didn't have very much, somehow we made it through, like so many others. My father was unemployed most of the time and was not able to provide for us adequately. Sometime in the 1930s we were on relief, much later they called it welfare. I remember my mom getting a box of groceries, which included canned goods, peanut butter, prunes, and other things. I was rather young at the time and knew we were getting free food, but I didn't understand the full implications of welfare or just how poor we were. However, very soon after that I learned that we didn't have much money.

My mom saved a penny whenever she could. I quickly learned to turned the lights off whenever I left a room and I do so to this day--seven decades later. On those occasions when we had butter, I was reminded politely that butter was expensive, so I took a little less for my bread and potatoes. Whenever I ate watermelon or cantaloupe, I ate every bit right down close to the rind. Many years later when I had a family of my own, I still ate watermelon down beyond the red part. One day Chris, our youngest son, asked me why I did that. After all, we were well off financially and Chris never saw the need for us to save pennies. I just smiled at him and tousled his hair a bit. Incidentally, Chris never turns off any lights at all; he lets them on all night! However, hard lessons learned early in life often stay with us all the way.

When I was just a kid, I saved every penny I got or earned. I'm sure it was a trait I got from my mother. When I earned a few cents shoveling out our neighbor's walk or doing some other chore, I also put that money away. Whatever I earned I always placed in a small box in my room where I slept. To tell the truth, I was sort of stingy. Many times I would just count the money in my box; it gave me a good feeling that I had "something."

Growing up in Big Mine Run wasn't an easy thing to do. When the other kids once overheard my Aunt Pauline Skocik calling me "Sonny Boy," I quickly got that as one of my nicknames. I didn't like it because it was a "sissy name." The other kids used to call me "sonny" when they wanted to tease me. When the guys learned that I was taking violin lessons, that also added to my woes. My violin teacher, Mr. Joseph Seder from Centralia, was a friend of the family so it didn't cost much for my lessons. The other kids in the neighborhood would tease me when they heard one of my sisters calling me to come home because my violin teacher came and it was time for my music lesson.

Harry age nine.   Harry age ten.

I was also called "Ruby" because somebody heard that a guy named Dave Rubinoff was a violin player and the name stuck. For many years that was my nickname. Most of the guys in the coal region had a nickname and it was especially true of the kids in Big Mine Run. In many cases, only small numbers (usually those who knew the person well) actually knew where the nickname came from. Often, when we wanted to get another kids attention; we would just call out, "Yo Billy, Yo Johnny or Yo so-and-so." Girls generally weren't given nicknames, but were often called by some other form of their regular name. That is, Mamie for Mary or just "mare."

We were somewhat isolated and didn't see or know much about the outside world. When we said we were going to town, we always meant Ashland, just one mile away. For the most part we just hung out in Big Mine Run. We thought golf and tennis were "sissy" games and laughed at people who played those sports. While we were naïve, we were comfortable with it, and that's the way it was in Big Mine Run.

Peddlers came around from time to time and they were always of interest to us kids. The "umbrella man" came around fixing and selling umbrellas. A "scissors man" also made his rounds and he sharpened and sold scissors. Many times we would follow them around the patch until they left. Sometimes a poor shabbily dressed man (never a woman) came around looking for something to eat. He was simply a poor guy who was non-threatening and wanted a handout. Even though we were poor ourselves, my very busy mom always found something to give him.

We always enjoyed the day when a large truck called, "Store at Your Door," visited Woodland Heights. The truck was roughly the shape of a fairly large moving van, which contained all sorts of ordinary groceries; it was something different. When it stopped in front of our house, my mom and I would go out and actually step inside the truck from the rear. When she made purchases, I would carry them into our house. A man named Joe Morris drove the truck for his father who had a grocery business in Girardville. Our house was his last stop at Woodland Heights. If we happened to be tossing a football around when he was through with his last customers, he would leave his truck and join us. However, all he wanted to do was kick our football. Every time he kicked the ball, we would retrieve it for him and that went on for about 15 minutes. When he was through, he would give us several tasty kakes, and then he would be on his way. I believe he played football at some college in Philadelphia, because he always wore a college football jersey.

Some families would cook in their basement during the hot summer months. In some cases they would also eat there because it was too hot in their regular kitchen. Even though our basement had whitewashed walls, a concrete floor and was quite cool, we didn't eat there during the summer; but we did use it to do some cooking during the hot weather. We used it mainly for storage, washing clothes, bathing, putting up a variety of preserves, making wine and also homemade whiskey.

During the summer all the kids wore sneakers (running shoes) and overalls (blue jeans) all day long. We spent a great deal of time outdoors during the summer playing games that lasted well into the evening. There were no organized games for kids supervised by adults, and there were no playgrounds. We just made up our own games. The summer was also nice because we could pick huckleberries and make some money. It was the most desirable season of the year. Many people had dogs and they were allowed to roam all over the place, especially during the summer. I never saw a dog on a leash.

However, at mealtime the doggies always seemed to find their way home.

The fall meant a change from those good old summer days to school and cooler weather. We had to get washed, cleaned and dressed up as we trudged off to school. Our lives were more structured in the autumn and we had to spent more time at home.

Election Day came late in autumn and before the real winter set in. I recall that almost everyone was a Democrat in Woodland Heights in those days. Just before Election Day, Our well-liked local politician, made his rounds visiting various homes in Woodland Heights. We were paid two dollars to vote the Democratic Ticket, and I presume that was the fee paid to other households he visited. The first national election I remember was the 1932 election when Franklin Delano Roosevelt was elected to his first term in office as President of the United States.

We looked forward to winter, and we always got excited about the first snowfall. In the evenings we had a habit of standing next to a telephone pole and looking upward toward the light at the top. In this manner we could see a beginning snowfall that often looked like a light blizzard because of the lighting effect. However, if you turned your head and looked out into the night, you would hardly be able to see any snow at all.

During mid-winter when we got a huge snowfall, schools were closed and we would play out of doors all day. We also had to shovel a lot of snow: making a path to our neighbor's house, clearing out the area in front of our own home, and also making a path to the outhouse.

There were no plows available to clear off the roads where we lived, so Woodland Heights would be isolated for a while. A vehicle had to climb two steep hills to get from the main road in Big Mine Run up to Woodland Heights and that was very difficult to do.

Christmas, of course, was the big event and we all looked forward to the big day. We would look in the Sears and Roebuck catalog and say, "I want this and I want that." Our expectations were always high but we never seemed to mind that it didn't work out that way. Sometime after Christmas we wold begin to look forward to spring and the warmer weather. The cold winter days seemed to drag on and we always wanted the warm weather to come sooner than it did.

Easter was also a nice time of the year. Jelly beans, homemade Easter eggs, and a milk chocolate rabbit or figure were the main items in our Easter basket. We enjoyed dyeing eggs various colors and would make a mess all over the kitchen table. We competed with each other to see who could make the looking colored egg, and there always were some arguments about that.

There was very little supervision of children. Even though I was reared in somewhat of a responsible family, I was more or less allowed to come and go as I pleased. Even when I was about ten years old, I would sometimes wander off on a summer morning and not return until the evening at dinnertime. In most other families the kids were allowed more leeway. It seemed that some guys only went home to eat and sleep.

There just weren't that many things to do in Big Mine Run, but we didn't seem to mind. On any hot summer day, someone in a group might casually mention that we should go for a cold drink of spring water. We all knew that the person was referring to a spring that was located at the base of a mountain about a mile away toward Homesville. The next thing you knew four or five of us would start walking along the railroad tracks headed for the spring. Several of us would play a game to see who could walk the farthest on top of a track without falling off. Of course there was some cheating going on, but it was okay to do that.

When we reached the spring, each person tried to drink more than anyone else. The spring never seemed to run dry and it always had very cold water running from it. After drinking all that we could, we simply walked back home. Again, we would see who could walk on top of the track the farthest distance without falling off.

For the most part, Sundays were quiet days. The day started with everyone getting dressed up and attending mass at the local Catholic Church. We always bought The Philadelphia Inquirer Sunday newspaper on our way home from church. I enjoyed reading the funnies—we never said comics. Dick Tracy, Popeye, Superman, Joe Palooka, Tarzan, Little Orphan Annie, Li' l Abner, Blondie, Bringing up Father (Jiggs and Maggie) and of course the Katz and Jammer kids were some of the characters I liked. Reading about some of the same characters in the funnies in the daily Shenandoah Herald was also a fun thing to do. Most of the day was spent just sitting around and talking, going for a walk or taking a ride. Sometimes we would visit friends or relatives would visit us and stay for dinner. There was no shopping, or working other than cooking meals. On occasion I would get involved in some activity and was politely told to stop it because it was Sunday. It was especially true that you were not to do any chores of any kind before noon on Sunday when masses were being read in church.

When I was in seventh or eighth grade, I was the only boy student who wore very expensive Florsheim shoes. However, they were second-hand shoes that were given to us. I was a little embarrassed about it, but I wore them anyhow because we didn't buy new shoes very often during those days. When shoes were getting worn-out, they were taken to a shoemaker who put on new soles and heels.

In some cases, families bought soles and heels and mended their own worn-out shoes. We had a small iron pedestal-like device shaped like a human foot called a "last" that was about two feet high, which we used to repair our shoes. Another small iron piece, shaped like a shoe, was placed upside down on top of the last. The worn-out shoe was then placed on top (upside down of course) and then you proceeded to nail on the new sole and heel. No one has any of these devices anymore, and I'll bet there are very few in antique shops.

Shoemakers did a brisk business then, so my mom thought it would be a good idea for me to be an apprentice to the shoemaker. It was a sign of the times, because people in Big Mine Run only thought about getting a job and making some money. Little attention was paid to getting an education beyond high school. I was happy that I never got talked into that business.

Education wasn't a high priority in Big Mine Run. Only about one-half of the guys finished the eighth grade, one-quarter attended some high school and one-quarter graduated from high school. It was a common practice for many kids to "bag" school; that is, they were absent form school without permission. And it was the always the same kids who bagged school—I never did. The school district had a truant officer who investigated unauthorized absences form school, but nothing much ever happened.

If you were a good student you were considered to be the "sissy type" and the other kids teased you about it. I encountered some name calling because of my interest in school. There was little encouragement or support for academic work. For example, parental expectations were not high and that wasn't a good thing. The advice we got from the older guys in Big Mine Run before we attended our first year in a new consolidated high school in Fountain Springs, was to start a fight with other guys that were also being bussed in from other neighborhoods. That way (we were told) we would show them we were tough.

During those formative years while I was in grade school, there were many opportunities to get into trouble. Drinking alcoholic beverages was common throughout the coal region, and Big Mine Run was no exception. Even though we were only a patch town, we had a saloon that sold beer and whiskey. Coal miners in general worked hard and drank a lot, so

Harry age 13.

beer and whiskey were plentiful. Even kids tried to act grown up and started cursing and drinking as youngsters.

My mom often praised me, especially when we had visitors. That was always nice to hear and I liked that. I always wanted to please my mother and I think that motivated me to act in such a manner so that she was proud of me. One day she asked me to write a letter for her since she never attended any school at all. While I felt good that I was able to help her, I realized the limitations of not having an education. On the other had, it was simply amazing that she could do so much without knowing how to read or write; but then, she was a special person. I was determined to do as well as I could in school. That, as it turned out, made all the difference in my life.

One day after being away from Big Mine Run for many, many years, I turned home, as we tend to do when we get older. I wanted to visit the place of my birth after being away for so long. As I drove up the hill from Big Mine Run to Woodland Heights, I thought of my past life there and all the things I did as a kid. As I drove slowly by my former home, I felt a close attachment to it and yet in a way estranged. Everything seemed to be as it was back then, and in another way everything seemed to have changed. All those years, all had gone by so very fast. I turned my car around slowly and looked again at my old home. I stopped, paused for a moment or two staring at that old familiar house I knew so well—my childhood home--then I drove away and did not look back. However, hardly a day goes by that I do not take some time to reflect and sort out thousands of old memories.

Chapter 2

STORIES ABOUT THINGS I REMEMBER

My Father's Lunch Box

The Bast Colliery, which was located in Big Mine Run, was a major employer for most of the men who lived in the vicinity. For a period of time, my father worked there as a coal miner. When I was a child I would wait for my father when he came home at the end of the workday. I would always reach out for his black lunch box (which was roughly the shape and size of a loaf of bread) and quickly open it to see if there was anything "good" left in his lunch box that he didn't eat. It was always nice to get a piece of cake or pie. A piece of fruit wasn't too bad, but I never ate a cheese or liverwurst sandwich that he brought home. The metal lunch box has a small thermos bottle held in by a clasp just under the cover; however, I never looked in the thermos bottle.

Duley Boxes

In the coal region we said "duley" for dynamite. You won't find it in the dictionary, but everyone knew that a stick of duley meant a stick of dynamite. The duley boxes contained sticks of dynamite, which were high explosives that the miners used in blasting coal. The words "HERCULES POWDER; high explosive-dangerous" were clearly printed in red ink on the side of the box so everyone knew what was inside.

I was always happy when my father brought home empty duley boxes from the Bast Colliery where he worked. A duley box was about the size of an ordinary breadbox. If you're not sure what the size of a breadbox was back then, how about the size of a small microwave oven?

The box was made of a good quality wood and the four sides were held together with V-shaped wooden joints. I remember stacking them on top of one another and playing various games with them both indoors and outside. At the time we lived in a company house in Woodland Heights and we didn't have much furniture. We used the duley boxes as stools, chairs, small tables and storage containers. Since the boxes could easily be taken apart, the wood was also used to build simple furniture, shelving and toys.

The Miners' Lunch Boxes

When I was about ten years old, I would find a buddy and we would go for a walk in the afternoon toward the Bast Colliery. The colliery was about a quarter-mile from my home. We would walk along the railroad tracks for a while and then stop to look at the mules in the yard next to the large stable that belonged to the colliery. Mr. George Kimmel was in charge of the stable and mules. Sometimes we would gather up a handful of grass and feed it to the mules. The mules always came over to us when they saw us holding the grass in our hand. However, just as the mule opened its large mouth and showed its teeth, we became frightened and pulled our hand away. Sometimes the mules managed to get the grass and other times it just fell to the ground.

After we got tired of looking at the mules, we would play in the large sand pile that was located between the railroad tracks and the stable. Then we would walk a little farther toward the colliery and sit down on the railroad tracks and wait for the miners as they walked home from work.

All miners carried a lunch pail or a lunch box. Some miners had a black rectangular lunch box with a rounded top like the one I described that my Dad had, and others had a round lunch pail. I little later I learned that a miner's lunch pail was called a "jelly bucket." The miners also carried an oval shaped water can that had a tapered top. The water can had a loop of thin rope for a handle, which the miners used to carry it over their shoulder.

When the miners left the colliery and started to walk home along the tracks, we would ask if they had anything left in their lunch boxes. Sometimes we would get a slice of cake, a piece of pie or some kind of fruit. If they didn't have anything they would say so in a friendly manner, and in most cases even show us their empty lunch can. Just imagine, after working hard all day for little pay, the miners took time to be nice to us—they were never rude.

One day as we started to walk up to the colliery, we noticed that there had been a fire and the stable had burned down. Later we learned that "Pickles" Neary, who was our neighbor, managed to get to the stable while it was still burning and led all the mules out to safety. Everyone said Pickles was a hero because he saved the mules.

My Father Taking a Bath

A coalhole was a small bootleg mine run by just several miners. Big Mine Run had many coalholes and it was common to see miners walking around all dirty on their way home from work. I remember my father coming home all dirty after working in a coalhole just like many others.

The first thing he did was to have a beer or a shot of whiskey—sometimes both. After that, he took a bath in a large round wooden tub in the cellar. We had no running hot water, so a large container of water was heated on the coal stove in the basement. He would strip down to his waist and my mother would wash his back as he kneeled on the floor with his arms resting inside the tub.

If by chance they were having a different opinion about something (O.K. an argument then), they would generally speak in Ukrainian. However, I still knew it wasn't just an ordinary family conversation. On those days, my father's back got scrubbed very clean, because my mother would rub harder and faster than normal.

My father went to work on a Monday with clean working clothes. However, working in a coalhole was a dirty business and his clothes became dirty very quickly. The next day, he would put on his dirty work clothes again and go to work. While my father's working clothes got washed weekly, he got washed daily.

Drowning the Poor Kittens

One summer day our cat had kittens. My parents didn't want the kittens, so my mom put them in a cloth bag and told me to drown them in the crick (we never said creek). At the time, it was not an uncommon practice to get rid of newborn puppies and kittens that way.

As I was walking off with the kittens, my mom reminded me to put several rocks inside the bag so it would sink to the bottom of the crick. I didn't like the idea, but went ahead and put in several rocks rather carefully so as not to injure them.

For the entire time I was carrying the kittens I could hear them meowing inside the bag and I felt very sad. When I got to the bridge, which was about fifty feet above the crick, I stood there for quite a while staring down at the water. Finally I tossed the bag over the railing and for some reason I watched it falling down to the water. It hit with a sickening thud; I turned around and ran away from the bridge.

I felt terrible about what I did. I was about eleven years old at the time and I did what I was told to do. I simply didn't question my parents. When I returned home I was sniffing and sobbing a little, so my mother tried to console me; however, that didn't seem to help very much. Afterward I felt that I did a foolish thing and that I should have left the poor kittens go free. When I think of the incident now, I can almost hear the kittens meowing as I did way back then.

The "Tin Lizzie"

During the middle 1930s there were a number of Model T fords running about in Big Mine Run--we called them "tin lizzies." Of course they weren't new, nor were they even second hand cars. They were cars ready for the junkyard or were actually purchased from the junkyard owner for about $20 or even less. I was too young at the time, but some of the older guys were able to save enough money to purchase one. Sometimes several guys would get together and buy a Model T and then they would take turns joy-riding celebrating their big purchase.

The Model Ts were simple in construction and it wasn't difficult getting them running again if they broke down. The guys who owned them were always tinkering with the engine and it seemed that all the tools they needed were a pair of pliers, a screwdriver and a set of adjustable wrenches.

All the Model Ts that I remember had a crank insert at the front of the car near the bottom of the radiator. Someone (usually one of the older guys) would get the crank handle from under the driver's seat and go to the front of the car to crank the engine to get it started. It took a fairly strong person to crank or turn the engine over as they used to say. The engine didn't always start with the first turn of the crank. Sometimes the crank handle would turn or spin in the opposite direction, and if you didn't release the crank fast you could easily inure or break your arm. You were always told that whenever you cranked a car, you should never hold the crank with a normal grip, That is, you only held the crank with your hand and fingers, but kept your thumb straight out and not in a clenched manner.

The tin lizzies or "flivvers" as we sometimes called them were not only easy to drive but inexpensive to operate. No one bought a license plate or a driver's license for the vehicle. The guys just drove their Model Ts around all the dirt roads in Big Mine Run and nobody bothered them. Gasoline only cost about fifteen cents a gallon.

1925 Model T Runabout with Pickup Body.

The most popular Model Ts running about in our patch when I was a kid were similar to the 1925 Model T Runabout in the photo. We would get free rides by sitting in the back part of the tin lizzie. The driver would go around turns very fast and even go up a steep hill where there was no road. Once in a while one of the kids would fall out because the driver would try to "show off" his driving skills. It was a rough scary way to get a free ride.

Flat tires however, were very common. When you got a flat tire, you had to jack up the car and remove the wheel. Then you had to separate the tire from the wheel, which was somewhat difficult. After that, you had to remove the inner tube (there were no tubeless tires then) from the tire and look for the hole in the inner tube. In some cases you had to inflate the inner tube, which had a stem about two and one-half inches long, with a hand-operated air pump. The inner tube was placed in water to look for tiny bubbles because that's where the hole was. Then you had to scrape and clean the area around the hole and apply some glue to the cleaned area. At this point you took a match and lit the glue and let it burn with a pretty good flame for only a few seconds. The heat from the flame made the glue very sticky. After blowing out the flame, you applied a patch over the hole and pressed down hard to make sure the patch stayed on. The repaired inner tube was put back into the tire and the tire placed back on the wheel. Then you had to fill the inner tube with the air pump and that wasn't an easy thing to do. Sometimes the older guys would let us kids use the air pump to fill the tire, and then they would laugh when they saw how we struggled. As we quickly learned, It really took an adult to do the job satisfactorily.

The Model Ts were also used for hauling all sorts of things including coal. When I went to pick coal at a local strip mine I would hire some guy to haul my coal. The tin lizzie could carry almost a quarter of a ton and it cost me twenty-five cents to haul my coal home.

If you had suggested to the guys in Big Mine Run who owned these Model Ts that they would be worth a lot of money sometime in the future, they would have said that you were crazy.

Remembering Penny Candy

Back to the good old days and penny candy. There was a small grocery store that sold penny candy in Woodland Heights owned by Jacob (Jake) Bielarski. Jake was a very large man with huge hands and fingers. I always took notice of the difficulty he had in picking up some small pieces of penny candy that you told him you wanted. (When I was in college, my sister Mary married Jake's son, Amil.)

The candy in Jake's store was displayed in a large wooden case with a glass front and top. I always enjoyed visiting the store to look at all the candies even if I didn't have a penny or two to spend. When I had a few pennies to spend it was still difficult to decide what to choose, because there were so many choices. However, I always looked over all of the penny candies before deciding what to buy. When Nicky Pechansky had a few pennies to spend, he would invite me to go along to the store when be bought candy. We often shared candy with other kids (dirty hands and all), but we never shared pennies.

In this short story I'm going to describe the different kinds of penny candies I remember.

Tootsie rolls were a dark, soft caramel-like candy about two inches long and about one-half inch in diameter. They came in a brown and gray wrapper with the words "Tootsie Roll" printed on them. They were nice and chewy and they didn't stick to your teeth as much as some other candies. If you liked tootsie rolls, you probably liked tootsie pops, the sucker with a tootsie center.

Licorice candies were not only popular, but there were a variety of different kinds that you could choose. One kind was called licorice laces, which were strings of red and black licorice about two feet long. They looked like strings of spaghetti and it seemed like you were getting a lot for a penny or two. Licorice pipes were fun because you pretended to be smoking them and therefore they lasted a long time. Sometimes there were tiny red candies at the top of the bowl of the pipe to give the appearance of red-burning tobacco. After you showed off your pretense of smoking long enough, you just started to chew up the pipe and eat it.

Also, there were red, black and brown strips of licorice about eight inches long that were somewhat flat and tubular in shape. I liked the brown strips better than the black. Licorice snaps were another kind of licorice candy. They were small pillow-shaped candies with licorice in the middle and coated with a fairly hard colored coating. Some of the colors I remember were: pink, green, orange and white. The ends of the snaps were not coated so you could see the licorice at each end. Lastly there were crows, which were licorice-flavored gumdrops. I think they were the least tasty of all the licorice candies.

Ah, Dubble Bubble Gum. The gum was cubic in shape and about the size of a small die. It had teeth-like marks embedded in it, which probably came from the manufacturing process. The gum came in a grayish wrapper with two twisted ends. Bubble gum cigars were also popular. They were about three inches long and came in various flavors. They had a nice colored cigar band on them to make them look real. You pretended to smoke them until you got tired, and then you chewed them because they were plain old chewing gum. Also, there were bubble gum cigarettes that came in a box, and I believe that each one was wrapped in paper. As you can imagine, they suffered the same fate as the bubble gum cigars. Then there was a teaberry flavored penny gum that you could buy. It had a nice teaberry flavor and it came in sticks like the more expensive chewing gum.

I also purchased bubble gum cards that cost one penny. The wrapped chewing gum and card were about the size of baseball cards that kids collect today. I was more interested in the picture card than the chewing gum, although the gum had a pleasant sugary taste. The earliest cards, which I collected were in color and depicted scenes of the Japanese invasion of Manchuria in 1937. I can remember one card in particular that showed bombing scenes of Nanking. Oh! Where are those cards now? Later on I collected cards of boxers and baseball players.

There were several choices of plain chocolate and chocolate-covered penny candies that I liked. I remember buying small flat squares of milk chocolate that had the word "Klein's" or "Grade A" stamped on them. Solid milk chocolate pieces in the shape of coins were popular. They were about an inch in diameter and wrapped with "gold" foil. The gold-looking coins came in a small mesh bag. Chocolate covered raisins called Raisinets were also tasty. Milk chocolate covered peanuts called Goobers were even better. Both Raisinets and Goobers were sold in small cardboard boxes. The chocolate candies were mainly sold during the colder months of the year.

Round lollypops were always popular. It was a common sight to see a kid walking around with a sucker in his or her mouth. They came in many flavors (cherry, lemon, chocolate, root beer, lime) and lasted a long time, so you got a lot for a penny. Sometimes more than one kid shared a lollypop. Kids in Big Mine Run never worried about germs. Sugar Daddy's were a different kind of lollypop. They were about two inches long and about one inch wide. They were made of tasty milk caramel and lasted a long, long time. Sometimes I bought flat multi-colored lollypops, but they were the kind that you licked like an ice-cream cone.

Everyone remembers plain old round jawbreakers. They were about three-quarters of an inch in diameter and came in various flavors. They too lasted a long, long time. It was impossible to crack them with your teeth so you just held them in your mouth until they got quite small. One day I actually got one stuck inside my mouth between my jaw and teeth for a little while. The only way I got it loose was by reaching in with my finger and giving the jawbreaker a good pull. If a jawbreaker accidentally slipped out of your mouth and landed on the ground, you would just pick it up, wipe it off, and put it back in your mouth. Root beer barrels were also hard and lasted a long while. They weren't quite as large as jawbreakers so they were easier to keep in your mouth. Most kids liked the root beer flavor so the tiny shaped barrels were popular.

There were several novelty items made of wax. One popular item was a mini six -pack of tiny wax bottles filled with various colored fruit flavored drinks called Nik-L-Nips. They were about two inches in height and came in various colors--green, red, yellow, orange, and blue. After playing with them for a little while I just bit off the tip of the wax bottle and drank the colored drink; sometimes I would also chew on the empty wax bottles.

Huge wax lips were a novelty. They were ridged so that you could simply put them on top of your own lips. Then you walked around showing off and looking for attention. The fact that you looked silly didn't matter. After a while you would chew on the wax like it was chewing gum; however, you soon learned that it was more difficult to chew wax than to chew regular gum. Chewing plain wax was never popular, because it didn't have any flavor.

Tiny red-coated candy hearts were sold in a small box. They had a cinnamon-like taste that left a slight burning sensation in your mouth. Since the bright red color easily came off the candy, we would color our lips with it. Small valentine shaped hearts with tiny messages also came in small boxes. We would always read the message on the candy heart before eating it. We would also ask others what the messages were on their candy hearts.

Cigarette candy also came in a small box. The tip of the cigarette was colored a slight pink to simulate a burning cigarette. After we walked around long enough pretending to be smoking, we chewed up the candy cigarette and ate it. Today they are called, "candy sticks." Girls bought candy necklaces more than boys did. They were small hard candies threaded on an elastic band. Of course, after the necklaces were worn for a while, they also got chewed up.

When I first saw candy buttons on paper tape they looked neat. The paper strips were about eight inches long and one inch wide with tiny colored candies pasted on them. There were two candy buttons along side of each other, which were pasted at the top and near the edge of the strip. About an inch below that, there were two more buttons pasted on and that pattern repeated itself to the bottom of the strip. Unfortunately, when you tried to chew off the candy buttons you also chewed off tiny bits of paper at the same time. Sometimes you even ate small pieces of paper and then other times you would spit them out.

Squirrel Nut Zippers were rectangular shaped tan colored candies with tiny nuts embedded in them. After taking off the wrapper, it took a few minutes for them to soften up in your mouth. They were chewy, nutty and most of all tasty. Bit-0-Honey was a similar kind of taffy, only they were smaller and flatter. They were tan colored, chewy and smooth in appearance. They had a honey nut flavor with very tiny almonds bits in them and were wrapped in a yellow and red paper with the words "Bit-0-Honey" in blue printed on them. Both of these tan colored taffy candies stuck to your teeth.

There were a variety of caramels with different shapes, which ranged in color from light tan to a dark brown color. The one kind that I seem to remember the best was called Bulls Eyes. I don't know how many people would remember them by that name, but they were also called caramel creams, which was a more familiar name. They were shaped liked a wheel. The sweet cream in the center was wrapped in a circular fashion with light colored caramel. The other kind that I enjoyed was a small cubic shaped milk caramel about the size of a small postage stamp. Also there was a small, square-shaped flat dark caramel I liked. It seemed to me that I got a lot for a penny since about six of these tiny wrapped dark caramels came in a small boat-shaped box. I think that was another reason I liked them.

Coconut strips were about three inches long and an inch wide. They were flat like a leather belt and each strip was colored white, pink and brown. They not only looked very appetizing in the box but they were sweet and tasty.

There was another candy, which we simply called peanut squares. They were about one and one-quarter inches square and one-eighth of an inch thick. They were held together by some sort of molasses or taffy like substance and loaded with peanuts. The peanut squares were tan colored and similar to peanut brittle but much harder. Nobody thought much about the damage that they did to our poor little teeth.

Gumdrops came in all sorts of colors and sizes. They ranged from those that were quite soft to others that were somewhat hard and gummy, which were not so easy to chew. The one specific name that I can remember was gummi bears that came in various colors. They were only about one half inch long and were relatively hard and gummy. Another gummy candy was called Jujy fruits. They were chewy fruit candies that came in various colors. Green leaves were roughly the shape of a very small leaf but much thicker. They were soft, somewhat gummy and sprinkled with sugar, and they had a mint flavor. Orange slices were similar to green leaves but with an orange slice shape. They were also soft and gummy and sprinkled with sugar. What did they taste like? Well, better than an orange, because they were candies. Gumdrop candies were generally more popular during the summer months.

Then there were pumpkinseeds that were also included with the penny candies. All I can remember about those is that they came in a small box with a nice colored picture of an Indian head on the box. They were very salty so I never bought many of them.

Finally I come to what is arguably the best known and best tasting penny candy of them all. Can you guess what it is? Yep, good old Mary Janes. They were roughly the shape of a domino, rectangular and flat. Mary Janes were tan colored molasses taffy with peanut butter on the inside. They came in a yellow wrapper with a picture of Mary Jane herself. They were not only "yummy" but they also stuck to your teeth, and that was also part of the fun.

It is not easy today to find penny candy sold as it was years ago, except for some specialized stores that still do that sort of thing. Of course, you can buy penny candy that is packaged in boxes or bags. However, that's not the same thing as going into a candy store and asking for one of those for a penny and one of them and so on. Good old-time penny candy is gone, and likely pennies themselves will soon disappear.

Our Early Family Car

The first car I remember that my father owned was a mid-1920s model Whippet. I don't remember very much about it, because I was only about three years old.

However, I do recall the next car he purchased because it had an unusual name; it was a Jewett. It was 1931 and I was seven years old. When I first started to write this story I didn't know what year our car was made, but I did remember that it was a four-door green sedan. My oldest sister, Hattie, also confirmed the green color. She also told me that it had two small flower vases (one on each side) that were located inside the car behind the two doors just behind the front seat. I can't recall the vases but the car had six cylinders and had a 40 horsepower engine. Whenever I mention the Jewett name today, no one recognizes that it was actually the name of a car.

After searching the Internet, I learned that The Jewett Car Company was a subsidiary of the Paige Motor Car Company located in Detroit, Michigan. The first Jewett was made in 1922 and the last one in 1926. I would guess that we had a 1925 model since that was the only year (as far as I could tell) in which Jewett made autumn green satin finishes for their three standard model cars. The average price of a new 1925 four-door sedan model was about $1550 and that equates to about $31,000 in 2005 dollars. Even though they went out of business, the Jewett car was considered to be a good automobile.

One day when I was writing this story, our youngest son Chris reminded me that it would have been a good idea to keep the old Jewett. However, we were probably glad to get rid of the Jewett back then, because they weren't making them anymore. It was almost an embarrassment to own one, because no one else in Big Mine Run had one. I think we all felt then that it would be nifty to buy a "real" car like others had--you know, like a Ford, Plymouth or Chevrolet.

One day my father and a group of his male friends were returning to our home from a picnic in Centralia where they had a little too much beer and whiskey to drink. My father turned off the main highway and then drove up the first steep hill to Big Mine Run. He stopped at a short flat part in the road before driving up the second steep hill to Woodland Heights. He pretended that the car stopped and that he needed a push to get going again. Well, everyone got out enthusiastically and started to push at the back of our old Jewett car. Just about that time, my father started up the car and drove swiftly up the hill to our house. His friends quickly realized that he played a joke on them, so they started the long slow walk up the steep hill to Woodland Heights. When they finally got to the top of the hill, they saw my father sitting on a rocking chair on the porch drinking a beer with his feet resting up on the banister. They started to shake their fists at my father and curse him at the same time. However, after having a drink or two they laughed about the whole matter. And after a few more drinks, everyone thought it really was a good joke.

Here's another similar incident about Steve Beckno who owned a large black Pierce Arrow car with bright red wheels. It was a neat looking car and got a lot of attention when he came to visit us. That's another one of those old cars that would be worth a lot of money today. Steve lived in a small patch named Oakland just about one-half mile west from Big Mine Run. Mr. Beckno had several of his drinking friends with him when he came, and during the course of the visit they all had a few too many drinks of whiskey.

When they were getting ready to leave, Steve got into his car and proceeded to turn his car around and return home. There wasn't much room for just an ordinary car to turn around near our house, because there was a steep hill close to the road itself. So it was much more difficult for a person to turn a large car like a Pierce Arrow around at that point. However his friends decided they would give him directions in turning the car around. They purposely kept urging him back to up, back up, and back up some more. The long Pierce Arrow went over the bank and down a steep hill. A towing truck had to be hired to retrieve Steve's car. Since they all had been drinking, they thought it was funny. Frankly, it was their own way of having some fun and they actually laughed about the incident. Somehow, even as a kid, I thought it was just dumb.

Those Damn Knickers

I never liked wearing knickers. They were loose-fitting full pants that only came down to or just below the knee. The balloon-like trousers never seemed like pants to me, but as a kid I had to wear them.

As I remember, very few if any of the other kids in Big Mine Run had to wear them. The other kids naturally teased me for wearing sissy balloon-like pants. Walking past a group of other kids while wearing them was just awful. The kids in Big Mine Run often used graphic language to describe things. For example, they referred to those damn knickers as "sh-t holders."

Why did I have to wear knickers? There was no "why" about it. My mom bought them and told me to wear them, and that was that. Even though I complained about wearing them, no one seemed to understand. I was told that the knickers looked nice and that the other kids were just jealous. Well, you can imagine how well that went over with me. I somehow toughed it out, but it was no fun.

Then sometime during the mid-1930s, knickers seemed to lose their popularity and went out of style. Thank God, long pants were in and knickers were out. You just don't know how good I felt to get my first pair of long pants, and of course to walk around outside so others could see me.

Making Bums' Soup

There were times when some of us kids would just "hang around" looking for something to do when someone would say, "Let's make some bums' soup." Each of us would then go home and quietly put some potatoes and other vegetables into our pockets and meet later to see what we collected. The person suggesting the idea would often bring a pot of water and a knife. The rest of us would bring our own spoon and a cup.

Then we would hike off to the woods and find a suitable place to build a fire. Several kids would agree to collect wood and get a fire going. The others would peel the vegetables, cut then up and put them in the pot of water. Nobody thought or cared about cleanliness, dirty hands were okay. Bums' Soup was made mostly with potatoes, carrots, onions and any other vegetables we could find. I suspect that we got the idea from watching the bums over in the hobo camp making soup when we went to visit them.

It was fun just sitting around the fire waiting for our soup to be done. When we first tasted our soup, It seemed we could never decide when it was ready to eat. However, after waiting a little while, each of us would take turns sampling the soup again and everyone would say the same thing, "I think it's done." However, I felt that we always ate our soup too soon.

When we ate our own special bums' soup that we made all by ourselves, we thought it tasted just great. I think it gave us a sense of accomplishment. However, if our moms would have fed us that same bums' soup, it's likely we would have made all sorts of excuses to say that we were not hungry for soup.

Roasting Potatoes

One of our favorite things we did on an autumn night was to roast potatoes in an outdoor fire. It didn't take much coaxing to get four or five guys together to have a roast. Each of us would then go home and sneak out a few potatoes.

We had a favorite place where we roasted our potatoes so everyone knew where to meet. Some of the boys' names that I roasted potatoes with were: Charles (Gyppo) Young, Joe Young, George Chuplis, George (Baxie) Mickle, Charlie Mickle, Stiney Bielarskie, Billy Kroh, John Horvath, and Nicky Pechansky.

Gathering up wood and building the fire was fun, but we couldn't wait to toss in our potatoes. We always covered them with the bright red ashes at the bottom of the fire because that was the best way to roast them.

It was fun just sitting around the fire with the other kids and watching the potatoes getting roasted. Naturally, there was a lot of talking going on. After a while the potatoes turned black, and we knew they were done. Sometimes friendly arguments would start because the potatoes would get mixed up in the fire and everyone would claim the biggest ones. Someone would say, "That big one is mine." Then somebody else would say, "No it's not, it's mine." That's how the conversation went for a while. And if you didn't watch your potatoes carefully they would burn to a crisp and you would have nothing to eat.

We used a stick to remove the potatoes from the fire and let them cool for a few minutes. However, we were always eager to eat them so we would pick them up while they were still hot. Then we would have to toss them from one hand to another trying to cool them off and getting slightly burned in the process. We enjoyed eating the over-roasted potatoes because we made them all by ourselves. It never occurred us to us that our hands were very dirty. We didn't have any butter or sour cream, but sometimes some kid would bring a salt shaker along and then everyone wanted to use it.

When we finished eating our wonderful potatoes, we just sat around the fire chatting and watching the flames die down. Smoke got in our eyes and our clothing, but we didn't concern ourselves about things like that. We would just sit next to the fire and talk about all sorts of things. Then someone would get some more wood and get the fire going again and we would sit and talk some more, not noticing that it was getting late. Finally someone would say it's time to go home, and one after another we would leave. The last person attending the fire put it out, but by then it was not much of a fire. Sometimes the last one at the fire would pee on it to put it out.

When I returned home after the roast, it was always evident to my family that I was hanging around a fire for hours because my clothes reeked with smoke. I didn't detect the smoky odor of my own clothing because I was close to the fire all night. When my family asked if I had been around a fire, I would always say, "I wasn't near any fire."

Visiting the Bums' Camp

My first experience with the bums' camp (or hoboes' jungle as we sometimes called it) occurred in the early 1930s when I was about twelve years old. One day when we were looking for something to do, someone said, "Let's go over to the bums' camp." The camp was about a quarter-mile from Big Mine Run and only a short distance from the main Reading Railroad line that ran from Girardville to Ashland.

The bums had a network of camps that were always located near railroads. They would hop off the freight they were riding and after spending a short time in camp they would be on their way again. The bums rarely went to town and they never stayed in camp very long. They were men who were unemployed, and I suppose there were also a few who didn't want any work at all.

They were dressed very shabbily and looked rather scary. They gave me the impression that they were loners and didn't care to develop close friendships, even with other hoboes. Although they appeared to be rough and tough, they were somewhat friendly to us. Maybe some of them looked at us kids and thought back to a more pleasant and innocent time in their own lives when they too were kids. Although I visited the bums' camp many times, I never knew a person who became a bum and rode the rails.

The bums' hangout in Big Mine Run had cool running water (as all hoboes camps had), which came from an underground spring. It was one of our favorite places to stop for a drink on our way home from picking huckleberries. Most of the time when we visited the bums' camp there would be several of them sitting on the ground heating a small tin pot of coffee or cooking some kind of soup. Just imagine, many times a hobo or two would hop off the freight they were riding just to see if he could get a free cup of coffee at the Big Mine Run camp.

After visiting the bums' camp for a while and talking with them we would head back home. We didn't think about our own home as anything special, we just went home. However, the hoboes who rode the rails, could only look ahead to the next camp and the one after that. Sadly, most of them probably didn't have any home to go to.

Picking Huckleberries

The huckleberry season was a big time for us kids and we all looked forward to it. Most of the huckleberries we picked grew on small bushes about a foot high; some also grew on bushes that were almost two feet high. While they were two different types of berries, we simply called them huckleberries. We picked berries every day during the summer except on Sunday. The berry-picking season lasted about three months. It was the only activity we could do everyday and earn some money.

Sometimes Nicky Pechansky (my buddy) and I would sleep outside on the front porch of our house in order to get an early start to pick huckleberries. We would get up about five in the morning while it was still dark and start out for the hills without eating breakfast. The bushes were always very wet at that time in the morning and it was cold and uncomfortable. Our sneakers and socks would get soaked first and in a little while we would be wet from the waist down. We would stay wet until eleven in the morning when the hot sun would finally dry things out, and by noon the sun would be too hot.

We always tied a small can (usually a quart can called a picker) around our waist and then we could pick berries with two hands. When the picker was full, we would dump the berries into a larger container, which held about eight quarts that we carried by hand. We would place the large container on the ground and wander off and pick berries in the nearby area. Then we would return to empty the picker into the large container and then move to another spot to pick more berries. By noon, if we were lucky, each one of us would have picked

Harry M. Bobonich, Ph.D.

about six quarts of berries. We would be tired, hungry, and thirsty and we were ready to go home. Of course, we always ate some of the huckleberries that we picked.

When we got home, we ate a hasty lunch, consisting of mainly a baloney sandwich with ketchup or mustard, a glass of milk or a cup of coffee and a piece of jelly bread. We always had plenty of huckleberries at home to eat, but they didn't seem to be as tasty as they were when we were out picking them in the hills. However, blueberry pie and blueberry perogies were very tasty and we enjoyed those when my mom made them. The blueberry perogies were sweet and more like a dessert, but we ate them as a regular meal.

As soon as we finished our lunch, we would head off to sell our berries. Most of the time we sold our berries to George Chuplis in Woodland Heights, who purchased them for an out-of-town buyer. However, the buyer didn't always pay the best price since he was the only purchaser in town. In the beginning of the season we got about eighteen cents for a quart of berries and then the price would drop to as low as five cents a quart at the end of the picking season. It was an early lesson in supply and demand. On an average day you could earn about seventy cents and we considered that pretty good.

When we felt the buyer's prices were just too low, we would stand alongside the highway and try selling our berries to passing motorists. When we were fortunate in making a sale to those motorists who stopped, we always got paid well for our berries. The drawback was that you might have to wait quite a while before you sold all the huckleberries you had.

One of the fun things about picking huckleberries was that everyone supposedly had a secret place, called a "kutch" (another one of those coined words we made up) where the berries were big and plentiful. For the most part, the kutches never existed. However, it was fun to talk about the secret place you found that you kept from everyone except your best buddies; a place where the huckleberries were as big as marbles. In some cases we would spy on each other; that is, we would watch where others would go picking berries believing that indeed they may have found a good kutch that nobody else knew about—you could never sure.

Huckleberries were generally small (about the size of ordinary beads) and grew on small low bushes. Sometimes you would get lucky and find some large huckleberries, but not very often. Blueberries, which were cultivated, were about twice the size of huckleberries but they did were not grown in the Big Mine Run area.

While huckleberry bushes grew in many places in our area (even close to our home) it seemed we always wanted to walk some distance looking for really big berries. Our region was somewhat hilly but it didn't bother us at all to climb a big hill if we thought there were berries to be found. There was a large mountain range located about a quarter of a mile to the south of Big Mine Run that had a huge rock which was situated at the very top of the mountain. We called it "The Big Rock," since it was visible from over a mile away. Many times we would hike right up to the Big Rock before we would start to pick huckleberries.

I recall how surprised I was the first time I climbed to the very top of the Big Rock and looked down at Big Mine Run and the surrounding area. It was the first time that I ever saw Big Mine Run from such a lofty position. Everything looked so small— almost miniature in size—like tiny houses under a Christmas tree. Big Mine Run and the entire area seemed so different.

Whenever I visited the top of that mountain, I would always stop picking huckleberries for a little while and sit down to take a rest. I enjoyed the feeling of just sitting on top of the mountain and looking down at that miniature world of houses, which looked like a toy land to me. Even though I had visited the Big Rock many times, I enjoyed not only looking down at Big Mine Run but at Oakland, another patch just west of Big Mine Run, as well as Ashland one mile to the West and Homesville another patch just to the east. However, the nine double-houses at Woodland Heights always caught my eye. In particular, I focused on my own home and I always looked to see if anyone was walking in or out of our house.

Picking Mushrooms

My father liked to pick mushrooms (hryby) and he was very good at it. He was a coal miner who contracted miners' asthma, and since he didn't work regularly he would walk the woods looking for mushrooms. They grew in abundance in the coal region and most people liked to eat them. However, my father didn't bother to pick mushrooms near our home because they were the common variety and not very tasty.

After traveling around in his car for sometime, he was able to locate several wooded areas where he always seemed to find mushrooms that were delicious to eat. Sometimes he took me along, but I never really enjoyed it. He carried a ten-quart empty water bucket and a knife as he walked through the woods and I would trail along a little behind him. I don't know how he learned to pick the edible mushrooms from those that were poisonous. As for me, I never showed any interest in knowing the good ones from the bad. On the other hand, my oldest sister, Hattie, liked to pick mushrooms. She not only went with my Dad to pick them, but she went by herself. She was always proud of the fact that she knew which ones to pick. I never heard of anyone dying from eating mushrooms in the area, but on occasion, I would hear about someone who got sick from eating some non-edible mushrooms.

I just never liked anything about mushrooms and I never liked picking them. They grew in dark areas very close to the ground and often they were partially covered with dirt, leaves and other debris. Sometimes we would see snakes lying close to them. Mushrooms never got any sunshine and they didn't appear to be food to me.

The mushrooms that we picked came in various colors and assorted sizes. Some were red, others white, but they mostly ranged from light brown to dark brown in color. Whenever my father would find a large mushroom as large as eight inches in diameter he would always place it on top of the bucket full of mushrooms so it could easily be seen. The average size of mushrooms we picked was about two to three inches in diameter, while the smallest ones were only about one inch or so in diameter.

The tastiest ones were the smallest ones, which I believe, were called "pit pen ka." Sometimes I was required to help clean and cut the damn things in preparation for drying or cooking them. One variety we called "sponges" had a fairly thick sponge-like undercoating, which had to be removed in the cleaning process. I believe I was given the cleaning chore because I fussed so much about not eating them.

My father enjoyed giving mushrooms to other relatives who liked to eat them. My Uncle Bill, who lived in Frackville, was especially fond of mushrooms. When my father would bring my Uncle Bill a bucket full of delicious mushrooms, Bill would reward him with a bottle of whiskey.

My mother did many things with mushrooms. She made delicious mushroom soup. (At least that's what others told me.) My mom also put mushrooms in diced potato soup that she made. While I ate the potato soup, I always left the mushrooms behind. She also made a mushroom and gravy mix that was used as a topping on other dishes. Everyone enjoyed eating all her mushroom dishes that she made except me.

In addition, she would thread mushrooms on a string about three feet long and then make it into a loop. After making several loops, she would hang them behind our kitchen coal stove to dry out for use in cooking future meals.

Sometimes my father would simply place cleaned, raw mushrooms on top of the coal stove and heat them on both sides. Then he would sprinkle salt on top and eat them. No matter how they were prepared, I said, "They're still mushrooms and I say to hell with them." Actually, I said it to myself.

The Old Swimming Hole

We had a favorite swimming hole that was situated in a wooded and isolated area that was located about one- half mile from Big Mine Run. It was not a regular swimming hole, but just a large oval-shaped hole in the ground made by nature that filled up with water from an underground spring. There weren't any large trees alongside the swimming hole; however, we had to clear out a small area where we could build a fire to keep warm and a place to pile our clothes. The water had a blue-green color so we called it the "bluey." It was near the site of the former commercial swimming pool at Woodland Park, which was a well-known recreation center in the early 1900s.

Whenever we felt like swimming on a hot summer day, several of us would hike to the bluey. It didn't take much coaxing, just a suggestion and off we would go; sometimes we went swimming twice a day. When we got to the swimming hole, one or two guys would start a fire so we could dry off and keep warm after we left the pool. The rest of us would take off our clothes and put them on a pile and then walk over and check the temperature of the water, which was always cold. Since nobody had a swimsuit, we went swimming naked. After splashing some water on ourselves, we would dive in and swim across to the opposite side to reach a large tree that fell over during a bad storm. The tree was situated at the far end of the swimming hole and provided a good place to rest after swimming across the pool. After resting on the tree for a while, we would dive in and swim back again. The bluey was quite deep so it was considered a feat if you could dive to the bottom and pick up some debris and raise your hand as you came to the surface to show that you touched bottom. Whenever we left the pool, we always stood around shivering and huddled around the fire to dry off and keep warm.

Huckleberries grew in the area and it wasn't unusual for us to hear berry pickers calling to one another while we were standing around the fire and chatting. Now and then someone would holler, "Hey you guys, some girls are coming." All of a sudden six or seven stark-naked kids, who were standing around the fire, would make a dash for the water. It always turned out to be a false alarm, and we would laugh and giggle about it later.

The big thing each year was to see who was brave enough to go for the first swim very early in the spring when the water was unusually cold. Whenever that happened, the word soon spread and then we all knew who took the first swim. The guy, usually an older person, was considered to be a hero. He was someone we looked upon as having done something great.

Sleigh Riding

Any youngster who grew up in Woodland Heights remembers how exciting and sometimes scary it was to go sleigh riding during the wintertime. Of course, we never had a sleigh pulled by a horse. We had sleds and went sledding, but we never called it sledding. We always said, "Wanna go sleigh ridin'?"

There was one steep hill from Woodland Heights down to Big Mine Run. After reaching the bottom of the first steep hill, there was a short flat run of about fifty feet and then you could go down another steep hill to the main highway running from Ashland to Girardville.

Both boys and girls participated in sledding, and often they both rode down the hill on the same sled. Sometimes Margie Colahan, Betty and Helen Monahan, my neighbors, and I would go sledding together. Even those kids who didn't have a sled could always hop a ride down the hill with somebody else. I had a sled called "Lightning Guider" and another name I remember was "Flexible Flyer." It was common to see several kids piled on top of one another flying down the hill. Some kids used a large piece of tin with the front part turned up (toboggan–like), while others used a large piece of cardboard as a sled.

Both hills were quite steep so there was no problem going fast. In fact, we probably went too fast for our own safety. Most of the time I would go sledding down the hill "belly bumper" style. That is, I would lie flat on my stomach on the sled as I went down the hill. Most other kids also went belly bumper style. Smaller kids, who were with their parents, just sat on their sleds going downhill.

On occasion you would get pummeled with snowballs from the other kids as you were sledding downhill. However, you rarely got hit because you would be going too fast and the snowballs were thrown too late. The kids didn't realize that they had to throw the snowballs before the sled was upon them.

There were times when I went so fast that my eyes teared up so bad I could hardly see. Often I had to turn off the road and into a snow bank to slow down or stop. It was somewhat dangerous since cars would also be coming up and going down the hill and there wasn't much room to get out of the way. Whenever anyone saw a car approaching he would holler out the number "59." Then others would also call out the number to let everyone know that a car was coming. I don't know the origin of the number but it was our own special warning system. While there were minor accidents from time to time, nobody ever got seriously hurt.

Most of the time we made it down to the bottom of the first steep hill. However, it was considered a big thing if some one would also go across the small flat section at the bottom and then start down the second steep hill. That part was really scary since the road was quite narrow and there was very little room to get out of the way of a car that was coming up the hill. In fact, the road was only wide enough for one car. If it happened that two cars got on the road at the same time (one coming up and the other going down), one of the cars would have to back away to let the other car proceed.

After reaching the bottom of the first steep hill I had a long walk back up the hill pulling my sled behind me. That was fun too because everyone would brag about how his sled was the fastest. As I slowly walked back up the hill, I would often have to jump out of the way of some kid who was sledding down at pell-mell speed. When I got back to the top, I would rest for a few minutes and then go back down the hill again.

Sledding was one of the most enjoyable things I did as a kid. The steep hill made it a lot more fun. After sledding most of the day or if it was getting dark, I would slowly start walking home. As I got close to our house I would think about how nice and warm it was inside since. As I got closer, I also wondered if there would be something good to eat. After all, I expended a lot of energy playing (serious stuff) and I was hungry.

When I got home, I would take off my hat and coat and then take off my shoes. I had a habit of opening the oven door on our coal stove in the kitchen and then sitting in front of the stove and placing my feet at the edge of the oven door to get warm. Sometimes my mom would even give me something to eat while I was getting warm in front of the open oven door. Aren't moms' wonderful? The only damn problem is that when we were kids we were too dumb to know it.

Playing Athletic Games

Most of the outdoor games we played involved running, jumping, pushing and shoving. Many times we made up our own games and our own rules.

I wheeled an old discarded automobile tire about for fun. Other kids did the same thing. We would race each to see who could go the fastest. Then we would bump into each other to see if we could knock the other kid's tire down.

Playing hoops (not basketball) was also popular. We all had our own iron hoop, which was about two feet in diameter and about a quarter of an inch round. Each one of us would push our hoop with a stick that had a small nail in it to guide the hoop. Some kids were very clever and were able to all sorts of tricks with their hoops. I know it sounds sort of silly, but that's what we did.

We also played a game called, "nipsey" that involved only two kids. The game began with one kid using a sharp stick to mark out a circle on the ground about three feet in diameter. Then we took a small square piece of wood (called a nipsey) about two inches long and about one-half inch wide and shaved each end to a sharp point. Each of the four sides was marked with a one, two, three or four. One person would toss the nipsey into the circle to begin the game. The other person would take a narrow stick about two feet long and using one hand tap lightly on one of the pointed ends of the nipsey. As the nipsey flipped into the air, he would try to hit it (baseball style) as far as he could. He would get as many chances to hit the nipsey depending on the number that faced up on the nipsey when it was first tossed into the circle.

When the batter was through hitting the nipsey, he challenged the other person who tossed the nipsey into the ring. The batter then tried to determine how many giant steps it would take his opponent to jump from the circle to where the nispey finally landed. The object was to slightly underestimate the number of jumps and challenge the other person so that he could not reach the nispey in that number. If the batter won, he would continue to be the batter, if the tosser won, then he became the batter.

Of course we played the usual game of marbles. We used the familiar multi-colored glass "knuckler" to shoot at the marble with our thumb over the bent forefinger. Everyone had his own little bag of marbles. The newly purchased marbles were shiny and brightly colored, and we would always try to win those first. However, after playing in the dirt for a few days they looked like the rest of our regular dirty marbles.

In addition, we also used a ball not quite as large as a billiard ball instead of the knuckler. We would roll the large ball, which we called a "dobber" in a similar fashion that one would roll a bowling ball. Playing with dobbers and the usual size marbles was fun because there was a lot more hitting and the marbles would go flying quite a distance.

We also played a game called cops and robbers where we pretended to shoot at each other. It started with about five players on each side. Each group would hide in a place where they felt they couldn't be seen, but that had a good view of the other side.

Someone would then call out, "O.K. we're ready" and the game would begin. Whenever anyone recognized a member of the other side moving or not, he would holler out, "Bang, bang 'so and so' hiding under the steps (or wherever the location was) you're dead." That player was then eliminated from the game. The game went on that way with each side trying to outshoot the other group. The last kid who didn't get shot won the game for his team. Of course there were all sorts of arguments, about who was shot and who wasn't, and sometimes the game would break up over a prolonged argument. However, everything would soon be forgotten and we would start playing some other game.

We played baseball and football, but these games are so well known that I won't go into much detail here. It was always easy to find a baseball of some sort along with a paddle for a bat to start playing a game. The type of ball that we generally used was a sponge ball that we called a "spongy." As we got a bit older we would play hard ball using a regular baseball and a regular bat. However, we rarely had more than one or two gloves.

Football was also popular, but most of the time we used a small empty condensed milk can for a football. It was hard on the hands but nobody seemed to mind. If someone got a regular football for a present we all wanted to get our hands on the ball. One Christmas day I did get a new football, and when I took it outside I was afraid to let it hit the ground so it wouldn't get scuffed. One older guy gave it a kick and I got quite mad at him because I thought it would damage my football. Sometimes we would challenge another patch town to a game of football and that was always fun.

Another game we played was called "kick the can." It was similar to baseball, but also different. The kicker at home plate placed a partially crushed condensed empty milk can on top of his shoe and tried to send the can as far as he could with a football-like kick. He would then run to first base and was safe, unless the lone fielder retrieved the can and touched home plate before the kicker reached first base. Other kickers would take turns stepping up to home plate trying to move the runner or runners around to home. If the fielder caught the can on the fly or reached home plate with the can before a runner reached his next base he would be out. Then the person who was the fielder becomes a kicker and the person making the out would become the fielder.

We played another game that also used the same type of condensed milk can that we used when we played football. The can was placed on the ground and then we stomped down on the can with our foot so the sides of the can caved in and became attached to our shoe. We did the same thing for each foot. So now we had a crushed can underneath each shoe. Then we would walk around on the pavement or road making a big racket. We probably looked silly, but we didn't know it at the time and besides we probably didn't care if someone felt that way.

We also played a game called "blacksmith" but I don't know the origin of the name. To begin with, a circle about fifteen feet in diameter was marked out on the ground. The person who was "it" or the "tagger" was outside the circle and all the other players were inside which was the safe position. The tagger could only tag someone if he was outside the circle. Those inside the circle could leave it and run as far and as fast as they wanted. It was up to the "it" person to tag anyone outside the circle. After a person was tagged, he and the tagger would race back to the circle to see who would get there first. The loser then became the tagger. The game went on in this fashion for hours and involved a great deal of running.

During the winter we would build snow huts (igloo style). Sometimes we would divide up into two groups and each group would build a snow fort to defend from an attack by the other group. At first, we would throw snowballs at each other and then duck down behind our own fort for protection. Sometimes some mean kid would take a 'gooney" (a small stone) and wrap it up in snow. If you happened to get hit with a "snowball gooney," it would really hurt. After we got tired of throwing snowballs, we would charge the enemy fort and try to knock it down. Generally we were able to ward off the initial attacks, but eventually each side would charge full-speed and destroy the other fort.

We played a game called "horsey." Ordinarily you needed about four players on each side. One group was called "horses" and the other was called "riders." To begin the game, the first person on the horses' team would wrap his arms around a sturdy up-right object, like a telephone pole. Then he would bend over and keep his back parallel to the ground. The second person would wrap his arms around the hips of the first kid and also keep his back level with the ground. The next two persons would assume a similar position. After all four of the players were lined up, they resembled a long multi-legged horse. That is, all four persons were lined up in a single file and their backs parallel to the ground.

Now it was the riders' turn to participate in the fun. The first person of the riders group would take a running start and place his hands on the hips of the last person and leap up as forward as far as possible landing on the backs of the other kids. The idea is to land as close as you can on the back of the first person, so other members of your team can follow behind. The other riders follow suit, all landing on the backs of the other kids. The trick is to find a weak spot on one kid and try to pile up as many riders as possible in that area to cause at least one person to collapse and break the connected four persons.

The two groups then reversed positions. The kids who were horses now became riders and the riders became horses. The team that caused the biggest collapse of the connected kids won. One final point, when you were a rider you pretended to be actually galloping on a real horse in an attempt to get the kid underneath you to collapse. It was always fun to jump on top of some kid that you didn't like. Then you pretended you were galloping on a real horse to try to knock him down. Of course, he remembered that, and when it was his turn he did the same thing to you.

Playing Other Games

Most kids in Big Mine Run didn't have the luxury of playing with many store bought toys. So we played with simple toys that we made ourselves. However, we did have playing cards, board games and some small toys that were purchased at the store.

During the summer I liked to toss around my homemade paper airplane. I used a sheet of tablet paper about seven by ten inches to make an airplane. Each kid would try to design a plane that would fly higher and longer than anyone else's plane. Surprisingly, the paper planes lasted for quite a while. However there were times when one of my airplanes would land in some water puddle, get stuck high up in a tree, land on a roof of some building or a doggie would get hold of it. For some reason, it seemed that my best plane always ended up in one of those situations. Then I started over again and made a new one.

I also made small paper boats from ordinary sheets of school tablet paper. The tiny boats were constructed to look like canoes. I would put several small stones in the canoe for ballast and then place it in a creek that ran past the schoolyard. As the little paper boat was being carried along with the current, I would run along side the creek following its progress. The tiny boat would generally sail for some distance before capsizing in rough water. Most of the time I would race my boat with another kid's boat to see which one traveled the fartherest. The creeks in Big Mine Run were all polluted from the Bast Colliery. The water was often black in appearance and the edges of the creek were always lined with yellowish sulfur compounds as well as rust colored iron chemicals.

We made our own "peashooters" from a hollow or tubular plant. We cut off a tube about one-foot long and blew small green wild cherries (pellets) at one another. Sometimes we would shoot pellets at some older kid and that usually turned out to be a mistake. If he did not like getting hit with the pellets, he would come over and take the peashooter and break it in half. After a while (usually when the older kid left) we would make another one.

I also made an inner tube gun from a solid piece of wood. The gun was an inch wide, two or three inches high and about 10 or 12 inches long. A separate narrow strip of wood one inch wide and four inches long served as the trigger.

The so-called bullets (rubber bands) were made from an old discarded inner tube that came from the inside of an automobile tire. I cut off rubber bands about one-quarter of an inch wide (they looked like garters) from the inner tube. Then I took several of the rubber rings and stretched them length-wise on the gun to hold the trigger in place. The rubber band (the bullet) that I shot was inserted between the end of the gun and the trigger to hold it in place. Then I stretched the rubber ring from the trigger to the full length of the gun. When I pressed the trigger, the rubber ring would go flying off some distance; it was surprising how far the rubber band would fly. Sometimes the rubber ring would slip out from the trigger when I was loading the gun and the ring would hit me right in the face. When that happened, I would look around to see if anyone saw that I did such a dumb thing.

Most of the time we would play games shooting at each other. When you were hit at close range by a rubber ring, it would really sting. However, we also shot our rubber bands at other things, and we were always losing them. Our rubber bands landed in trees, or on roofs of shanties, porches and garages—perhaps some of them are still stuck in some crevice or rainspout somewhere.

Small hand held water guns were popular during the summer. The water guns were purchased items, however they were cheap. In order to load the gun, you had to pull back on the trigger and then immerse the barrel of the gun into water. As you released the trigger, a small amount of water was drawn up into the gun. The gun was now loaded and you could give someone a good long squirt of water. The other kid you were shooting at would then shoot back at you. The only problem was that you had to have a source of water to load your gun. Later on another model of gun was available, which held a larger amount of water that allowed you to shoot more water and that was much better.

I also made a small wooden toy from an empty spool of thread. I put an ordinary rubber band completely through the hole of the spool and fastened it to the outside flat edge of the spool. At the other end, I inserted the rubber band through a small thin wax washer. I made the washer from an ordinary piece of wax, which I got from the top of a jar of jelly. Then I placed a short thin pencil between the rubber band itself and twisted it until the pencil was flat against the wax washer. When I placed the spool on the floor, it would travel some distance, like a small wind-up toy. Then I learned that if I notched the edges of the wooden spool, it would run across the floor much better.

Board games were popular since they could be played both indoors and outdoors and they were relatively cheap to purchase. Monopoly was the most popular board game we played. Of course anyone who ever played Monopoly remembers that the object of the game was to control the high rent real estate squares in order to win. So everyone wanted to purchase Boardwalk, because you collected the highest rent if you owned that property. The other thing that was important was not to land on the square, which said, "Go to Jail."

We also played checkers and it was always fun to be able to jump your opponent's checkers more than one jump. Double jumps were not too common and generally won the game. However, triple jumps were rare and always won the game.

Pick-Up-Sticks was also another game that we played. The game consisted of twenty-five sticks, which were approximately eight or nine inches long. The needle-like sticks were various colors (blue, green, red and yellow) and were roughly the shape of a round toothpick. To begin the game a player would hold all the sticks upright (except for the lone black colored one) in his hand on top of the table. Then he would open his hand quickly so that the sticks would scatter about on the table in roughly the shape of a circle. The player who started the game would try to pick up one stick at a time, without causing any other stick to move except the one he is attempting to pick up. If he erred, the next person took his turn at picking up a stick. The lone black stick could be used as a moving tool. The colored sticks were each worth a different number of points, and the first person to get 500 points won the game.

I also played "jacks." It was a game played mostly by girls with a set of small six-pointed metal objects and a small ball. The object of the game was to pick up the pieces in a prescribed manner while bouncing a small rubber ball. My three older sisters liked to play jacks, so that's how I learned to play the game.

Then there was hopscotch. It was a girls' game in which an object (usually a small flat stone) was tossed into succeeding sections of a geometric figure that was drawn on the ground or pavement. The person who tossed the stone would then hop through the figure, pick up the stone and continue hopping back on one foot. I also played hopscotch with my sisters.

Jumping rope was also a game that was mostly played by girls. However, I did some rope jumping but my sisters were always better at jump rope than I was. Sometimes the girls turning the rope would sing a song, and often the "jumper" would also sing along. On occasion, my sisters used two ropes and they called that "Double Dutch." Needless to say, I wasn't very good at that at all.

I was the youngest child with three older sisters. Now you can see why I learned to play jacks, hopscotch, and jump rope. In a way, I had no choice. Of course, I could be just saying that so I don't have to admit that I was playing girls' games by my own choice. On the other hand, I was always careful, and why do I say that I was careful? Well, I never wanted the other kids to see me playing those games with my sisters.

Young girls didn't play as many outdoor games as the boys did. The girls had to help out more with the domestic chores than the boys. However the girls did play some baseball but not football. When playing baseball the girls always used a solid rubber sponge ball or sometime a hollow rubber ball. They never used a regular baseball bat, but instead they used a flat board with a narrow handle. The girls held the bat straight upward over the top of their head. The pitcher would the toss the ball about three feet over the batters' head because that's where the flat part of the board would come in contact with the ball. Of course, there were always a few girls that could play boys' games as well as any of the boys. We called them tomboys.

Going to the Movies

There were two movie theaters on Center Street in Ashland. The Roxy Theater, which was open every night, was located near Fifth Street. The Roxy always showed movies (we called them love stories) that the adults attended. On the outside of the theater, the placards, which were enclosed in glass cases displayed the big Hollywood stars in the featured movies that were currently playing. As you entered the theater, there was a large candy stand in the lobby. The entire interior of the theater was elegantly decorated with fancy lighting fixtures. And you were allowed to choose the main floor or the balcony for seating.

The Temple Theater, located near Sixth Street, only showed westerns movies. It was our theater—the one where all the kids went to see their western heroes. One of the big days we looked forward to was going to see a matinee, which cost ten cents. We always looked closely at the outside posters of our cowboy heroes before go into the theater.

When we got a little older, we were allowed to go on Saturday night to see the westerns. Generally a small group of us kids got together and walked to the Temple Theater, which was about one and a half miles away. The walk to the theater was fun because we would talk about what we thought was going to happen in the new serial, since there was a serial film that continued from week to week. All the guys in Big Mine Run always sat in the same place in the theater. It was our way of "sticking together." At first we sat at the very rear of the balcony, then we changed to the very back of the main floor. When we got to theater, we always knew just where to go for our seats because some of the other kids would already be there.

Before the movie started we would talk with one another and look around to see who else was there from Big Mine Run. If someone were sitting in front of us and blocking our view, we would keep changing seats so we could see the screen better. Then suddenly the theater lights dimmed and a faint bluish light beam slanted down from the upstairs projector room onto the screen—the movie started. We would clap our hands and shout, but then we would quiet down quickly. It was time to settle down in your chair and watch the magic unfold on the movie screen.

Our cowboy heroes were Tom Mix (a very early western cowboy star who was born in Pennsylvania), Buck Jones, Ken Maynard, Bob Steele, Harry Carey, Tim McCoy and others. When one of our cowboy heroes kept on shooting his six-shooter more than six times, we would laugh and tell each other that his gun only held six bullets—how could that be? But that was okay, because it was our hero.

Sometimes we would boo and hiss when coming attractions of feature films were shown that were not strictly westerns, or if there was a short documentary on ladies' fashions.

The weekly serials were always fun to watch. At the end of each serial the hero or heroine would be facing extreme danger and you were given the impression that they would be killed. But the following week they always miraculously escaped and we would clap and laugh. Each week we went through the same thing.

After the movie, we would all walk home together. When we got to the edge of town and away from the last houses, all the kids would start urinating on the macadam road that we were walking on. If you weren't careful someone would even pee on you.

Then for some reason, the kids would start throwing rocks at the large overhead light that was nearby. More often than not, someone would hit the bulb and it would blow up with a flash. We would all start running toward Oakland, a small patch between Ashland and Big Mine Run, which was about a half-mile away. After running for a while, we slowed down and just started walking again. Then one of the kids would shout, "someone's coming" and we would all start running again until we found out it was a false alarm and we would all laugh and just continue to walk on home.

Wow, going to see those cowboy movies with the other kids really was fun. Sometimes you had an extra nickel to visit the five and ten cent store for a bag of candy—that was living.

When the Junkman Came Around

A junkman from Pottsville came around every Saturday to buy all kinds of old junk. He had a large open truck, and as he drove slowly through Woodland Heights, he rang a bell and called out, "Any old rags, any old junk, any old iron." I was about eight years old when I started collecting items to sell to the junkman. I was always glad to see him because it was only one of just several ways I could earn a few pennies.

Since my mom made homemade braided rugs, she always gave me small pieces of cloth that she no longer needed. I stuffed all the small pieces of cloth that I gathered up in a large burlap bag. I also picked up other old clean rags that were lying around the house and put them in the bag.

I also collected various types of metals that I knew I could sell to the junkman. When I took a walk along the railroad tracks, I would look for pieces of scrap iron that the railroad workers discarded after doing some repair work and carry them home. Old pieces of scrap iron were not too hard to find; however, the junkman paid the least amount of money for iron. On the other hand, he paid the highest price for aluminum. However aluminum was very light in weight--and besides, how many aluminum pots can you find in a week?

I knew the price per pound the junkman would pay for aluminum, brass, copper, and iron. I collected all these junk metals and kept them separated, because they varied in price and each pile had to be weighed individually.

When I waved for the junkman to stop, he came over to see what I had to sell. First of all, he looked through by bag of rags to see that they were clean. He had a scale with a hook on the bottom, which he stuck into the bag of rags. He lifted up the bag of rags with the small hand-held scale to see how much it weighed. Then he looked at the small piles of metals I had and handled the pieces to get an idea of how heavy they were. He then made an estimate and told me what they were worth. He only weighed a metal pile if I had a rather large amount of a particular metal. I generally got fifteen or twenty cents for my junk and I always showed my mom what I earned.

For the most part, it was only kids that had stuff to sell to the junkman. I only saw adults sell to the junkman when they had an old motor, stove, mattress, bed or some other large object that was worth more money than the small junk items we sold.

I was about ten years old when the Bast Colliery shut down. When I took a walk around the colliery area, it was easy to see many odd pieces of iron, copper and brass lying about. However, the Coal and Iron cops patrolled the area and you were not allowed to take anything, even though most of the items were just plain junk.

One day I took my wagon and went for a walk to the colliery grounds. After a while, I helped myself to several pieces of iron that weighed about 100 pounds. As I was leaving with my wagon and junk iron, a Coal and Iron cop caught me and threatened to take me to jail. Of course, I didn't know at the time that the cop was primarily trying to frighten me--and he did. The cop had his 15 year-old son along (a kid that I knew) and he asked his son if I should be put in jail. I was frightened and must have shown it, because the son told his father to let me go. The cop agreed, but told me to return the pieces of iron and not to take anything anymore. I started on my way back to the colliery as they were leaving. As soon as the cop and his son were out of sight, I dumped the pieces of iron on the ground and scooted home with my empty wagon. I never told anyone about this incident

Playing Cards

There wasn't that much to do in a small patch town like Big Mine Run. However, playing card games was the most popular indoor game we played as a family and with friends. Pinochle, in particular, was a game we played all the time. The most common pinochle game we played involved two players who were partners (or buddies) who played against two other two players. Another pinochle game we played involved four players as I just described above; however, we played with a double deck where we tossed out the nines. A third type of pinochle we played also involved four players using a single deck, however there were no partners. In this game, it was difficult for the person getting the bid to collect many tricks, since there were three players playing against one. Another variation of pinochle was a two-player pinochle game that I sometimes played with my father.

Hearts was also another game we liked to play. Generally we would have four or five players to start the game. It's a trick-taking game in which the object is to avoid winning tricks, which had hearts on them. The terrible queen of spades was to be avoided at all costs, since it counted for the most points of any one card. The game ends when someone reaches one hundred or more points. However, the winner is the player with the lowest score. One interesting facet to the game, which was difficult to do, occurred when a player would collect all the heart tricks and also the queen of spades. When that happened, all the other players received points.

We also played other card games such as: old maid, go fish, poker (jacks to open), rummy, solitaire, fan tan, black jack, and red dog. We even played euchre (a little more sophisticated game). Another game that we played was called hasenpfeffer (we called it "haw-zee") where jacks in the trump suit were the premium cards. Of course all kids played war, you know, highest card wins.

Mr. and Mrs. Harry Boris, who lived in Ashland, were friends of my father and mother and they would often come to our home to play cards. While they often played pinochle, they mostly played a game called "hola." My mother was always the partner with Mr. Boris, while Mrs. Boris was the partner with my father. Johnny Boris, the oldest son of the Boris family that visited us, was a well-known barber in Ashland and later served in the legislature in Harrisburg.

Card playing went on in our home from as early as I can remember. There were times when my father and his friends would start playing poker on a Sunday afternoon, and when I got up for school on Monday morning the players would just be leaving to go home. Charles (Chick) Medrick and Mickey Yuhas were two younger guys that were regular poker players at our house. So it wasn't unusual for me to be able to play all kinds of card games even as a youngster.

Wanna Fight?

Sometime during the summer months outdoor boxing became a popular form of entertainment for the older guys and adults. They simply chose two of us kids to put on boxing gloves and told us to box each other—we didn't have a choice. There was always a number of people watching so it was difficult to say that you didn't want to fight. If you refused, it was embarrassing to be called a coward and a sissy.

There was no boxing ring; we just fought outdoors on the dirt road with all the older guys standing around in a circle. There was no set number of rounds either, but once in a while you would get a rest. You fought until they called a halt to the match or if someone just quit.

The first time I was chosen to fight, they matched me with another kid (his name was Joe Young) who was bigger than I was. I didn't want to box, but I had no choice. However, I had read about boxing and knew some of the skills of how to fight defensivley, so that was helpful. As it turned out I did pretty good, and even though I did well I didn't enjoy the experience. I was glad that my turn to box was over with for a while.

No one ever got hurt in the boxing games, since the boxing gloves were large. However, if you didn't do well, your feelings were certainly hurt, especially if you got knocked down. After one fight was over, another couple of kids were selected to put on the gloves.

By the way, none of the older guys did any fighting—only us kids.

Making Homemade Candy

I remember that my three older sisters made homemade candy and I always enjoyed watching them make it. The most popular candy they made was a molasses candy, which we called "mozhee." The principal ingredients in the candy were molasses and sugar with peanuts or coconut being optional.

The ingredients (except for the nuts or coconut) were cooked on the coal stove until it came to a rolling boil. After a while a small portion was taken out with a teaspoon and put in a glass of cold water. My sisters would then allow me to reach into the glass and take out the cooled candy to taste it. When the candy had a certain consistency and was chewy it was done. Others also got a chance to test the candy to see if it was done and at times we all had a different opinion. Someone would say, "It needs to be cooked more." Another would say, "No it doesn't, it's done."

When they decided that it was done, the mixture was poured into a buttered tin pie pan so that the candy was about a quarter of an inch thick. If we had any peanuts or coconut we would add those. The candy was then placed outside on our porch banister or in the basement to allow the mozhee to cool and slowly become solid. My sisters always allowed me to check the hardness of the mozhee by pressing my thumb on top to see it was hard enough to take out of the pan. Sometimes I checked too early and my thumb would form a slight depression in the candy and that meant it wasn't hard enough. Eventually the mozhee turned solid and I was happy to carry the pan into the kitchen.

One of my sisters would take the pie pan, and turn it upside down and a large round chunk of candy would plop onto the kitchen table. Sometimes we had to bang on pie pan to get the mozhee out. Then we would break it up into smaller portions and we would all have a piece. It was similar to a very hard caramel that would soften and get chewy after you had it in your mouth for a while. Sometimes I would take one of the larger pieces and would put it in my mouth and it would last for hours. However, I soon learned to just take regular size pieces.

At Easter time, my sisters made coconut Easter eggs. I always sat close by watching them put in the ingredients (powdered sugar, grated coconut, vanilla and some of the liquid from inside the coconut) into a bowl and then shape the mixture into white Easter eggs. They made the Easter eggs about the same size as regular eggs. Sometimes they would let me make a few, but I wasn't too good at it. That is, mine didn't look like Easter eggs. After making a large number of them, they would dip the coconut eggs into hot dark chocolate and place the eggs on wax paper to cool and harden. While mine didn't look like Easter eggs, they nevertheless all tasted the same.

They also make peanut butter eggs using the same ingredients but substituting peanut butter for coconut. I enjoyed eating the peanut butter eggs more because they were not quite as sweet as the white coconut Easter eggs. And we all know that all kids like peanut butter. However, both types of Easter eggs were the same size and coated with the same dark chocolate, so that posed a minor problem. When I took a bite of an egg and it wasn't peanut butter, I would put it back in the large bowl of Easter eggs. More than once I was reminded that when I took an Easter egg I was to finish it and not put it back if it wasn't peanut butter. After that, I took a knife and carefully sliced the Easter egg in half. If it was peanut butter, I ate it; however, if it was white coconut I carefully pushed the two half portions together and put it back. When my sisters found out what I did, they called me "a sneak."

My sisters also made a white taffy candy with walnuts, but for some reason they didn't make it very often. I don't remember too much about all the ingredients they used. However, I recall that they pulled the taffy to soften it and that was fun to watch. When it was done, It was tasty and chewy like all taffy candy.

They also made plain fudge with and fudge with nuts. Most of the time I couldn't wait for it to harden and I would take some while it was still soft. I always seemed to enjoy sampling the candies before they were ready to eat.

Making homemade candy was fun because I could watch the entire process from beginning to end. Besides, I got to taste some candies before anybody else—like eating a small Easter egg before it was coated with chocolate. After all, I was the only little baby brother my sisters had.

Making Moonshine

Moonshine is a slang word for illegally distilled whiskey made "in the light of the moon." Popular culture has it that moonshiners lived chiefly in rural areas of the southeastern United States. I can attest that making moonshine was not only a southern Appalachian endeavor. Since the statue of limitations has run out, here goes.

When I was a youngster of seven and growing up in Woodland Heights, a section of the patch called Big Mine run, in northern Schuylkill County, I helped my mom make homemade whiskey. We made real moonshine, but we were indoor moonshiners. Our house was at the end of the road and somewhat isolated. That made it ideal for a manufacturing operation such as ours.

The stereotype of a typical moonshiner is one we are all familiar with from print, film and television—the still that was set up in some rural isolated wooded area next to a stream. The male moonshiners—never women—were shabbily dressed and tending to business. To complete the picture, there were always several good old hound dogs that knew how to bark and yelp when anyone came around.

History shows that making moonshine was not uncommon in Pennsylvania. A government tax on whiskey in the very late 1700s led to "The Whiskey Rebellion" in the western portion of our state, which in turn led colonists taking matters into their own hands. They started making homemade whiskey by the light of the moon—moonshine. Other settlers moved form Western Pennsylvania to the Appalachia area and started making moonshine there.

Moving forward to 1920, Prohibition came into effect in the United States. Illegal drinking places called "speakeasies" became common and popular. Making whiskey illegally on a major scale (bootlegging) became a major problem. Rum-running, that is, transporting illegal whiskey cross borders was routine. Not only was Prohibition a failure, it was repealed in 1933 by the 21st Amendment.

As I recall, my three older sisters occasionally helped with the Big Mine Run moonshine operation. I was the chief assistant. My mom always got me involved in helping her in one way or another. She believed n learning by doing—she had no other choice. My mom never attended school. She neither read nor wrote.

Our still was not the stuff of which stereotypes are made. We had a 60-gallon wooden barrel in which we fermented all the ingredients. We started by adding 100 pounds of sugar, three water buckets full of washed rye, several large cakes of yeast, ripened fruit (optional) and enough water to almost fill the barrel. The very ripe fruit, which generally consisted of peaches, plums and grapes, was added for its sugar content. The 60-gallon barrel sat beside the burning coal stove so the entire mixture in the barrel would become warm and ferment. In other words, the sugar would become alcohol. The process takes several weeks.

Several times a day, I would stir the contents of the barrel with a long wooden paddle to mix the ingredients, which helped the fermentation process. You had to be careful, because as you stirred the liquid mixture, carbon dioxide (a gaseous by-product from the fermentation process) was generated and a mass of gas bubbles would rise rapidly from the bottom of the barrel. On several occasions I stirred the fermented liquid too vigorously and some of the contents bubbled up and spilled over the top of the barrel.

Once fermentation occurred, we separated the residue of grain and fruit from the liquid in the barrel. We added about 20 gallons of the fermented liquid to the copper boiler or until it was about two-thirds full. Then we placed the copper boiler on top of the stove. The water-cooled condenser rested on a wooden stool and the jug was placed on the floor. The warm water outlet was hooked up to a hose and ran off to the cellar drain. The complete still apparatus was set up as shown in the drawing below.

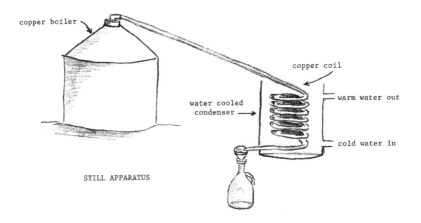

Our still set-up. Drawing by Lucas Kalathas.

After a while, the liquid in the boiler, which is continually being heated on the coal stove turns to a vapor. The vapor or gas is mainly ethyl alcohol, which has a lower boiling point than water. The vapor passed out from the boiler and down through the copper coil where it was converted back to a liquid by the cold water in the condenser. The condensed liquid (somewhat warm at this point) comes out from the spout or bottom of the coil in a small steady stream and into a gallon jug as shown. It always my job to change the jug when it was full.

The heating process continued for several hours until all the ethyl alcohol is boiled off and no more liquid comes through the spout into the gallon jug. For each batch that we distilled, we generally collected about three gallons of ethyl alcohol. There would be, of course, some water remaining in the boiler, which was discarded. We repeated this process of adding fermented liquid to the boiler and boiling off the ethyl alcohol until all of the fermented liquid in the barrel was consumed. At this point, we ended up with about12 gallons of alcohol.

Then we poured the 12 gallons of alcohol back into the empty boiler and started the heating process once again. This final phase of distillation is necessary to acquire a good quality of whiskey. We would end up with about six gallons of 180-proof alcohol.

Since 200 proof means 100% alcohol, we used water to dilute the 180 proof to 90 proof. Note, liquor purchased at a Pennsylvania "state store" is 80 proof, so our moonshine was stronger. Regular whiskey drinkers liked that. To measure the proof, I used a hydrometer, an instrument similar in shape to a thermometer. The instrument is weighted on one end and sinks into the liquid so you can read the proof similar to the way you read a thermometer.

After diluting our 180-proof whiskey to 90-proof we ended up with about twelve gallons of good quality moonshine. Since all whiskey is colorless (like water) when it comes off the still, we colored it with caramel (burnt sugar) to give it the usual light brown color. Then we stored it in a large barrel to age, which improves the taste.

There were other names for moonshine: "white lightning," "rot Gut," "happy Sally," and others. We generally called our homemade whiskey, "hooch," a common coal region term. The synonym hooch apparently came from the Hoochinoo Tribe of Alaska, noted for its homemade whiskey. However, the agents who worked for the Bureau of Alcohol, Tobacco and Firearms called it, "non-tax-paid liquor."

One day my brother-in-law, Amil Bielarski, asked if he could watch us make hooch. He just couldn't wait to taste the alcohol as it came off the still for the last time— when it was ready to drink. Normally, at that point we stored it in barrels for aging. However, Amil started to sample the hooch early and often. He humorously said, "I'm just taking a swig now and then to see if it's good." As you can imagine, he was tipsy—no, drunk by the time the distillation process was complete. It seemed he was always around to "help" when we made whiskey.

At the end of the distillation process I would dispose of the solid residue that remained in the barrel after the fermentation process was completed. It was mainly spent rye and some very ripe fruit we often added. I chose a rocky place outside our back yard to dump the rye and then covered it up. My oldest sister, Hattie, recently reminded me that Pechansky's chickens, one of our neighbors, kept pecking away until they found the rye and ate some of it. It turned out to be somewhat of an unexpected but humorous event. The chickens got tipsy. In fact, they could not stand up straight and were wobbling around the back yard. (Note: intoxication is not an exclusively human condition. Birds and animals will sometime feed on fermented fruits and grains and become intoxicated.)

When I buried the rye I was sure nothing would grow there since the soil was very bad. I was amazed the following year to see rye sprouting up from the ground. I didn't think it was a good idea to have rye growing just outside our back yard, so I quickly chopped it down and also dug up the roots. In the future, I found a place much farther away to get rid of the damn rye!

Since we made homemade moonshine regularly, we always had a fairly large amount on hand at all times. It was not unusual for us to have 40 or 50 gallons of moonshine stored in barrels in our basement. We always had several quart bottles of hooch in our kitchen cupboard. When a bottle was empty, I was usually the one who would go down to the cellar and fill up the bottle from a gallon jug. When the gallon jug was empty, I would fill it using a siphon hose from one of the 20-gallon barrels of whiskey that we always had in storage.

Even though homemade whiskey was readily available to me, I rarely drank any hooch, even when I was older. However, when I had a toothache as a kid, I would take a swig and keep it in my mouth until my jaw was numb. The moonshine left a burning sensation in my mouth, but it always dulled the pain.

We often had friends and relatives visiting us, and of course, we served them our good old homemade hooch. Since our homemade liquor was stronger, someone would usually remark how much better it was than "bought" liquor. And why not, they were getting it free?

Small whiskey glasses (shot glasses) and large whiskey glasses (double shot glasses) were always available and used at our house. We had a nice mailman who delivered our daily mail. On cold winter days, my mom would invite him in for a shot of whiskey—sometimes two. Technically, he wasn't supposed to drink on duty, but on those cold days I recall how he really enjoyed a shot of whiskey and always thanked my mom and then he was on his way.

We also sold our hooch to our friends and relatives. Some customers would bring their own bottle. My mother would often ask me to fill a small size bottle for a customer. I would place a small funnel into the small bottle and fill it from a quart bottle, which we had on hand. My mom charged them 25 cents for the small bottle and one dollar for a quart of hooch.

My impression is that most of the moonshine manufactured in the coal region was made in ordinary homes. However, we did not make homemade whiskey in large quantities for sale elsewhere simply to make a profit. Making hooch was a matter of economics (as bootleg mining was) and not a moral issue for us.

State store liquor was costly because of the high tax placed on it by the government. Consequently, most people in the coal region could not afford to pay the high price of commercial liquor. Our relatives and friends were glad that they could buy good quality hooch at a very reasonable price. I believe that was the main reason that no one ever reported us to the authorities.

To the best of my knowledge, we were the only ones in Big Mine Run that made the quantity of moonshine that we did. I'm quite sure though, that there were several other families in Big Mine Run that also made much smaller quantities than we did. However, I did know of others in the area that made homemade whiskey. Their neighbors and friends also protected them. My best guess is that there is very little homemade whiskey being made in the coal region today; although making boilo and tasting it is a cultural art and a culinary science in the Schuylkill County area during the winter holiday season to this day.

One time when we were transporting our moonshine to relatives in Philadelphia, we hid the containers of whiskey under the back seat of our car. At some point in Philadelphia a policeman stopped us. A relative of ours who was riding in the back seat quickly gave my father a piece of chewing gum to mask any liquor odor that might be on his breath. We were nervous since we didn't know why the cop whistled us to stop. As it turned out, my father made an illegal turn. When the policeman learned that we were "coal crackers" from up state, he explained what we did wrong and then let us go. That incident was the topic of conversation for several days.

We obviously knew that it was illegal to make moonshine— so we had to exercise caution. Whenever a stranger knocked on our door, we could not be sure that it was not someone checking on us. On several occasions I dumped good homemade rye whiskey down the drain in the cellar floor to destroy the evidence. I often wondered whether the alcohol affected the rats in the sewer system and I wondered if the rats looked forward to the next time I dumped some hooch down the drain.

A local Democratic politician (who was a friend of our family) would often warn us that "someone" might be coming around to check on people making homemade liquor. When we received that information, we stored our still in a pit, which we dug out in the cellar floor. Then we covered it over with old boards and placed ordinary storage boxes on top. We also hid any other items that we used to make hooch.

After all, it was us against "them revenuers."

Boozing in the Coal Region

Boozing in the coal region was quite prevalent. Barrooms were popular places where miners gathered to talk, argue and drink. Coal miners were tough and they worked hard and drank a lot; it was part of their social life. A familiar expression of the miners after a hard days work was—"a shot of whiskey with a beer chaser to wash down the coal dust."

When the anthracite industry was doing well, practically all the towns in the coal region had an unusual number of "so-called saloons." Dr. Harold W. Aurand wrote: "In the 1880s, for example, Hazleton, with a population of less than 12,000 people, maintained eighty-five taverns . . . Despite Prohibition, the small town of New Philadelphia in Schuylkill County (population 1,500) boasted thirty-five bars during the 1920s."

Dale Freudenberger of the Delaware & Lehigh National Heritage Corridor said, "Mahanoy City, with a population of about 4500, according to the 2000 Census, once boasted more than 120 bars. [It] was the barroom capital of Schuylkill County."

In other words, there was a barroom on every corner. However, at the time there were many small drinking places that weren't what we would generally call a typical or traditional saloon. They perhaps could better be described as drinking spots or crude saloons. I suspect the large number of saloons that were often reported included all types of drinking places.

During the mid 1930s, when some collieries were only operating time, the heavy drinking still went on. Many young adults in Big Mine Run, who were bootlegging coal or doing other jobs, were attracted to saloons. The ones that were particularly heavy drinkers were called "boozers."

Someone told me that Minersville had thirty-seven taprooms sometime around 1930 when the town only had about 6000 people. The number of saloons recorded from about the 1930s on would be more representative of what we generally regarded as traditional saloons. While the numbers have decreased from previous years, practically all the small towns in the coal region still had a large numbers of barrooms.

Girardville, which was just a small town about two miles away, had an unusually large number of saloons. In some places, like Second Street in Girardville, taprooms were operating right next door to each other. Many of the guys in Big Mine Run frequently visited a popular taproom in Girardville called Whitey's Place. Whitey was a popular saloon owner and when he visited my sister Hattie's saloon in Big Mine Run he would buy the drinks for everybody as long as he was there. When the word got out that Whitey was going to visit, everyone was sure to be present. Girardville was somewhat typical of all the small towns and patches in the region. They all had their share of barrooms and they all seemed to do a good business.

The young men in Big Mine Run not only drank on weekends, but many of them went to saloons during the week. Since Big Mine Run had at least one saloon, the local guys also spent time drinking there. It appeared to me that peer pressure played a big part in their behavior—it was cool to drink.

Even though Big Mine Run was just a patch it always seemed to have a saloon. Someone told me that there was a hotel and saloon (operated by the Sweeney family) located at the corner of Big Mine Run Road and Bast Avenue. I recall that it was a large brown building where people voted on Election Day. To the best of my knowledge it opened as a hotel and barroom sometime prior to 1920 and closed down about 1935. The building remained vacant until sometime in the 1950s when my sister Mary and her husband Amil Bielarski purchased the property. After tearing down the old building, they built a ranch type house on the site, which still exists to this day.

Barney and Mary Dumboski operated a saloon in Big Mine Run from about 1918 to 1988. It was a popular place since it was the only saloon in our patch during most of that time. It had an attractive bar with large mirrors and several side rooms for seating patrons. Mary Dumboski would often serve as the bar tender and sometimes her daughters would also serve behind the bar. It wasn't unusual for women to sit and drink at the bar. The saloon was located at the eastern end of Big Mine Run next door to my good friend Frank (Frankie) Adamavage. (Frankie and I played on the same high school basketball team at Butler Township in the late 1930s and early 40s.)

As kids we would stop in Dumboski's saloon on Halloween to sing and dance for a few cents. Those who wore dresses, with bloomers underneath, were told to kick their legs high up in the air when dancing. I still remember a silly little song we sang which went, "North, South, East, West, Barney Dumboski's hooch is best." We simply dressed up in any old type of clothing we found around the house. We had no store-bought Halloween outfits.

In 1946 my oldest sister, Hattie, and her husband John Pahira opened a barroom in Big Mine Run at the old Cannon residence. The saloon was about three blocks down the street from Dumboski's barroom. It was a popular drinking place since many women from the Ashland Shirt and Pajama factory frequented the barroom, and the men followed. Hattie had the usual large jars of pickled eggs and pickled sausage for customers to eat; in addition, she also served ham sandwiches and other snack foods.

All barrooms at that time were closed on Sundays. My sister Hattie's saloon (where I worked for a while before going to college) was also closed on Sunday—well, technically. However, everyone in Big Mine Run knew the back door was opened, and it was the same as if a sign was hanging on the front door that read, "Closed on Sundays, but go around to the back door." A good poker game would get started on Sunday afternoon that would go on until the wee hours of Monday morning. My sister closed her taproom in the early 1950s.

It shouldn't be too surprising that the coal region also had an unusually large number of breweries. Towns the size of Pottsville, Shenandoah (we said Shan' a door), Mahanoy City (we said monnoy city), Shamokin and Mount Carmel (we said Mon Carmel) had at least one brewery. Even a small place like Fountain springs had a brewery. Now they're all gone except for the Yuengling Brewery in Pottsville, the oldest continuing brewery in the country, and arguably one of the best.

On the other hand, the coal region also had many, many churches. Each ethnic group seemed to have its own church.

Sometimes there would be divisions and new churches established within an ethic group. The churches played an important role in the culture of the people. Even though the parishioners were poor, they supported their churches financially and also by their attendance. However, the coal region had many more saloons than churches—and the attendance in saloons was even better.

Superstitions

Superstitions originated with our ancestors and in some cases those "folk beliefs" are probably as ancient as human curiosity itself. As a child, like many others, I believed in some superstitions. And I always preferred those that brought "good luck" rather than the other kind. Some good luck superstitions that I remember were:

Finding a four-leaf clover was fun, however it was hard to find one. Of course, some cheating always went on. Someone would call out, "I found one." When we checked it out, it was always a three-leaf clover. Sometimes someone would hold several two-leaf clovers to make it look like a four-leaf clover.

Pulling apart the dried breastbone of a chicken until it cracked and broke was a favorite one. Each person would make a wish and the one who got the larger half of the wishbone would get what he or she wished for.

Losing a tooth as a child was a little disconcerting. As a reward for being "good" about it, you were told to place the tooth under your pillow when you went to sleep. Then the good fairy (usually a parent or more likely grandma) would leave you a gift of money.

Blowing out all the candles on your birthday cake with your first breath meant you would get your wish. Sometimes you got a little help in blowing out the candles, but that was all right.

Hanging a horseshoe over a doorway was supposed to bring good luck. I recall that we had one hanging over our cellar door. Do you remember though, the horseshoe had to be hung with the open end facing upward?

Carrying a rabbit's-foot was considered a good luck charm. I never had one, but some of the neighborhood kids did. One time I asked one of the kids to hold his rabbits' foot; however, after looking at it closely and touching it I was glad to hand it back to him.

Here's a few more good luck ones: At the end of a rainbow, there's a pot of gold; having a cricket in a house; crossing your fingers; an apple a day keeps the doctor away; knocking on wood and if your palm is itchy you will get some money. This one I recall was very popular and is probably so even today— for a happy marriage the bride should wear something old, something new, something borrowed and something blue.

However, I took bad superstitions more seriously. Remember the ones that were supposed to bring "bad luck?" Here are some of them: Opening an umbrella indoors; walking under a ladder; having a black cat cross your path; breaking a mirror (seven years bad luck); looking at a person who had an evil eye can do you harm; if you heard a dog howling at night, it meant that someone was going to die; stepping on cracks in the sidewalk; killing a ladybug and Friday the 13th is an unlucky day.

Some more superstitions: A cat has nine lives; If a groundhog sees its shadow, there will be six more weeks of winter; If you spilled salt, you should toss a pinch over your left shoulder to avoid misfortune.

Although many superstitions have their origins from the past, many continue to be believed even today. Consider these two for example—fortune telling and astrology. Fortunetellers have prepared answers to questions that people who come to them always ask. Of course, the customer generally gets some good news about something that will happen soon. Astrology also continues to be popular. Just look at the thousands of newspapers that regularly print an astrology column for those who believe their fate is written in the stars.

My mom was a superstitious person, and that's where I got some of my early beliefs in superstitions. However, I think it was somewhat common for immigrants of her time who didn't have a formal education to be superstitious. MY mom felt that some dreams could be interpreted to mean good things, while others could represent bad things. I remember my mom saying that dreaming about coins would bring good luck, but dreaming about paper money would bring bad luck. Dreams about clear water were good, but dreams about muddy water were bad. Also, dreams of green grass, or a field of growing crops like a field of grain was good. When I told her about a particular dream I had, she would tell me what it meant. Both of us were always glad when the dream meant that something good was going to happen, like getting money. However, I sometimes worried when she told me that a dream I had meant that something bad was going to happen. When I learned about the bad dreams, I never mentioned them to my mother because I didn't want to bring her bad news.

My mother believed if a man was the first to enter our home on New Year's Day, it was good luck. On the other hand, if a woman was the first to enter, it was bad luck.

I know my mom talked to other women about their superstitions. It was my impression that after their discussions, they all came away with even more things to be superstitious about. One of their favorite topics they talked about was fortunetellers. It seemed that there was always someone who just learned about a new fortuneteller who was very good. Pretty soon one story led to another, and after a while the name of the new person became known to everyone in the group. Since the new fortuneteller was supposedly able to see the future, many of the women felt that she could really help them with a problem.

I recall that there was a woman named Mrs. Ann Weber in Big Mine Run who was known to be a fortuneteller. She lived in a different–looking house situated all by itself across the main road in Big Mine Run. Mrs. Weber was a Protestant, however most of he customers were Catholic women. I don't know if the women considered it sinful, but in any event they went to fortunetellers. I know that some of my mother's friends went to see Mrs. Weber and they would talk to my mom about it afterward. They mentioned how she read cards and also read the palm of their hand. In particular I remember one woman saying, "She's very good." (I'll bet she was told what she wanted to hear.) I know that on occasion my mom would go to see a fortuneteller when she was seeking an answer to a difficult situation. However, as far as I know, men as a rule did not visit fortunetellers.

One summer day, when I was a young teenager, a man came to our door selling a homemade "medicine drink" he prepared. He spoke in Ukrainian, and as you can imagine he was a fancy talker. I remember him asking my mother if she ever got a pain in her shoulder and then sometimes does she get a pain in her back and so on? Well, of course she did, all hard working women experienced those pains. He said that his medicine could cure this and that; you know, a cure-all for everything. He was a slick talker and soon had my mother convinced that he knew what he was talking about. It was an example of my mother's good nature and willingness to believe in people and sometimes be deceived by them. When I realized that my mom was ready to buy his medicine, I spoke up and told the peddler that he shouldn't be practicing medicine without a license. It didn't take long for him to leave the premises fast.

When I got a little older and thought I was smarter, I tried to tell my mom not to believe in superstitions. I told her that fortunetellers could not predict future events. I told her to be wary of slick peddlers telling stories that weren't true. However, I never felt that she listened. Anyhow, who was I to tell her what to do?

Do you think there's any truth to these old superstitions? Well, as I grew older I certainly didn't think so. I said to myself that not being superstitious is what brings good luck. I believe I can live with that—or until my luck changes. Yeah! But then— why does washing my car always seem to bring on the rain?

Lastly, there is this story told about visitors who always asked a Nobel Prize winning scientist why he displayed a good-luck horseshoe above the door of his cottage. His reply was, "Of course it's nonsense, but I am told that it works even when you don't believe in it."

Second-Hand Furniture

My mom did housecleaning for three different families in Ashland for a number of years. They all liked my mother and treated her well. At times they would give my mom some furniture and other items they didn't want anymore.

One day they gave her some pieces of quality furniture, which included a desk, a Victorian sofa, several marble top tables and a marble top commode. I wanted to keep everything, because I liked old furniture, especially marble top pieces. However, my sisters didn't care for the furniture because they thought it was all old-fashioned. In fact, they left the bright red-colored Victorian sofa outside on the porch where it go wet and eventually got chopped up for firewood. I know that it doesn't make sense, but that's what we did.

In its place they bought a "modern" box-like parlor suite which was dumpy looking from my point of view. This was about the mid-1930s. It was a time when my sisters started to work in the local factory and began to earn a little money, so they wanted to buy some new furniture. The large sofa and one smaller chair were one color and the other chair was another color and that seemed to be the fashion. Also it was also a time when my three older sisters were beginning to date and they wanted new furniture to show off when their boy friends came to visit.

The families that my mom worked for also gave her old religious statues, such as St. Ann, St. Anthony and other saints. I liked them all and repaired those that were damaged and also painted some of the statues. She also brought home old dishes, glassware and similar household objects. I think that many times we gave my mom the impression that all those things were "second-hand," and not new stuff. In reality, many of them would now be antiques.

However, when I was somewhat older I made a similar mistake my sisters did. I sold some marble top pieces of furniture that were given to my mother who in turn had given them to me. They were unusual pieces and I should have kept them. However, at the time I felt that I needed some money and sold them for just a few dollars, and it was a dumb thing to do. To this day, I do not have a single piece of furniture my mother gave to me and I regret that.

St. Mary's Church in Centralia

St. Mary's Church in Centralia. Courtesy of Diane Rooney.

The official name for the church at the top of the hill in Centralia is "Assumption of the Blessed Virgin Mary Ukrainian Greek Catholic Church." However, most people in Centralia call the church St. Mary's Greek Catholic Church or simply "St. Mary's." It is located on the northern most end of the town and situated near the top of a rather steep hill facing South and overlooking Centralia. It's a white wooden church with the typical three-cross bar on top as you can see in the picture.

Construction of the church began In the fall of 1911 after an active committee received approval from bishop Soter Ortynski to build a church to accommodate the Ukrainian residents in the town and nearby communities. In order to save some money, the parishioners dug the foundation of the church themselves. The church was completed in 1912.

Several years later they established a Day School and purchased a hall and convent. It was a progressive parish that conducted concerts and put on plays. However, the parish school closed in the mid-1950s due to the lack of sisters. Later, the school building and other church properties were torn down when most of the town was demolished on account of the underground mine fire.

In reading over the history of the church I noticed a list of people who served as chairmen of the church committee from the beginning of the parish. As I read over the list I was surprised to note that I recognized the names of four of them (John Cheppa, Hryhori Bazan, Wasyl Mikash, Washl

Wolchansky). I actually knew two chairmen (Hryhori Bazan and Washyl Woclchansky) personally.

As a young child, I recall my father driving two miles to St. Mary's in Centralia where our family attended Sunday mass. There was no parking lot for cars, so we just parked our car along side of the road below the church with everybody else. It was a bit hazardous since you couldn't pull off the main road completely. However, there was not too much traffic on that road on a Sunday morning and drivers had to slow down when they saw the lined-up cars. After we parked our car, we had to climb about 25 steps to reach the basement level of the church and then another 12 steps to get inside the church. I always felt sorry for the elderly people who had to climb all those steps.

The mass at St. Mary's was almost two hours long. (The length of the mass in a typical Roman Catholic Church is about one hour.) The kids got restless and would begin to talk, but pretty soon we were told to be quiet (cicho buth). When I got bored during the mass, I would look around at the elaborate decorations and all the statues and paintings. I also would spend time looking at the icons, which were representations of sacred persons such as Christ, a saint or an angel that was usually painted on a wood surface.

The church service was in Ukrainian, and we blessed ourselves three times rather than once as they do in the Roman Catholic Mass. At one point during the mass, the priest says, "I will walk around the altar of God." At St. Mary's, the inside of the church was constructed in an unusual manner, it allowed the priest to actually walk around the altar, and he did.

After the mass was over, my parents always talked with friends outside the church. They usually chatted for a while because there were a number of different people they wanted to see. It was like a social gathering since it was the only time of the week when they got together to just talk about things in general. Meanwhile, I would roam around the church to find other kids to talk to and play with. There was a picnic ground behind the church and a cemetery just beyond the picnic area. While I played in the picnic ground, I never ventured near the cemetery because my grandparents were buried there and I didn't like visiting "that place."

One Sunday after mass, my mom and Mrs. Joseph Seder has a good laugh about something I said several days earlier. I was about eleven years old at the time and alone when Mrs. Seder came to visit my mom. I said to her, "Ya doma sa ma." That is, I'm home alone. She smiled in a comical sort of way and said good-bye and left. My mom told me later that I mistakenly used the feminine form like a girl would when I said to her that I was home alone. I guess I was trying to impress Mrs. Seder with my knowledge of the Ukrainian language, but apparently I tried too hard.

The church had a basement, which was used for social activities. It also has a stage on which plays were performed where the actors wore traditional Ukrainian dress and also spoke Ukrainian. I recall a scene in a play where a large fat man came on stage. After a few minutes he began to remove one vest after another and the audience began counting out loud—one, two, three . . . as the vests came flying off. After taking off about 20 vests, the fat man became a rather thin man.

My two older sisters, Hattie and Mary, walked to Centralia and back during the week to attend St. Mary's for religious instructions. They walked up the back road through Buck's Patch (a "real" patch that only had three or four houses) since it was slightly shorter than walking the main road through Ashland. It was a rather lonely road for two young girls to walk, but they did it. Incidentally, Buck's Patch no longer exists and a family by the name of Reilly was the last family to live there.

My mother would always take me to the cemetery with her on certain holidays when she visited our cemetery lot. It was quite common to see a number of families at the cemetery, not only to put flowers on the graves, but also to do housekeeping chores around the gravesites. I never enjoyed going with her because I didn't like visiting the graveyard, but I went anyway. I'm still that way today; cemeteries are not one on my favorite places to visit.

Many picnics were held on the grounds behind the church. These outings were held to support the church financially. You had to buy tickets to purchase a variety of Ukrainian foods along with hot dogs, hamburgers, soup, soda, ice cream, beer and other things. It seemed to me that more beer was sold than anything else and quite a few men got tipsy.

Centralia was a small typical coal region town until a minor fire in 1962, which got out of control and destroyed the town. After several decades of fighting the runaway underground coal mine fire, there was only a few houses left standing in the borough. One of the buildings that was not torn down was St. Mary's because it was situated near the top of a hill to the north, somewhat away from the main fire. However, as Centralia moved closer and closer to a ghost town, it became more difficult to keep the church open with a resident pastor, which they had for most of their history. The resident pastor lived in a home just a short walking distance to the church.

In1985, the church was placed under the care of St. Peter and Paul Ukrainian Church in Mount Carmel about two miles away. Priests from the Mount Carmel parish now administers to the congregation in Centralia. Many of the church members of St. Mary's, including my Aunt Frances Puketza, live in nearby communities and faithfully return to attend church services on Sundays and other holidays. In 1991 they celebrated their 80th anniversary.

It may see somewhat strange to people visiting the area to see a church sitting near the top of the hill with no other buildings near it. One could easily get the impression that the church is closed. However, St. Mary's is not abandoned and forgotten. It is alive and well, thanks to some strong supporters of the church who have attended services there since they were children.

Shopping in Area Towns

We always did our grocery shopping in Ashland, which was about a mile away. My mom shopped in the typical grocery store (like the A & P) in the down town area were all the stores were located. At that time you told the clerk behind a counter what you wanted and he simply reached up to a shelf and picked off the item you selected. If he had to reach for some item high up near the ceiling, he used a long handle stick that had a pair of tongs on the end to grab the item and bring it down. He continued to place your selections on the counter and checked you out when you were through.

One day a new Acme (we said Ack a me) Store opened up in town. It was located about half way up town on the right hand side somewhere near Tenth Street. The store stands out in my mind because it was the first one I remember that provided shopping carts for its customers to do their own shopping. Customers just wheeled their carts through the aisles and picked out their own groceries; it was innovative shopping at the time. Everyone was intrigued with the new way of shopping for groceries, and before too long the older smaller grocery stores where you asked for the items you wanted went out of business.

My mom always bought enough groceries for a week or so, and she referred to her large purchase as an "order." She was always surprised when the clerk totaled up the bill because it always seemed to high to her.

When it came time to buy shoes, we always went to Portz's Shoe Store in Girardville. The owner, Mr. Portz, was a friendly guy and would give my mom a small discount because we generally bought more than one pair of shoes. It was fashionable in those days for a shoe store to have some kind of x-ray machine so that you could see your foot with the shoe on, and Mr. Portz had one of those.

One day I heard my mom ask Mr. Portz why he charged $1.99 or $2.99 and so on for a pair of shoes rather than the rounded off figure of two or three dollars. He went on to explain the psychology of how people felt that $1.99 just seemed cheaper than two dollars. That is, the figure one was always larger and followed by two much smaller nines and that looked more appealing than the rounded off two dollar figure. They both had a laugh about that.

However the big shopping event was Friday and Saturday shopping in Shenandoah about eight miles to the east. When we went shopping to Shenandoah, we drove from Big Mine Run to Homesville (another patch) one-half mile away. One day my mom told me that a Roman Catholic cardinal named Dougherty was born in little old Homesville. Mary McDonald who was my teacher in the fourth and fifth grade also lived there. As we drove by her house I always looked to see if I could see her.

Then we drove on through Girardville, the home of a number of Molly Maguires who made history in the coal region about a century and a half ago. John Kehoe, one of the better-known Mollies, had a saloon in Girardville.

After leaving Girardvile we drove through Mahanoy Plane (another patch town), which was the birthplace of Jimmy and Tommy Dorsey. The Dorsey brothers moved to Shenandoah (about three miles to the east) as youngsters and were reared there. The Dorsey brothers went on to become famous musicians. Tommy (1905-56) was a trombonist and his brother; Jimmy (1904-57) was a saxophonist. Both Dorsey brothers were buried in Shenandoah Heights, just north of the town of Shenandoah.

It was over the Mahanoy Plane that anthracite coal was moved in cars from coal operations in the Mahanoy City, Gilberton, and Girardville areas. It was then hoisted up the mountainside to Frackville and delivered down the other side to coal yards in Saint Clair. From there it was put on trains and sent to city markets.

There was a colliery named East Bear Ridge in Mahanoy Plane that was built directly over the highway. I often wondered about the construction of that colliery as I drove underneath it on my way to Shenandoah. That colliery was the last place my father worked as a coal miner before becoming ill from miners' asthma.

From Mahanoy Plane we drove through Maizeville, another small village. It was a station stop for the train, which traveled from Philadelphia up state to the coal region. Girardville and Ashland were other station stops for the same train.

Finally, from Maizeville we drove up a rather steep hill to Shenandoah. At the time Shenandoah had a popular and thriving business district that included about six blocks on the main street. The population of Shenandoah was about 15,000 and the town drew shopping customers from the surrounding area. It was mainly a shopping center for blue-collar workers. That is, the type of shopping items and the prices were geared for the average family. On Friday and Saturday the main street was crowded with shoppers. The stores always advertised sales and everyone seemed to get caught up in the excitement of the bargains being offered. I remember a radio program, which played polka music that was sponsored by Siswein's Furniture Store in Shenandoah. When I was about eleven years old, my Aunt Mary, from Frackville, took me to see "Pygmalion" at the Strand Theater on Center Street in Shenandoah. The theater was located on right hand corner just as you entered Shenandoah from Maizeville. It was the witty G. B. Shaw play that became My Fair Lady. The only thing I remember about the movie is that I didn't like it.

Shenandoah had several places where people could play lottery games, which at that time were called "pools." The pool games were very popular because you could purchase a disk with a number on it for a dime. A writer would then record your name and address on a sheet of paper that corresponded to the number of the disk you purchased. The disk was tossed into a large barrel-like container. When the pools closed for the night, the large barrel-like container was revolved with a crank to mix up the disks. Individuals were selected to reach into the barrel and pull out a disk. If your number was selected you could win as much as much as one thousand dollars, which was the main prize. That was a lot of money for an average person in those days. There were other cash awards as well. The pool places were very popular and everyone played the lottery game. Other towns like Mt. Carmel and Mahanoy City also had pools.

My sisters and my mother did all the shopping. They mostly visited ladies' stories to look for bargains. The only shopping I did was to visit a large warehouse located below the Strand Theater to buy sugar or rye to make moonshine. After we were through shopping, we would get ready for our return trip home. Sometimes we would take the back road and go through East William Penn, William Penn, Lost Creek, Connerton, Girardvillle, Homesville and then to Big Mine Run.

On occasion, my sisters would go shopping in Mahanoy City, Mount Carmel or even Pottsville. However, Shenandoah was always the main shopping town for us. As the economic picture of the coal region continued to decline, the Shenandoah business district also went into a decline. The town never regained the reputation it once had as a busy shopping center for the surrounding area.

A Look Back at Woodland Park

When I was about ten years old, I enjoyed talking to our neighbor, Mrs. Bridget Colahan, who was an elderly Irish woman. She told me about Woodland Park, which was a well-known recreational area in the early 1900s located right in Big Mine Run. She said that a trolley car service brought many visitors from nearby areas to enjoy the facilities at the park.

I was surprised to hear what she said because there wasn't any clear evidence of any recreation park in the area. I became more curious about the park and wanted to know more about it. However, nobody ever talked about it or seemed to know anything about the park.

One day I recall playing in an area between Woodland Heights and Big Mine Run that had concrete foundation supports still sticking several feet above the ground and I asked Mrs. Colahan if she knew what they were. She said, "That's where the Woodland Park Theatre was." However, I didn't find out too much more about the park from any others.

However, I did find out a little more about Woodland Park by accident. As teenagers we went swimming almost every day during the summer at a place about a half-mile from Big Mine Run called the "bluey." We gave it that name because the water always appeared to be a dark blue-green color. Of course, it wasn't a regular swimming pool. It was an oval-shaped body of water, which was fed from an underground spring. As it turned out, the bluey was located close to the regular swimming pool that was part of Woodland Park in the early 1900s. However, over the years the swimming pool area had deteriorated and was completely overgrown with bushes and small trees.

One day after my swim in the bluey, I took a walk around the area and discovered the concrete remains of the Woodland Park swimming area. Most of the concrete was demolished and broken, but I could still make out the wall or breast of the dam. In fact, I walked across the top of the crumbled wall that was still there. As I continued to wander about, I was also surprised to find a cement water overflow that was also part of the pool structure, which was almost completely intact even after all those years. The concrete overflow was about ten feet wide and looked like a very wide sliding board. I remember seeing a date on the overflow and I know it was in the early 1900s, but I can't recall the actual year. I was told that a trolley car service brought visitors up to the swimming pool area as well as other parts of the park.

Some fifty years later, I was fortunate in communicating with Diane Rooney, a photojournalist and historian, who sent me the following two pictures of Woodland Park.

Entrance: This is the Woodland Park entrance from the grounds, 1906. Picture courtesy of Jean Watkins, Ashland.

Entrance to Woodland Park. Postcard, courtesy of Diane Rooney.

Woodland Park Dance pavilion, 1906.
Courtesy of Diane Rooney.

About the same time I made contact with Leonard Cooper who provided me with some information about Woodland Park. Leonard pointed out to me that even today (if you look closely) you can see evidence of the rail bed that is still visible where the trolley cars brought visitors to the park near the theater site. I was pleasantly surprised one day when Leonard sent me a picture post card (below) dated 1909 of the theater at Woodland Park. He was also helpful in confirming just where the theater was located. It was the area Mrs. Colahan had told me about some five decades ago and where I played as a kid.

Woodland Park Theater, 1909. Courtesy of Leonard Cooper.

I also learned from Les Meredith that the Schuylkill Traction Company built Woodland Park as a recreational area for its trolley customers sometime in the early 1900s. It was a popular place and people came from all over to picnic, dance, swim, and also enjoy vaudeville shows. He went on to say that the Lee Family, who owned the Lee Theater in Ashland, also conducted picture shows at the park. However, in 1929 a wage strike forced the Traction Company to go out of business and that also ended the trolley line in the region.

As times changed, Woodland Park lost its popularity and eventually the park closed. Today, there is essentially nothing remaining of Woodland Park--only memories of another time. The park has simply faded into oblivion. I'll wager that not many young people living in Big Mine Run today ever heard of Woodland Park.

Saturday at Ashland's Memorial Stadium

As a youngster I walked from Big Mine Run on Saturday afternoons to see the Ashland High School football team play their home games at Memorial Stadium. I would start out about noon and walk along the railroad tracks for about a mile before coming to Center Street at the bottom of town in Ashland. I always walked on the right hand side of Center Street, which was about a mile long and ran straight through town. I remember walking past the Mother's Memorial, then past Peter E. Buck's Hardware Store, past Dr. Robert Spencer's Office and then up to Hotel Loeper. The first seven blocks were relatively flat. I continued walking uptown (but from then on Center Street went uphill rather steeply) to the Acme Store then past the Johnny

Boris barber shop. After walking some more, I crossed over the road that went up to Centralia and finally to about Twentieth Street at the top of town where the stadium was located.

I never had money to buy a ticket so I would walk around the outside of the stadium and look for a way to get in free. A lot of other kids also did the same thing. Some youngsters who lived near the stadium would dig out crawl spaces under the solid wooden fence during the week prior to the game. Sometimes I was able to crawl in through one of the holes dug underneath the fence surrounding the stadium. However there were guards watching out for "sneak ins" on the inside, so you had to be careful not to get caught. As soon as you made it inside you would have to run and get lost in the crowd of people.

Sometimes I was even able to climb up on some piled-up boxes (with the help of other kids) and then climb over the fence, which was about nine feet high. Scaling the fence was difficult because several strands of barbed wire ran along the top, and more than once I got snagged in the barbed wire. In those cases, the guards on the inside hauled me down, scolded me and then tossed me out of the park with enthusiasm to set an example. However, there were times when I made it over safely and got lost in the crowd.

On occasion, there would be a promotional event where an adult could take a child in free. I would stand around the ticket counter looking for some guy who was by himself and ask if I could walk in with him. Sometimes the guy would laugh and say, "Okay kid, come on," and as soon as I got inside I would go off by myself. There were times when I was not able to get in, so I would linger around on the outside of the stadium because the guards always opened up the gates half way through the fourth quarter and then I would just walk right in.

When I got inside, I did not always watch the game. There was a lot of space inside the stadium and I would just wander around. Sometimes I would run about and play football with other kids. It was a lot of fun to run out on the playing field and play after the game was over.

When most of the crowd left, I would start walking back down Center Street on my way home. Sometimes people who were sitting on their front porch would ask me who won and I was always happy to tell them when Ashland won and to also tell them the score. As I continued to walk home I would start thinking about the next home game. At the next home game, I would do the same thing all over again.

Ashland High School Football—Its Greatest Year

It was 1935, a memorable year for the Ashland High School football team. The Ashland Black Diamonds played a difficult schedule and won every game; it was an undefeated season. Ashland was the eastern conference winner and traveled to Altoona, the western conference winner, to play for the state championship. All Schuylkill County was proud when Ashland defeated a very tough Altoona team in a close game to become state champions. It was arguably the best Ashland High School football team of all time. Here's how it all happened.

Ashland won its first game of the season with a 39-0 victory over Porter Township. While Ashland was favored, it was still an impressive win since the game was played on a very wet field. However, it was too early in the season to determine how good the Ashland team was after the first game. Scoring touchdowns: Simononis (2), Brunzdo (I), Reichwein (1), Joe Rettinger (1), C. Umlauf (1).

The following week Ashland traveled to Pottsville where they played before a record crowd of over 7000 fans. Ashland's coach, Alvin "Doggie" Julian, would have preferred to face a less formidable team so early in the season because Pottsville had a strong team and was favored to win. Pottsville scored early and led 7-0 at the end of the first quarter. Ashland came back to tie the score in the second quarter and the half ended 7-7. Both teams played hard, but neither team was able to score in the third quarter. Ashland scored in the fourth quarter to upset Pottsville and win by a score of 13-7. Brundzo and Bogachinskie both played well on offense for the Black Diamonds. Scoring touchdowns: Bogachinskie (1), Brundzo (1).

Ashland won its third game of the season against the Pennsylvania Institute for the Deaf (PID) by a score of 34-0. In the mid-1920s, the PID had a remarkably strong team. In a four-year period, they won 33 games and only lost three. They managed to score 826 points against their opponents 93.

However, this year Ashland had a powerful team and won an easy victory. The score was 26-0 at the half, so Coach Julian was able to play many of his substitute players in the second half. Scoring touchdowns: Simononis (2), Bogachinskie (1), Campbell (1), Umlauf (1).

The following week Ashland played Reading, a city ten times the size of Ashland. The game was played before a large crowd of over 5000 fans at Ashland's Memorial Stadium. Ashland led 7-0 at the end of the first quarter. Then Reading came back to tie the score 7-7 at halftime. Ashland went on to score in the third and also in the final quarter to win by a score of 20-7. It was an impressive victory and Ashland was beginning to get more attention from other teams in the eastern conference. Scoring touchdowns: Simononis (1), Bogachinskie (1), Reichwein (1).

The next week Ashland played Berwick. The Black Diamonds were a solid favorite to win, so it was a surprise that the score was 7-7 at the end of the first quarter. Ashland roared back to score in the next three quarters including a 15-point spree in the final quarter. Ashland won convincingly, the final score was 36-7. Brundzo had an 85-yard run for a touchdown. Scoring toudhdowns: Brundzo (2), Simononis (2).

Ashland's next game was against Mount Carmel Township. After running up a 27-6 lead, Coach "Doggie" Julian put in some of his reserve players. Mount Carmel Township then scored several touchdowns, but the game was never in doubt. Simononis, Ashland's flashy halfback made a brilliant 85-yard run for a touchdown, the longest run in the game. The Black Diamonds won 27-20. Touchdowns scored: Simononis (2), Bogachinskie (1), Joe Rettinger (1).

The following week Ashland played Shamokin. The Black Diamonds were not able to get going offensively; however Shamokin did well and scored in the first and second quarters and led 12-0 at the half. Coach "Doggie" Julian must have had plenty to say in the locker room. Ashland scored a touchdown in the third quarter and then rolled up an additional 26 points in the final quarter to win 32-12. Scoring touchdowns: Brundzo (3), Bogachinskie (1), Reichwein (1).

Ashland's next opponent was Bethlehem, another city ten times the size of Ashland. Coach "Doggie" Julian's team was the underdog and many fans felt that this game would be their toughest they played all season. Even though Bethlehem won the state championship the previous year, they were no match for Doggie Julian's team. Ashland led 7-0 at the end of the first quarter and continued to dominate the game leading 20-6 at halftime. Ashland's offensive was impressive; they scored in the last two quarters and won the game by a score of 32-6. It was a major upset and a telling game for the Black Diamonds. Scoring touchdowns: Simononis (2), Bogachinskie (1), Brundzo (1), Joe Rettinger (1).

The following week Ashland played Shenandoah at home before a record-breaking crowd. Shenandoah had a strong team and they were determined to defeat the Black diamonds who were on their way to an undefeated season. The game not only drew a great deal attention since they were evenly matched, but there was a lot of betting on the game. Brundzo scored in the first quarter and Ashland led 6-0. In the second quarter, Brundzo threw a pass to Simononis for touchdown and Ashland led 12-0 at the half. The game went back and forth in the second half with both teams moving the ball but unable to score. Ashland dominated the game making 18 first downs to only one for Shenandoah. The Black Diamonds stunned the Shenandoah Blue Devils with a 12-0 victory. Scoring touchdowns: Simononis (1), Brundzo (1).

Ashland traveled to Minersville for its final game of the season. The game was played before a crowd of over 5000 fans in a drizzling rain. The inclement weather resulted in the game being played mainly on the ground with Ashland's powerful running game taking over. Bogachinskie scored in the first quarter and Ashland led 6-0. Brundzo then scored and Coach Julian's team led 13-0 at the half. Ashland's running game continued to prevail with Brundzo scoring in the fourth quarter. The final score was 19-0. Scoring touchdowns: Brundzo (2), Bogachinskiie (1).

It was an unforgettable season for Coach "Doggie" Julian and the Ashland High School football team. Ashland, the smallest town in the eastern conference, was now selected to play Altoona for the state championship. It was a coach's dream come true.

Ashland High School record for the season:

Ashland 39	Porter Township 0
Ashland 13	Pottsville 7
Ashland 34	P I D 0
Ashland 20	Reading 7
Ashland 36	Berwick 7
Ashland 27	Mt. Carmel Township 20
Ashland 32	Shamokin 12
Ashland 32	Bethlehem 6
Ashland 12	Shenandoah 0
Ashland 19	Minersville 0

The powerful Altoona team also went undefeated and had an impressive year. Altoona High School record for the season:

Altoona 34	Williamsburg 0
Altoona 27	DuBois 0
Altoona 54	Westmont 0
Altoona 26	Lewistown 7
Altoona 19	Lock Haven 0
Altoona 6	Clearfield 6
Altoona 18	Pitt South 7
Altoona 7	Johnstown 7
Altoona 26	Huntingdon 0
Altoona 27	Portage 0
Altoona 54	Tyrone 0

Ashland was now facing its biggest game of the year. Everyone agreed that the game would be very close with Altoona being a slight favorite to win. For all you football buffs out there, here is the starting lineup for the state championship game with Altoona.

Position	Ashland	Altoona
L. E.	Joe Rettinger	Lloyd Ickes (C)
L. T.	John Rettinger	Tony Grassi
L. G.	John Umlauf	Harold Klein
C.	Harvey Bennetlhum	Mike Patronik
R. G.	Marlin Quick	Tom Corbo
R. T.	Edward McCutcheon	Bob Thompson
R. E.	William Rothermel	John Carothers
Q. B.	John Bogachinskie	Kenneth Simms
L. H.	Charles Umlauf	Leroy Patterson
R.H.	John Simononis	Ernie Harf
F. B.	Brundzo (C)	Bill Hardaker

Ashland Coaches: Alvin F. "Doggie" Julian, Russell Crosby, and Lloyd Daub. Altoona Coaches: Edward F. (Snaps) Emanuel, Kenneth Bashore, and Richard Bartholomew.

The Championship Game

This championship game (although I did not see it) stands out in my mind more than any other game. The game was played in Altoona on December seventh on a Saturday afternoon. It was a wet drizzling day and that held down the scoring.

Ashland won the toss and elected to receive. Altoona kicked to the Ashland six-yard line where it was picked up by Brundzo and retuned to his own 16. After one running play. Simononis's kick went out of bounds on the Ashland 45-yard stripe. After two running plays, Altoona punted to the Ashland ten-yard line. Ashland punted right back, but Simononis's kick was blocked and the ball rolled into the end zone and resulted in a safety for Altoona. Even though Ashland got off to a poor start early in the game, the rest of the first quarter was hard fought with neither team threatening to score. The first quarter ended with Altoona leading 2-0.

The second quarter got under way with Ashland starting on its own 27-yard line. The next play was the highlight of the entire game. Bogachinskie skirted right end and raced down the field for fifty yards. It was considered to be one of the most sensational runs ever seen on the Altoona field in sometime considering the poor condition of the field. Another nice run around right end took the ball down to the Altoona three-yard line. On the next play Brundzo crashed through for a touchdown. The try for the extra point failed, and Ashland led 6-2. Neither team was able to put on a sustained drive for the remainder of the second quarter. The half ended with Altoona in possession of the ball on its own 32-yard line. Ashland led 6-2.

The third quarter started with Altoona returning Ashland's kick off back to their own 37-yard line. Three running plays took the ball to the Ashland 31-yard line. Ashland called time out. Several more running plays advanced the ball to the seven-yard line, where Altoona's sustained drive was finally halted and Ashland took over. After making a first down, the Black Diamonds punted out of danger to the Altoona 22-yard line. The rest of the third quarter was mainly a kicking game with neither team threatening to score. The third quarter ended with the score 6-2 in favor of Ashland.

The fourth quarter started with Ashland holding the ball on its own 32-yard line. After making a first down, Ashland punted to the Altoona 28-yard line. Again, both teams punted back and forth with neither team being able to maintain any consistent offense. Late in the game Altoona returned a punt to the Ashland 45-yard line. Then Altoona put on a nice drive and the Altoona crowd roared sensing it was their last chance to score. Altoona advanced the ball to the Ashland 35-yard line. However, time was running out. Altoona drove to the Ashland 19-yard line where they lost the ball on downs. The Black Diamonds took over but were unable to move the ball. Ashland punted out of danger once again to the Ashland 48-yard line. With very little time remaining, a Patterson pass completed to Peters took the ball to the Ashland 28-yard line. With only seconds left to play, Patterson faded back to pass, but Reichwein intercepted Patterson's pass on the18-yard line and returned the ball to the Ashland 25-yard line as the game ended. Scoring touchdowns: Bogachinskie (1).

Ashland narrowly defeated a powerful Altoona team by a score of 6-2. It was the fewest points either team had scored all year. It was the biggest victory in the history of Ashland High School football. The entire coal region was proud that the Black Diamonds won. I was 11 years old and I was proud too.

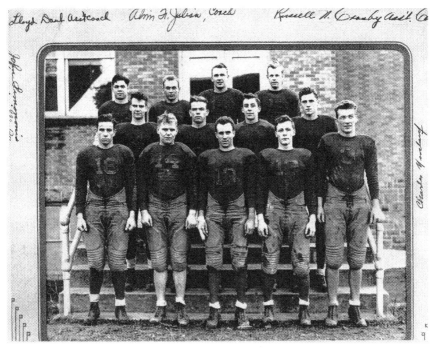

Ashland High School State Championship team—1935. Courtesy of Dottie Miller, North Schuylkill Jr./Sr. High School. Members of the team. First row, left to right: John Rettinger, Edward McCutcheon, Harvey Bennethum, John Umlauf and Marlin Quick. Second row, William Rothermel, Joseph Rettinger, Charles Umlauf and William Sell. Third row, John Simononis, John Bogachinskie, William Brundzo and Francis Reichwein. Names: Courtesy of James Klock, Ashland Area Historic Preservation Society

This contest was the 13th state title football game to decide the Pennsylvania conference champion since the conference was organized in 1922. Ashland was the second coal region team to win the state title. Mt. Carmel, the first coal region team to win defeated Bellefonte 7-6 in 1927.

An understandable error occurred during the championship game. The drizzling rain and soggy field made playing condition difficult. In addition, the players' uniforms were covered with mud and their numbers could not be read clearly by the press. As a result, Simononis was given credit for the 50-yard run that Bogachinskie had actually made that paved the way for the only touchdown scored in the game. However, the next day's edition of the Pottsville Republican newspaper corrected the error.

The best high school football player I ever saw was Al Simononis, who played in the mid-1930s, and was one of the many heroes in the championship game. I felt that if "Simmy" (as he was called) had gone on to college, he would have been a star football player. Simmy was also a very good baseball player and had a tryout with the Boston Red Sox as an outfielder.

I remember seeing Simmy and Brundzo in Big Mine Run often. Why was that? Well, Simmy had girl friend named Evelyn Dumboski, whose parents had a saloon in Big Mine Run. Brundzo, the captain of 1935 championship team, was dating Irene, Evelyn's older sister. So Big Mine Run played a role (in a way) in this greatest of all football seasons for Ashland High School.

Alvin "Doggie" Julian was the Ashland High School coach in basketball, baseball and football from 1933-35. After leaving Ashland, he went on to have an extraordinary successful career in coaching sports at other schools including the college ranks and even at the professional level.

Ashland's Mothers' Memorial

Ashland's Mothers' Memorial. Courtesy of Diane Rooney.

After writing about my own mother, I thought I would write a short story about a very special memorial that pays tribute to all mothers. The memorial that I'm proudly referring to is unique, and it's only found in Ashland, Pennsylvania, my hometown.

The dedication Of Ashland's Mothers' Memorial ceremony took place on Sunday, September 4, 1938 at the 38th reunion of the ABA. Mrs. Mary Wilson (91) and Mrs. Elizabeth Schmidt (88), two of Ashland's oldest mothers unveiled the monument, which is a replica in bronze of Whistler's painting of his mother. Immediately after the unveiling, a hush came over the crowd and then there was cheering and applauding. At the time, I was fourteen years of age and beginning my sophomore year at Butler Township High School.

The impressive monument, a bronze figure almost twelve feet high, is set on a five-foot granite base weighing over eight tons. The memorial, which is located at the northern end of Hoffman Boulevard and Center Street, sits on a hillside overlooking the town. It stands as a perpetual tribute to the mothers of Ashland.

Mothers' Memorial. Courtesy of Vincent J. Genovese.

The Ashland Boys' Association (ABA) was chiefly responsible for raising $6000 for the erection of the monument. The

Mothers' Memorial was designed by Emil Siebern and sculpted by Julius C. Loester. They were from New York City, and they both attended the dedication ceremony. The Honorable M. M. Burke, of Shenandoah, a former Ashland resident who was Chancellor of the Schuylkill County Bar Association delivered the dedication address. The distinctive stone construction and steps that lead up to the memorial from street level were built as a project of the Works Progress Administration (WPA) during President Franklin Delano Roosevelt's Administration.

The inspiration for the memorial came from James Whistler's well-known painting, often referred to as "Whistler's Mother." An inscription on the memorial reads, "this is a reproduction in bronze of Whistler's famous painting. It honors all mothers, past and present and is the only one of its kind in the country." It was the first time that a well-known painting was depicted in bronze.

James Whistler (1834-1903) originally called the painting of his mother, "Arrangement in Grey and Black." It's an 1871 oil painting approximately four and one-half feet by five and one-half feet. The famous painting resides in Paris, but occasionally goes on tour worldwide.

In the fall of 2003, Mary 0. Bradley of the Harrisburg Patriot-News, interviewed James Klock one of the founders of the Ashland Area Historic Preservation Society. Klock said, "The memorial is a popular attraction. It's unique. We feel it's the only one in the world dedicated to mothers." He also pointed out that, "In 1994 the statue was cleaned and the green patina was removed. [Then] a was coating was applied giving the memorial a dark bronze color."

For almost seven decades, this work of art at Ashland stands majestically as a tribute to motherhood. Perhaps it's best said by a quotation at the memorial adapted from a poem by Samuel Taylor Coleridge which reads, "A mother is the holiest thing alive."

Bradley, Mary 0. "Ashland's Mother's Memorial stands as tribute." The Patriot-News, 12 Sept. 2003, Sec. E p.1.

Chapter 3

STORIES ABOUT DUMB THINGS I DID

As you soon will see, sometimes I'm wrong, and sometimes I even admit it. One day I got to thinking about some dumb things I did as a young kid. Then I thought how dumb it would be to write about such things, but as you can see I changed my mind. On the other hand, St. Augustine said, "The confession of evil works is the first beginning of good works."

Stuck on the Bridge

One very cold winter day, when I was about ten years old, I was walking across a railroad bridge in Big Mine Run. I stopped to touch the gray galvanized steel pipe railing with my bare hands. The three-inch diameter pipe seemed colder than the weather itself. Then for some unknown reason, I stuck out my tongue and placed it on the pipe and a damn funny thing happened. My tongue was actually stuck to the pipe. I became quite scared and tried to glance about but no one was around. But then, what could anyone do? All I could do was to just stand there and wait.

After what seemed a very long time, but probably was only fifteen seconds, the heat from my tongue was enough to warm the pipe a little and my tongue came loose. For sometime, my poor tongue felt very, very numb inside my mouth. For a while I wasn't entirely sure that I got all of it back. As I looked about,

I didn't see anyone and I was glad that nobody saw me. I don't believe I ever told anyone about this incident, and I think you can easily see why.

Challenging a Freight Train

In Big Mine Run, one railroad track crossed another at right angles; however, the upper railroad was about fifty feet above the lower one. The upper railroad ran across a bridge that was constructed in such a manner that you could see directly through the bridge down to the railroad below as you walked across.

One summer day as I was walking across the higher railroad bridge, I noticed a freight train on the lower railroad track a short distance away. It appeared to me that the smokestack on the approaching engine below would only have a small amount of clearance when it passed underneath. I was curious as to what it would feel like to stand directly over the huge smokestack on the engine as it passed directly below me.

I quickly positioned myself so I was standing at a point where I would be right over the blast of hot air and smoke coming directly from the smoke stack on the engine below. The chugging train was hauling a long line of freight cars and a lot of dark smoke was shooting upward from the smokestack of the engine. As the train got closer, I felt myself holding on to the railing of the bridge as tight as I could. However, I became frightened as the huge train came huffing and puffing right toward me. It was too late to run, so I actually closed my eyes and held on for dear life. The train made a deafening noise and the tremendous blast from the engine was much, much greater than I had anticipated. In a moment I was completely enveloped with a terrific rush of hot air, smoke and soot. I surely thought I was going to be blown high into the air, but it was over quickly.

After the engine passed, I opened my eyes for a second but couldn't see anything and I found it difficult to breathe. It was a very scary event and I walked away feeling very foolish. Later on when I felt safe, I somehow felt a little better about my experience. Still later when I came to my senses, I realized that it was not a very clever thing to do.

Smoking as a Kid

I was about seven years when I had my first experience smoking a pipe with, my buddy, Nicky Pechansky. We got some corn silk that turned brown, and since it looked like tobacco we tried smoking it in a corncob pipe that we made ourselves. We soon learned that it didn't taste very good; however, we saw the big guys doing it (they actually smoked tobacco) so we thought we would also try it. As it turned out, my mom caught us and took away the pipe but didn't scold us.

Practically every young kid in Big Mine Run smoked at one time or another. At that time a cigarette or "ciggie" cost one penny. However, if we didn't have any pennies—and that was usually the case—then we would walk along side of the highway looking for partially smoked cigarettes that passing motorists threw out the window. We called them "stumpies." One kid would walk on one side of the highway and another would walk on the opposite side of the road. If you happened to find a discarded ciggie that was only half smoked, you would call out to your buddy about the good luck you had.

After walking for about a half-mile, we would have a pocket full of cigarettes that we picked up so we would start back. When we got home we would tear off the cigarette papers from the stumpies and end up with a small pile of cigarette tobacco. We put the loose tobacco in a pipe and smoked it. We also took the loose tobacco and made it into homemade cigarettes. It did not take us too long to figure out why grown-ups smoked tobacco and not corn silk. While we did smoke, we did not smoke seriously; it was more of an experiment or a "copy cat" thing we did since we saw adults do it all the time.

Then we got the bright idea of trying to hitchhike a ride as we walked along the highway looking for stumpies. We would stick out our thumb at the passing motorists to see if anyone would give us a lift. Of course, none of the cars ever stopped to give us a ride. However, in a few cases we would get a lift from some slow moving pick-up truck that was hauling some junk. The driver would tell us to jump in the back and off we went. In those few cases when we did get a ride, we found that we always had to walk back home.

When the Farmer Came Around

Farmers came around regularly in small pick-up trucks peddling their produce in Big Mine Run. They sold live poultry, eggs, a variety of fruits and all kinds of vegetables at reasonable prices. It was a convenient way for families to purchase food items without going to town. However, the kids in the neighborhood also took advantage of the farmers' visits, but in a different way.

My mom would leave our house and walk out to the farmer's truck to see what kind of produce he was selling. Other women would also do the same thing. In most cases, they always bought something. Whenever anyone made a large purchase like a sack of potatoes or a bushel of apples, the farmer would carry it over to the yard in front of the house or sometimes take it into the cellar for the customer.

When the farmer left his truck unattended for just a little while, we would steal apples and run off somewhere to eat them. Sometimes we would take other kinds of fruit, but it was always something small. We never really thought it was outright stealing. The farmer had a lot of apples and it did not seem like a terribly bad thing if we took an apple or two. In a twisted sort of way, we probably looked upon the farmer's visit as a "meals-on-wheels" opportunity for us!

Sometimes the farmer would bring his young son along. He would serve as a watch person when the farmer had to leave his truck unattended for a short time. However, the farmer's son was usually a young kid so that did not bother us. Besides, we were good runners and we felt we could outrun someone if we had to.

The farmer, who was a nice guy, noticed that it was always Nicky Pechansky, George Mickle and myself that always stole his apples. One day he gave each of us an apple and told us to keep an eye on his truck and not let other kids steal anything. That's all that it took, we got a free apple and we also felt important. We were the police now, and yes, we chased the other kids away.

In Big Mine Run there was a custom that was generally followed when eating an apple. If someone asked for "cobbs" while you were eating an apple, you would have to leave a bite or two on your apple and then pass it on to the person who asked for cobbs. Rarely did anyone eat an entire apple if someone else asked for cobbs—it just wasn't done. Once in a while a second kid would call out cobbs, so then one apple was shared with two other kids. I don't know where the term cobbs came from, It seems that it was just one of a number of slang words we used or made up in Big Mine Run.

One day I noticed a farmer trading a sack of potatoes for a bag of coal. I was only a youngster, and it was the first time I saw two adults barter. While I was curious and surprised about trading one item for another, I learned later that it was not an uncommon thing to do in the coal region at that time.

Riding the Freight

Fast freight and passenger trains used the main Reading Railroad Line that ran east and west about a quarter-mile from Big Mine Run. The track line ran along the base of a mountain and could readily be seen from Woodland Heights. I was about twelve years old when I heard the older guys bragging about hitching a ride on one of the fast moving freight trains. Something told me it wasn't a good thing to do. However, it sounded like an adventurous thing to try, but I did not realize then that it was a dangerous thing to do.

It is difficult to appreciate how fast a train is moving unless you're standing right next to it. On occasion a fast freight train would slow down for a short while (but still going pretty fast), as it went past Big Mine Run. That was only time we were able to climb aboard to get a free ride.

After the train speeded up, it was difficult to jump off safely. On several occasions we had to stay aboard until the train got to the next town when it would slow down or come to a stop. It was a scary feeling for a young kid to be aboard a fast moving train and not being able to get off. When we were finally able to hop off, we were damn glad to leave the train and did not mind walking several miles back home.

There's a correct way to hop on and off a fast-moving freight train. When attempting to hop aboard a freight train, you have to run very fast along side the train. Then as you reach up and grab the rung on the car you have to be prepared for a good tug you get from the moving train as you're pulled aboard. When getting off (which is much more difficult), you have to be ready to run fast in the direction the train is moving the moment you hit the ground; otherwise, you could easily tumble over and land under the moving train. I had several bad experiences when I fell after jumping off a moving freight because I did not know how to get off properly. On at least two occasions I tumbled over as I hit the ground and almost rolled under the train. Those two scary incidents I had leaving a moving train were a good teaching lesson for me to mend my ways.

It seemed that every time I hitched a ride on a train, I was seen by one of my three older sisters or someone else "snitched" on me. When I returned home, one of my sisters would always ask why I was riding the freight and then reprimanded me before I could answer. After several scoldings, I stopped riding the trains. I don't believe it was my common sense altogether, but also my fear that my sisters would tell my parents, especially my father.

Playing With Torpedoes

One of the tough characters in Big Mine Run was a guy named Charles "Gyppo" Young. He always seemed to be doing things that eventually got him into trouble. One day while walking along the railroad tracks with several other kids, I saw him throwing rocks at a small object on top of the railroad track. It looked like a strange thing to do, but suddenly something even stranger happened next. Gyppo hit the object on the track and it exploded with a flash and a loud bang. For some unknown reason we called the device that exploded "torpedoes."

The torpedo that Gyppo exploded was about two inches long and as thick as a ballpoint pen. The torpedoes were wrapped with a thin lead sheet, and each one had a short twisted portion of lead at each end, which was used to fasten it to the track. They resembled salt-water taffy candies in appearance and size.

The torpedoes were exploding devices that railroad workers fastened across the track to send a signal to other trains that came along later. For example, when the next train ran over one exploding device, it would go off with a loud bang. When two torpedoes were spaced slightly apart on the track, the engineer would hear two consecutive bangs.

These exploding devices were not to be tampered with, removed or destroyed because erroneous information would then be sent to the passing engineer. It was a serious matter since the misleading signal could possibly result in a train accident. But Gyppo would simply take them off the tracks and carry them around in his pocket, or he would explode them by throwing rocks at them.

I often noticed them lying on top of the tracks as I walked by. On one or two other occasions, some of my buddies and I also threw stones at torpedoes that were fastened on the tracks; however, we never hit any causing them to explode. At the time we did not know how dangerous it was to tamper with them.

I recall Gyppo giving me one and I just stood there holding it in my hand and looking at it. These exploding devices would not explode by themselves. Nevertheless, they were not things that kids should handle. When they exploded, small pieces of lead metal went flying all over the place and if by chance one would explode in your hand, you would be seriously injured. When I finally found out what the torpedoes were used for and how dangerous they were, I did not handle them anymore. I did not bother with Gyppo anymore either. Could it be that I was getting more common sense?

Looking for Fruit Trees

It seemed that we always had plenty of time on our hands so we were constantly looking for something to do, We were never lacking for suggestions, because someone would say, Let's do this" and another person would say, "No, Let's do something else" and so it went. One thing we generally agreed on was to search for fruit trees growing in the wild. Apple, peach, plum and pear trees were the most common ones we found.

Not far from our home there was a huge pile of discarded slate and rock (culm bank) from processing coal at the breaker near the Bast Colliery. It was as large as a mountain and we would climb it to look for peaches. For some reason, several peach trees with nice peaches started to grow at the very top. The trees probably got started when some breaker boys tossed peach stones into the slate pile and they ended up at the top of the rock pile and flourished. When we finally reached the peach trees, we would start eating them until we were full. Then we would stuff our pockets with some more and climb back down the mountain.

Most of the time we would eat the peaches before they were ripe. We called the small, green, hard unripe peaches, "colliery marbles." Even though we knew they were not ripe, we ate them anyhow. Of course, there were times when we got sick, but somehow we toughed out the stomach pains. Then next year, we did the same thing all over again.

It was also common for many families to grow fruit trees on their own property. Can you guess what's coming next? Of course, we kept a close watch on those trees as the fruit ripened. When the time was ripe (pardon the pun), we would sneak in the yard at night and help ourselves to apples, peaches, plums, grapes or whatever fruit we found. Then we would find a quiet place to sit down and eat what we stuffed in our pockets, and we always ate more than we should.

Chewing Birch Bark

Another one of those silly things we did as kids in Big Mine Run was to chew on black birch bark. It was one of those peer pressure things we did to some extent; this is, if some kids were doing it then other kids also wanted to do it.

We would break off a small branch about the thickness of an ordinary pencil from a birch tree. Then we would put it in our mouth and turn it around to strip off the bark with our teeth, like you would eat corn off the cob. The bark, which had a dark black color, came off very easy. We chewed on it like you would ordinary food, but we did not swallow it right away. Sometimes we would strip off enough bark so that it looked like we had a jaw full of tobacco in our mouth. Of course, we would always spit a lot like the older guys that chewed regular tobacco.

The bark had a typical sweet birch-like taste and of course we talked our selves into believing it was better than it was. After chewing on it for a while, we would sometimes even swallow it. While we got some fiber content, we didn't know anything about that at the time. Oh, and by the way, we got one other thing—a good old stomachache.

Fighting With Slingshots

One of our favorite things that we made was a slingshot. The slingshot was a Y-shaped stick, which we cut from a branch of a small tree that had an elastic strip attached to each prong. The other two ends of the elastic strips were attached to a piece of thin leather or other material about one and one-half inches square. The material we generally used came from the tongue of an old shoe. If you look at the picture, you can see how a slingshot works.

You take a small round stone or similar object and place it in the leather pad and hold it together with your thumb and forefinger. Then you hold the lower portion of the Y-shaped stick with your other hand, and stretch out the elastic strips about two feet and let go of the stone. Wham—the stone flew like a bullet, but not always on target to the object you aimed at.

While a slingshot was not very accurate, it did shoot a small stone a considerable distance and with a lot of force. It could be a dangerous thing if you were careless, because the flying stone could injure a person. For the most part though, we shot stones at cans, bottles and sometimes at birds (although

Using a Slingshot.

we never hit one). There were times however, that we did shoot stones at each other and that was dumb, maybe stupid is a better word.

When we weren't using our slingshot, we carried it around in our back pocket with the two elastic strips hanging down outside the pocket. We always wanted to be sure that others saw it as we walked around the patch.

Chapter 4

STORIES ABOUT HARD COAL

The Rise and Fall of the Bast Colliery

The Bast Colliery. The photo is from 1885 by George Bretz.
Courtesy of Diane Rooney.

This brief history of the Bast Colliery mirrors the history of many other collieries in the anthracite region with some variation in dates of when things happened. The Bast Colliery was located one-quarter of a mile west of Big Mine Run. For many years it was the main employer for most men in Big Mine Run as well as others in the general vicinity.

The original digging to start the colliery occurred in 1853. And the first tenant houses were built for workmen in 1854. However, it was not until 1859 that the first shipment of over five thousand tons of coal was made. By 1890 they rebuilt the old breaker and new machinery was installed.

The Bast Colliery. The photo is from 1890 by George Bretz. Courtesy of Diane Rooney.

Safety procedures were not a top priority for the owners of the collieries. The owners were generally forced to comply with increased safety measures for miners; and in many instances, new safety programs were only introduced at the collieries after some mining disaster.

In the early years of mining, it was common to see precautionary multilingual information signs regarding safety which were posted in various places because workers came from different backgrounds and many could not speak English.

In some cases, early mine workers were known to use canaries to detect the presence of lethal gas. The canaries did not sing when lethal gas was present, because they were dead. Sometimes a dog or a lighted lamp would be lowered down into a shaft to detect poisonous gases. The older experienced miners (who were quite superstitious) would often say that you have to watch and see what the rats were doing. The miners felt that the rats could detect lethal gas or a creaking roof that was about to fall and that the rats would hurry out fast. If you were smart, you would follow the rats out.

Eventually fire bosses were employed who had the responsibility for determining whether conditions were safe for the miners to start their working day. They would inspect the mine for the presence of noxious gases, dangerous roofs or ceilings and other hazards. The fire bosses checked the mine for asphyxiating gases, which settled to the lower areas of the mine. They also tested for explosive gases that rose and collected in pockets in overhead regions where the miners worked.

Anthracite mining was always difficult and dangerous; it was not for the faint-hearted. It was perhaps more dangerous than any other occupation. Thousands of men lost their lives, countless others were injured and many thousands contracted the deadly black lung disease. However, it took many, many years before miners were able to achieve reasonably safe working conditions.

The anthracite strike of 1902 was a major event. It lasted for about five months and created a national crisis. Factories shut down, hospitals closed, schools closed and of course unemployment rose. It was the first time the President of the United States intervened in a labor management arbitration matter. President Theodore (Teddy) Roosevelt brought the two sides together in order to settle the dispute. After months of wrangling, both parties signed an agreement. While the miners did receive some benefits including a wage increase, management also got some concessions such as an open shop. John Mitchell and Clarence Darrow were the main advocates supporting the miners in their dispute with the coal companies.

In 1917, an electric lighting system was installed throughout the Bast Colliery. However, improvements in working conditions for the miners have always come slowly. And bargaining for better wages was just as difficult. It took many years for wages and working conditions to improve.

While mine workers felt that by going out on strike was one way of getting the coal companies to listen to their concerns, it did not always turn out that way. There were two long strikes, one in 1922 (163 days) and another in 1925-26 (165 days) that turned out to be serious setbacks for the Anthracite Industry.

Of course, there were numerous times when workers went out on strike for just short periods of time. As a very young kid, probably about seven or eight years old, I recall some old time miners talking about going out on strike because of some unfair practice by the coal operators. They would say, "Mus be strike! Mus be strike!"

The general public was beginning to become more and more concerned with continued strikes in the coal industry. Many consumers began to feel that the industry was not dependable since the unions could call a strike at any time they chose to do so. Gradually the demand for Anthracite Coal decreased and many collieries began to work only three days a week rather than full time. In addition, increased strip mining and other consolidated operations also led to many miners being laid off. So there was a serious depression in the hard coal region several years before the big depression hit the nation at large in the late 1920s.

The Bast Colliery, as I remember it. Circa 1920.

By 1928 the total shipments of coal from the Bast Colliery was over nine and one-half million tons! However, only six years later in the fall of 1934, when I was ten years old, the Bast Colliery closed down. Other collieries also followed or slowed down their operations and economic conditions turned bad. Ironically, some families that could afford it, switched to using oil burners to heat their homes. In Big Mine Run, as well as other places, the miners were unemployed and there was simply no other work available. In the mid-1930s, approximately 20% of the families were receiving some form of relief (more recently called welfare).

The people had to make a living somehow, so bootlegging coal or the beginning of individual coalholes got started. That is, former miners started to mine coal on property owned by the coal companies without authorization. While it was illegal, it was quite common to do so and the sale of coal produced in this manner was the only means that people had to feed their families and to stay alive.

The big coal companies, who owned the land, did take action and attempted to close down some bootlegging operations. However, there were many small independent bootleg coalholes and the coal companies could not close all of them. In many cases, the bootleg miners would just start another coalhole if the authorities closed down one of their operations. After a while the coal companies realized that it did not pay them to try to stop the bootlegging of coal completely; and besides they were not going to mine the coal in these areas anyhow since it was no longer profitable to do so. However, unemployment was still a major problem since the bootleg miners could not mine very much coal and at the same time coal was cheap. With the passing years, bootlegging in the anthracite region all but vanished.

For the most part, families in Big Mine Run just eked out a living but no more than that. Most households had a vegetable garden and grew their own produce. Also, women started to go to work in larger numbers at factories and mills in Ashland and Girardville. My three older sisters were employed at the Ashland Shirt and Pajama Factory, and their salaries contributed greatly to the support of our family.

After a decade or so, the factories and mills also cut back on their production so the number of unemployed women also increased. Many younger people, especially those who had an education, left to seek employment elsewhere. As a result, the population in the coal region has deceased every decade from 1930.

If you visit the area now, you can still see some of the remains of what was the Bast Colliery. The railroad beds for all the tracks are still visible as well as portions of concrete walls that have been crumbling for over a half-century. The culm banks that I once climbed as a kid are leftovers from the Bast Colliery. By now these culm banks have been so overgrown with trees and shrubs that some youngster walking by would not recognize that they are indeed just artificial hills. I seem to remember that it was always small birch trees with a light gray bark that were the first trees to grow and flourish on the culm banks.

During the years the Bast Colliery operated, a number of slopes were sunk with the deepest reaching almost twelve hundred feet from the surface. In addition, miners constructed many tunnels or gangways underground with some tunnels as long as three thousand feet. The colliery with all the tunnels, shafts, slopes, and gangways that were constructed over decades of work created an intricate structure of interconnecting passageways--like a giant maze. If you were to look at a map of the Bast Colliery showing all the underground passageways, it would look similar to the geometric pattern of streets in a photograph of a city taken from a great height. Many of these interconnecting passageways are now flooded with water.

In retrospect, the Anthracite Region thrived from the Civil War era into the early 20th century. Just before World War I, there were more than 189,000 men and boys employed in hundreds of mines. In 1917, coal production exceeded 100 million tons. Coal production dropped to less than five million tons each year in the 1990s. Since then, "King Coal" has continued to spiral downward to the present time. By the spring of 2004, according to Ford Turner, "There were [only] 16 functioning underground anthracite mines—with 200 or fewer working miners—left in the coal region."

So these few small family-type mine operations are all that remains. It appears that in the near future, these rugged independent miners will dwindle to just a hardy few. "But the line likely will end there. Underground miners in Pennsylvania's historic 'coal country' expect to be forced out of business in the next several years by ever-increasing pressure from the federal [mine] inspectors," according to Turner. Some of these hard-working small family-run mines who are facing hard times are: The RS & W Coal Company in Pottsville owned by the Rotherrmel family; The D & D Anthracite Coal Company in Good Spring, Schuylkill County owned by the Lucas family; and the RND Coal Company in Porter Township, Schuylkill County owned by the Himmelberger family.

Generations of strong, resilient hard coal miners helped shape this country into a great nation. It was anthracite coal that was the turning point in changing this country from an agrarian society to an industrial society. Sadly, the die is now cast. The glory days of King Coal are far in the past. However, its proud and important history cannot be denied.

Blasé, Frank. "The Bast Colliery." Internet note. Historian, Reading Anthracite Co. Historical Library.

Turner, Ford. "For Hard Coal, Hard Times."Sunday Patriot-News, 28, March, 2004, p.1.

Bootleg Coalholes

Bootlegging or mining coal illegally was a common occurrence throughout the coal region during the depression years. Several unemployed miners would get together to start a coalhole and begin mining coal on private land owned by a coal company such as the Philadelphia and Reading Coal and Iron Company.

In many cases, coalholes were started and operated by members of the same family. Most of the unemployed men in Big Mine Run, including my father and relatives, were bootleggers at one time or another. Technically, bootlegging was wrong but it was not considered just plain stealing from another person. For the most part, it was coal that would never be mined by the coal companies, and was one way the unemployed miners were able to feed and support their families.

In some cases bootleg miners had to pay a fee to the coal companies in order to continue bootlegging. In Big Mine Run the independent bootleg miners (to my knowledge) never paid any fees nor did the authorities dynamite their coalholes. The coal cops came around and harassed the miners, but for the most part the interruptions were only temporary. As long as the coalholes were small, the coal company police generally did not bother the miners in Big Mine Run; however, if the bootleg operation became large and too profitable they were likely to shut the operation down. However, in some other areas the big coal companies actually used dynamite to close down some bootleg coalholes.

Some of the earliest coalholes I saw were just vertical holes (shafts) that went straight down. The coal from down inside was hauled up in a large bucket with a windlass. It was very hard work, but that type of mining operation did not last too long.

A typical coalhole was a slope and would have one worker at the surface and a minimum of two miners down inside mining the coal. The worker on top controlled a small car or "buggy," which ran on tracks that was pulled up or lowered by a cable that was attached to the rear axle of a small stationary automobile on the surface. Sometimes the miners hopped on the buggy and were lowered down the slope to their working area.

When the miners down inside loaded up the buggy, which held about 300 pounds of coal, they signaled (using a small electric bell) to the worker on top that the buggy was full of coal. The buggy would then be hauled up, tipped over and the coal dumped into a large hopper that normally held about five to seven tons of coal. The empty buggy would then be lowered back down to the miners inside. When there was a truckload of coal in the hopper (about four or five tons) a truck would then pull under a chute at the hopper and get loaded up. The truck would then haul the coal to a local breaker for processing.

Big Mine Run and the surrounding area had many coalholes. There were at least fifteen coalholes within twenty minutes walking distance of our home in Woodland Heights. There was one as close as fifty feet away from our back yard. Billy Colahan, our neighbor, who was about eighteen years old, was killed working in a coalhole that was only 150 feet from our home. Hilbert Kroh, a kid I played games with and knew well, was killed in a bootleg coalhole when he was only sixteen years old.

A number of coalholes were located at the top of the hill beyond Woodland Heights in a region called the "flat." Ben, Charles and Andrew Medric had a coalhole there. At the end of the working day, they would walk down from their coalhole to Woodland

Heights past our home (all dirty and black) on their way home. The Young family: Charles, Joe and George also had a coalhole there. John Pahira employed Metro and John Pechansky to work for him in his coalhole in that area. George, Charles, and Mike Mikurak and John Turanko also had a coalhole nearby.

In addition, a number of coalholes were located just behind the back yard of the houses in Woodland Heights. Joe Petrusky and some neighbors operated a coalhole just across the dirt road from his own back yard. Mike and John Latsko had a coalhole across the road from their back yard fence. Roy Kroh also had a coalhole behind his house. Warren and Haven Wolfgang also had a coalhole behind their home. Amil Bierlaski, who married my sister Mary, had two different coalholes in the Big Mine Run area. One was located at the base of the South Mountain that was close to the Reading Railroad line and the other was in Bucks' Patch.

After grade school let out, I would go looking for coal at the different coalholes on the hill behind our home. When my 100 pound burlap bag was full, I would it put it on my wheelbarrow and wheel it home for our own use. Sometimes I would go around the neighborhood and sell my 100-pond bag of coal for twenty-five cents.

My father, and two of my uncles, John Skocik and Pete Daniels, ran a bootleg operation near Germantown about two miles from Big Mine Run. My father took me to their coalhole during the summer when I was about twelve years old. While I did not work there regularly, I helped my Uncle Pete who stayed on top and operated the buggy that brought the coal to the surface. At times he would have to drive to his mother's place in Germantown only a short distance away to get supplies for the coalhole. He was a hot rod driver and at times I thought we were going to crash and turn over. I went along because he would say in a rough voice, "Jump in." I recall one time when we went to Germantown for supplies that his mother was milking a cow. She gave me a glass of warm milk directly from the pail of milk she used from milking the cow. It didn't taste too good, but I drank it because I did not want to disappoint her. Then Pete would drive like crazy back to the coalhole.

At times I would go down inside the mine while my Uncle Pete worked at the surface. So I knew what it was like to go down a sloped coalhole several hundred feet below the ground. It is cold, damp and scary down there. Not only that, it is very hard work and also dangerous. I recall hearing strange creaking and crunching noises overhead while down hundreds of feet inside the coalhole. I could almost sense the weight of the dirt and rock now hanging over my head. Frankly, I often said my prayers wondering when all the thousands of tons of earth was going to come crashing down on top of me. A miner once told me, "You can't work in a coalhole and be afraid, you must just go down and do your job and that's that." I said to myself, "Oh Yeah?"

The miners who worked in coalholes faced similar hazards as the deep hard coal miners. In addition, many bootleg miners were generally not as experienced in mining operations as the professional miners were. Further, they did not have the fire bosses to check on underground hazards. Each coalhole miner operated individually and set his own safety standards for mining coal. Also, timbering and equipment were not as reliable as that of the deep coal miners. The bootleg miners did not use canaries because lethal gas pockets developed more readily in deep mine operations. However, the term "the canary in the coal mine" (which now describes a potentially dangerous situation anywhere) could also be applied in bootleg mining because other dangerous situations besides lethal gas were always lurking there.

As a youngster, I often visited my Uncle John Skocik and Aunt Pauliine in Germantown, which was smaller than a patch (only about ten houses) just outside of Ashland. There aren't any more homes in Germantown, apparently they were also part of the buyout program offered by the government to the Brynesville and Centralia communities.

My Uncle John had five brothers named: Bart, Henry, Joe, Oscar and Tom, some of them also lived in Germantown. The Skocik guys were all strong tough men, and they were also friendly. I always thought my Uncle John was a pretty smart guy. I felt he would have made an excellent engineer if he had the opportunity to go to school; however, he spent most of his years as a coal miner.

One summer when I was about fourteen years of age, John Skocik and I got together to start a coalhole near his home in Germantown. He said he knew a good place to dig and that we would hit coal. My Uncle John was a very hard worker, and I could not keep up with him. After using a pick and shovel all day, I was very tired and could not wait to go home. At the end of one week of just plain tough work, I decided never to go back again. What an important lesson for me to learn early in my life; I was more determined than ever to get an education.

Just prior to World War II, the number of bootleg coalholes began to decrease and before too long no one was mining coal that way any more in Big Mine Run. However, the coalholes were just abandoned and they became a potential hazard. This was especially true when the opening of the slope of the coalhole was overgrown with brush. An innocent person could easily tumble into and fall many feet down the slope. During the winter, the snow would also mask the coalhole opening and one could easily fall down into an abandoned pit.

When I got a little older I often wondered how the bootleg miners could work day after day under such harsh conditions for so little money. In thinking about it some more, I realized that most of them faced Hobson's choice—an apparent freedom of choice with no real alternative.

Stealing Coal

The main railroad line of the Philadelphia and Reading Coal and Iron Company, which ran from Girardville to Ashland was about a quarter-mile from Big Mine Run; however, a branch from the main railroad line ran directly through Big Mine Run to the Bast Colliery.

After the railroad cars (which held about fifty tons each) were loaded with coal at the Bast Colliery, the engine would slowly pull the loaded cars to connect with the main Reading Railroad line. This took a little while since the train moved slowly at this point and in some cases would come to a stop for a short period of time. Meanwhile, Frank and Andy Adamavage, Joe Grabowsky, Joe Baldino. George Mickle, and I along and others would hop aboard and throw off large lumps of coal. The railroad tracks were only a few feet away from the backyard of some families so they were able throw the lumps of coal directly into their own back yard. After the engine started to pull the loaded cars away from the Big Mine Run area, we would hop off the freight and pick up the coal and haul it home.

One day I happened to be on top of a coal car throwing coal off by myself. I thought it was strange that none of my buddies were doing the same thing. I got so absorbed in throwing off coal that I didn't pay attention to any cops that might be patrolling the area. Suddenly, I heard Joe Baldino shouting as loud as he could, "Cops, cops, run Ruby." When I looked around and saw two cops approaching—I froze for a minute (probably only a few seconds). I ran across the top of the coal car and then scrambled down the ladder rungs on the side of the car. When I got down to the ground, I ran as fast as I could. Even though I was running fast, I had a strange feeling that my feet were not moving at all. I was really scared and thought they were going to catch me. Somehow I eluded them, but I always remembered that it was Joe Baldino's warning that saved my hide that day.

Every once in a while the loaded coal cars were left standing on the sidetrack in Big Mine Run overnight. In those situations the coal cops would make periodic checks on the loaded cars because they knew from past experience that we helped ourselves to the coal. However, as soon as the cops left, we would hop up on the freight and start throwing coal off the cars. These were special opportunities since we were able to steal a lot more coal. We also had our own lookout, and if he saw anyone coming who looked suspicious he would holler "cops" and everyone in turn would call out "cops" and we would all disappear. Then later, after the authorities would leave we would haul our coal home. It was not too different from the old comedy short movie featuring the "Our Gang Kids."

There were times when I got quite dirty from throwing coal off the railroad cars. As I walked up the hill to Woodland Heights on my way home, I would often hear some adult say, "Yuz look like yuz were workin' in a coalhole."

The Poor Breaker Kids

There were many bad working conditions over the years in the coal region, but none was sadder than the story of the young boys (kids really) who worked in the coal breakers at the collieries. Boys from the ages of 10-14 were regularly employed to work in the breakers, and in some cases kids as young as six years of age were hired. While there were laws prohibiting employers from hiring youngsters under age, employers often disregarded them. In some cases, one-third of a family's income came from a kid working in a breaker, so a family would often fabricate a child's age in order for the youngster to be employed. It may seem cruel today, but times were hard back then. In any event, that's the way it was.

A group of breaker kids, circa 1900.

The colliery where the breaker kids worked is a major coal mine including all the buildings, equipment and surrounding land. A typical colliery always had a line of railroad cars stationed nearby. Empty railroad cars would generally be moving toward the colliery and loaded coal cars moving out. The breaker is the main central building sitting on top of the mine and it's surrounded by smaller buildings such as a fan house, engine house, machine shop, office and still smaller buildings called shops or sheds.

A coal breaker is a towering structure as high as 150 feet, and has a blackened wooden appearance with an unusual number of small windows lining both sides. While all coal breakers looked somewhat similar at first glance, no two breakers were exactly alike. The roof of a typical breaker has a tiered shape and was built to meet the need for that particular colliery. It's that part of the colliery where the coal is processed after it is delivered from the mine. If you draw an analogy with an iceberg, the tip of the iceberg is the breaker and the hidden part of the iceberg is the huge coal mine under the ground.

The beginning of the coal processing starts when large two-ton mine cars full of coal are pulled from deep inside the mine up a long inclined track to the top of the breaker called the tipple. At this point, the cars are tipped over and the coal and other impurities are emptied into chutes. The large lumps of coal are fed through powerful revolving cylinders with huge teeth that crush the coal. The fragmented coal is screened and sorted into different sizes as it moves downward to lower levels of the breaker.

The breaker kids sat on a board suspended over conveyor belts and reached down between their little legs to pick out rock and slate from the coal as it rushed along. The breaker kids, who were called slate pickers, often had to slow down the flow of coal with their feet so they could pick out the impurities with their tiny fingers.

Anthracite coal, as contrasted to slate, was shiny black and often had sharp edges. In only a few weeks their small fingers would be bloodied and raw from the sharp-edged coal. Their tiny bruised fingers were called "red tips." Mothers would often rub their sore fingertips with goose grease to soothe the pain. However, the kids soon learned that their bloodied fingers would heal more quickly if they urinated on them. Slate was a dull black color and had to be separated from the coal because it would not burn. Rock and other debris also had to be removed. The various sizes of coal, which were cleaned of impurities, were conveyed to storage bins from where it was loaded on to trucks or railroad cars for shipment.

Breaker boys picking slate.

The working conditions were unhealthy, dangerous and just plain horrible. The kids worked under the supervision of adults called "overseers," who were armed with a stick for hitting those not working hard enough. It was simply brutal and inhumane treatment of youngsters. The air was constantly full of coal dust and there was no fresh air to breathe. The faces of the breaker kids looked like adult miners--they were black and grimy.

The rushing coal, revolving wheels, crushers and screens inside the breaker made a deafening noise. During the summer the breaker was stifling hot and during the winter it was very cold. The slate pickers were too young to realize the danger of their environment. They would jump and leap about like monkeys inside the breaker often putting themselves in peril. In some cases, boys actually fell down into the machinery and were mangled to death. In other instances, the youngsters accidentally fell into the chutes and were smothered with crushed coal. A funeral procession of a breaker kid being carried by his buddies, who were hardly teenagers themselves, was enough to bring a tear to the eye of even the toughest adult miner.

The terrible working conditions went on for years with hardly any improvement. The boys worked ten hours a day, six days a week for about 45 cents a day, sometimes a little more. In short, it was a backbreaking job. It was a clear example of how prevalent the evil of child labor was at that time. In the early 1900s there were approximately18, 000 kids employed as slate pickers, and most of them were full-time employees.

Childhood ended early for the breaker kids. Many of them smoked and chewed tobacco, they also learned how to swear like men. They worked and lived more as adults than they did as kids. It was a time when they should have been in school but they were not. The breaker kids never had a chance to develop physically and mentally. Sadly, they did not have a chance to experience their youth on their way to manhood. In many cases, fathers worked in the same colliery as their children.

Why do I call these breaker kids children? Well, I remember my mother telling me that when the circus came to town, many of the breaker kids would skip work and go to see the circus. What else would we expect children to do? They were telling society in a poignant way, that it is the right of a child to have a childhood.

The "Little Miners"

Generally speaking, young boys had to be age 14 before being allowed to work down inside the coal mine; however, that age requirement was not always adhered to. They performed various jobs that the authorities at the time felt it was appropriate for them to do. Young boys were "nippers," "spraggers," and mule drivers; they were the "little miners."

Nippers were the youngest (age 11-13) of the boys that worked down inside the mine. A nipper's job was very boring and lonely because it required a lot of "just sitting" all alone. His job was to open the large wooden doors when he heard the coal cars approaching. Then he would close the doors after the coal cars passed through.

A nipper who was all alone down inside the coal mine, would often feed the rats a little of his lunch just to have something to do. The rats (who were always looking for something to eat) would come right up to the young boy for the food. Other times the young lad would whittle pieces of wood to stay awake. Generally the nipper shaped wooden stakes called sprags used by "spraggers" to slow down the coal cars as described in the following paragraph. Sometimes the poor young kid would get so bored that he fell asleep.

The nipper as a doorkeeper.

A "spragger" had a dangerous job because he had the responsibility for controlling the speed of loaded mine cars running on a downgrade. He had to be very fast, because his job was to run beside the loaded cars and jam a wooden stake (sprag) into the spokes of the wheels to slow down the cars if they were going too fast. While spraggers worked in pairs, slowing down a coal car was not an easy thing to do, and as a result many kids incurred injuries.

Young boys also guided the mules that pulled coal cars down inside the mine. A mule driver's job was more desirable than either a nipper or a spragger because they moved around a lot more. A mule driver also developed a special relationship with the mule—they were in many cases good friends. Sadly, the poor mules were often kept working underground for long periods of time. As a result, these hard-working animals never breathed fresh air, nor felt or saw the nice warm sun nor munched on grass for years. Ironically, when a mule died, the mining company paid to replace the mule. On the other hand, when a miner died, they just hired a new miner.

Young boy leading a mule inside a mine.
Drawing by Lucas Kalathas.

Chapter 5

STORIES ABOUT FAMILY AND FRIENDS

A Tribute to My Mom

My Mom.

My Dad.

My mom's maiden name was Pauline (Parania) Kostyrka. She was born on October 7, 1892 in the town of Sambir in Mainych, Poland. My mom arrived in New York on October 22, 1912 on the SS Kroonland. She married my father, Harry Bobonych, (ethnic names often varied in spelling) on July 29, 1917 in the Ukrainian Catholic Cathedral of the Immaculate Conception in Philadelphia, Pennsylvania.

My mother was a very industrious person. It seemed to me that she did the work of several people all of her working life. When I was a youngster she did housecleaning in three different homes in Ashland, in addition to all the work she did in our own home. At times she took me along to help her with the housecleaning. I think she felt it was good for me to learn how to do all sorts of domestic chores.

My Mom and Dad.

One of the households my mother housecleaned was a family named Frank Burke. They lived in a large three-story house on Center Street in the downtown part of Ashland; it was about one block from the town's most famous physician, Dr. Robert Spencer. Their eldest daughter (Marie) was my age and they also had two younger daughters (Peggy Ann and Frances). Everyone in the Burke family was always well dressed, especially their daughters. The girls' dresses were colorful and they looked expensive. The Burke home was furnished lavishly with lamps, rugs and furniture I've never seen before. Everything looked quite elegant to me. It was not what I saw everyday in Big Mine Run.

Many times my mother took me along to help her. When it came to housecleaning, my mother would always assign me to dusting. She would day, "Dust this and then dust that." To this day, seven decades later, I hate to dust; the damned stuff always comes back and settles in the same places.

Mr. Burke operated a successful funeral parlor business, and from time to time I did a variety of jobs for him. It seemed to me that every time I went there to help my mother, he had a dead body stored on a table in his working room in a large garage in the rear of his home. The place always had a stench of formaldehyde. Unfortunately, I had to walk through that area alone as a youngster and it bothered me. I walked very fast past the damn table where the corpse was and it seemed that I always glanced over at the body rather than looking straight ahead. There were times that I swear I saw the dead body move.

I soon realized that the Burke family lived differently from the families I was familiar with in Big Mine Run. The Burkes were well to do and seemed to have everything. At Christmas time they had magnificent oversize electric trains, which ran on wide gauge railroad tracks. I had never seen trains like that running around the Christmas tree on a large raised platform. I began to see first hand the difference in the standard of living between those who have money and those who were poor. Until my experience with the Burke family, I did not realize we were as poor as we were.

My mother also did housecleaning in the John Shovlin home, which was located directly across Center Street from the Burke residence. Mrs. Shovlin was Mr. Burke's sister. The Shovlin family also lived in a large three-story house and I had similar household chores to do there. Mr. Shovlin, who was a high school principal in Kulpmont, hired me as his chauffeur when I learned to drive. I liked that job much better than helping with the housecleaning.

One day when my mother and I were working there, Mr. Shovlin, who was eating lunch at the time, began telling my mother and me about a wonderful restaurant named "Childs" in Philadelphia. My mother was always "on the go" and she just kept on working while Mr. Shovlin kept on talking. My mother said, "Yes, yes, I know." Mr. Shovlin said, "No, no Annie" (he always called her Annie) "this restaurant is in Philadelphia, which is about 100 miles from Ashland." My mother then proceeded to tell him that she actually worked at that same Childs restaurant a number of years ago when she first came to this country. We all had a big laugh about that. My Mom always wanted to open up a restaurant but she never had a chance. She would have been a very successful businesswoman.

My mother also did housecleaning for Leo and Anna Almond. They lived in a corner house on Center Street but farther up town. My mother said that they lived off the interest and dividends from their investments and therefore did not have to work for a living.

In addition we did the laundry for all three families in our own home. My three older sisters helped with the laundry so it was common to see three ironing boards in use at the same time in our home. I helped iron flat pieces like pillowcases, sheets, towels and handkerchiefs; we ironed everything. After a while

I became pretty good at ironing and sometimes I ironed more complex pieces. Leo Almond picked up the laundry for his family at our home when it was finished. While Joseph Shovlin picked up his own family's laundry and also the laundry for the Burke family at our home when it was done.

It seemed to me that we always had enough to eat. My mom was very resourceful and was able to manage well, considering what little we had. She was an excellent cook and everyone liked her cooking. My mom always made tasty soups like: cabbage, potato, rice, vegetable, pea, bean, string bean, lima bean, mushroom, redbeet (borscht), and noodle. I also recall that she made a soup dish with milk, which had small dough balls in it. Sometimes we would take saltine crackers, crush then in our hands and then put them in our coffee. We called it "coffee soup" and we would eat it with a spoon like you would any soup.

My mom made her own noodles when she made noodle soup. She would roll out the dough on the table into a circle about three feet in diameter and only about an eighth of an inch thick. She would start at one end and fold the dough over about two inches at a time and keep on folding it to the end. Then my mom would hold her fingers very close to the end of the folded dough and begin to chop down swiftly with a sharp knife cutting off portions only about an eighth of an inch wide.

I always felt she was going to cut her fingers; in fact, I would turn my head away because I was sure that she was going to cut herself. However, when she was through cutting the dough to shreds (and all her fingers in tact) she ended up with the most wonderful homemade noodles. My impression at the time was that everyone made delicious homemade noodles like my mom did, but that was not the case.

We always ate our evening meal together and everyone had a regular seating place. As Catholics we did not eat meat on Fridays so we had perogies or (pyrohys), fish or some other non-meat meal.

My mom made delicious potato, cabbage (kapusta), prune and blueberry perogies. I also enjoyed the potato perogies the next day when they were pan-fried to a light brown crisp on each side.

She also made potato pancakes (bleenies), which were another favorite non-meat meal we ate on Friday. The main ingredients were grated potatoes, grated onion, eggs, flour, salt and pepper all mixed together. My mom would pour out the batter into a frying pan and fry them like you would regular pancakes.

During the hot summer days families kept their kitchen doors open. So on Fridays you could tell those families who were making bleenies, because you could smell them being fried as you walked by. It was common to see a youngster outside eating a bleenie and holding it with a piece of brown wrapping paper. The brown paper was used not only to hold the hot bleenie, but also to soak up the grease.

Instead of making potato pancakes, my mom would sometimes pour the entire potato pancake mix into a large frying pan and bake it in the oven. We called it "bobka." When it was done, it was crusty and brown on top and about ten inches in diameter and about three inches thick. We cut it like you would a cake or pie and serve it that way, but it wasn't dessert. We ate the bleenies and bobka with margarine and sometimes with sour cream, when we could afford it. By the way, the margarine that we bought was white in color with a small pellet of orange dye included inside a plastic bag. It was my job to squeeze the bag together until the pellet and the white margarine became a homogenous yellow color similar to ordinary butter. The two dishes (bleenies and bobka) were very tasty and we ate them both hot and cold.

Everyone loved my mom's stuffed cabbage rolls called holubtsi. My mom's stuffed cabbage rolls (sometimes called blind pigeons) were made mostly with rice and a little meat. On the other hand, my Aunt Mary (who was much better off financially) always made the point that her holubtsi were mostly meat with only a little rice. My mom's holubtsi were about four inches long and one inch in diameter with a rice-meat mixture wrapped in a cabbage leaf and cooked in a tomato sauce. She always made a large pot full that lasted several days.

My mom was a great cook but she did not bake many cakes or pies. Now as I think about it, where would she to find time to do any baking? She did however, make some apple pies during the fall season, and I suppose that was because apples were plentiful and cheap. I can still see her holding up the pie on her fingertips, twirling it around while she trimmed off the loose edge of the dough with a small knife in her other hand.

My mom also made a food dish, which is somewhat difficult for me to describe. To the best of my recollection it was called "studenetz." She generally made it on Saturday evening for Sunday breakfast. She boiled pigs' feet in a large pot until the meat softened. Then she took the pigs' feet out of the pot and picked off the meat and small bones. After that, she put the meat and small bones back in the same pot with the liquid in which she originally boiled them. Then she added garlic, celery, onion, and small portions of veal. My mom heated the mixture slowly and then poured it into soup dishes. The dishes were the placed in the basement to cool where the contents solidified. Some dishes had a few pieces of bones (pigs knuckles) and some had small pieces of meat; however, most of the dishes only had the solidified liquid, which had the consistency of Jello.

Everyone in my family ate it cold for Sunday breakfast. As I recall, they poured vinegar on it to make it taste better. I didn't like it and I rarely ate it. After I tasted it for the first time, I secretly hoped that I would never see the stuff again. It was the only food dish (besides mushrooms) that my mom made that I didn't like. I must confess that all the other members of our family liked it. Of course I didn't really understand that it was very cheap to make and did help feed the family.

Guess what? When I got married many years later, I never told my wife, Gloria, about making mushrooms or the pigs' feet dish because I didn't want her to make either one.

My mom had a garden and she planted a variety of vegetables. Some of the vegetables she grew were: lettuce, carrots, potatoes, peppers, cucumbers, corn, string beans, tomatoes, onions, red beets and a few others. She was fond of flowers and grew different varieties all around our house. She also kept many plants inside our home.

My mother could do almost anything with her hands and I learned a lot from her. She preserved all kinds of fruits and vegetables: tomatoes, cucumbers, peppers, onions, huckleberries, peaches, pears and probably a few other things. My mom made chili sauce, chow-chow, and ketchup. She made grape, peach, strawberry and cherry jellies. My mom also dried mushrooms (hryby) on long strings behind our coal stove. I felt it was a chore to help putting up all kinds of preserves during the summer. However, it was always nice to eat homemade huckleberry pie during the winter.

One day I saw my mother stuffing cucumbers (ohirky or ogorki) into jars and it looked like fun, so I agreed to help. Well, I soon learned that the "cukes" had to be stuffed together as close as possible so there weren't too many spaces left in the jar. It wasn't as easy as I thought it would be; it was tedious, tiresome and just hard work.

When we put tomatoes in jars, I helped my mom peel the tomatoes. The tomatoes were first soaked in very hot water, which made them easier to peel. It was difficult to hold a hot tomato in your hand and then peel it, but that's the way we did it. After peeling the skin off the tomato, we cut it up and then put the pieces in a jar. You probably guessed by now, I didn't like that job either.

I also picked elderberries, blackberries and grapes so my mom could make wine (my father never helped with these chores). We made a lot of wine that we stored in barrels, but it was mainly for our own consumption. We drank it with some meals and also when we had company. We also drank it with hot tea when we had a cold.

Sometimes we sold some wine in small bottles to our neighbors and friends. One neighbor, James Monahan, who liked wine, would stop in and my mother would sell him a glass of wine for ten cents. She always gave him a free glass of wine before he left. (My mom was a good businesswoman without taking any business courses.)

We also made a root beer drink that we put up in regular soda bottles. We bought a root beer concentrate, followed the directions and ended up with a batch of root beer. My mom taught me how to use a siphon hose to fill the bottles from the large container of root beer that we made. I had to be careful to squeeze the siphon hose very tight when the bottle was full, so I could move the hose over to the next bottle. In the beginning I couldn't squeeze the siphon hose tight enough and some root beer would flow over the floor. My mother didn't mind, she said, "Keep on going, you'll learn."

After all the bottles were filled, I would get ready to clamp caps down on top of the bottles. I would take one bottle at a time and place a cap on top of the bottle. Then I put the bottle under the bottle-capper and press down hard on a large handle to clamp the cap on the bottle. When I first started to cap the bottles, I cracked a few and they had to be discarded. I soon learned that you have to be careful how you placed the cap on the bottle, and how to press down on the capper without breaking the bottle. My mother had a lot of patience and never reprimanded me. She knew that was the way to learn, just do it. When I got finished, the bottles I capped looked like regular bottles of soda; however, they didn't have any labels on them. Our homemade soda didn't taste like the bought kind, but it was pretty good.

My mom also showed me how to make soap. She collected fat and fat-like substances until she had about eight pounds of solid fat. Then she heated the fat on our coal stove until all the fat liquefied. The liquid fat was very hot, so she placed it aside to cool down until it was warm but still a liquid.

At this point she allowed me to take over. I poured the liquid fat into a large porcelain bowl. Then I poured the lye (from a can) very slowly into the liquid fat. The mixture became quite hot, so I had to stir it with a wooden spoon to allow it to cool down. The mixture turned from the original brown color of the melted fat to a grayish color as the lye was added. The mixture also became thicker and was more difficult to stir. After all the lye was added and the entire contents stirred thoroughly, I put the porcelain bowl aside for several days to let the contents solidify.

After a few days the soap would harden. Then I used a large flat knife to loosen the cake of soap from the porcelain dish. When I turned the dish over I had a thirty-pound cake of light tan-colored soap, which I then cut it into bars. Since my mother took in washing for three different households, it was much cheaper to use homemade soap for washing clothes. It worked just as well as bought soap. My mom always told me I did well and I felt that she appreciated my helping her with her chores.

My mom also made beautiful braided rugs. She started by cutting strips of cloth about one-half inch wide from all types of colored clothing. The strips, which were various lengths, were sewed end to end and then made into a ball about the size of a cantaloupe. So each ball was actually one very long one-half inch strip with various colors. Then she would use the individual strips from three balls to make a tightly wrapped braid. The braid or plait was then stitched by hand and made into a round or oval rug about one-half inch thick. My mom always used a large needle and a waxed thread as she sewed the platted braid to the rest of the rug. She also kept her regular iron (which she used to iron clothes) on top of the braided rug to keep it flat while she made the carpet.

When I was a kid I would sit on the floor and play with some of the extra balls my mom made while she was working on her carpet. Sometimes I would unravel a ball by playing too rough with it, but she never scolded me. She would just reach down and wrap up the ball again. My mom's eyesight wasn't too good, and she would often ask me to thread her needle so she could continue her sewing.

When she finally completed a rug, my mom would simply lay it on the floor and we would start walking on it. She was always pleased when she finished one of her multi-colored rugs. She had every right to be, because it took a lot of work and they were beautiful. As I grew a little older and realized how much work went into making a rug and how attractive they were, I didn't feel we should just walk on then as we would on any other rug. So one day (about 1950) I put several of then away. No one has walked on them—nor will they. I treasure them because each one is unique; each one made by my mom's own hand.

Our attic had two brass beds with a thick comforter or bed cover filled with feathers on each bed. My mom saved the feathers (she never wasted anything) from the ducks that we raised and we used the feathers to make feather comforters; we called them "feather ticks."

When my mom collected a sufficient amount of feathers, we all got together for our first lesson on how to make a feather tick. I remember my mother giving me a small bag and telling me to strip the "down" off the feathers and put it in the bag. I held the feather (with the quill pointed downward) in my left hand between my thumb and index finger. Then I took hold of the tip of the feather and stripped off the down with my thumb and index finger of my right hand. It was a tedious job—picking, stripping, picking, stripping—it took a lot of work to just get enough down to fill a small pillow.

Eventually we stripped enough feathers to make several thick comforters; however, none of us liked that job. Of course, we all liked to sleep under the feather tick in the winter, and many times we would play on top of the bed, roll around on the feather tick and throw pillows at each other.

My mom often attended card parties sponsored by St. Joseph's Church Roman Catholic Church in Ashland. By selling tickets for the event, the church was able to raise money to offset expenses. She always got a free ticket from one of the women in the three homes she housecleaned. She was very frugal and never left anything go to waste, so she always used her ticket. Sometimes she would have an extra ticket and ask me to along with her since I was good at playing cards.

Surprisingly, my mom knew how to play all types of card games and she usually won a prize. The prizes usually consisted of ordinary household items such as towels, tablecloths, pillowcases, sheets and various household appliances. However, there were always a small number of more valuable prizes such as a set of dishes, a complete set of pots, or a large homemade quilt. It was one of the few social activities she attended in her very busy and hard life.

Somehow my mom found time to teach us to say our prayers in Ukrainian. She would ask my youngest sister, Ann and I to kneel down and say the Lord's Prayer. We started by saying: "ot ce nash sco jesy na nebesach . . . " That is: Our Father who art in Heaven . . . Sometimes we would start giggling but she never scolded us, she just told us to go on saying our prayers. My mother was a religious woman and had many religious calendars, paintings and statues throughout our home. It was also a time when religious medals were given to children on special occasions. Religious cards were also popular items that were given to children.

She also sent us to school so we could learn to read and write the Ukrainian language. We attended classes on Saturday morning that was taught by a professor from the Ukrainian Catholic Church in Centralia. The class, which was only about ten is size, was held in our local public school in Big Mine Run. When we were in class, some local ruffians outside in the playground would shout obscenities and other obnoxious remarks into the ventilating system that carried into our classroom. The professor would ask angrily why they were doing that, and we would tell him that it was just some bad boys. It was typical behavior for some of the rough Big Mine Run kids. Church services for Roman Catholic parishioners were also held in the same school building on Sundays.

Since my mother never went to school, she could not read or write. As I got a little older I often wondered how difficult it was for her not to be literate. It was only later in life that I was able to appreciate fully what my mom did under those difficult circumstances. It was simply amazing to me that she was able to do all the things that she did. When I was about 13 years old, she became a United States citizen. We were all proud, but my mom was the proudest one of all. I recall how she would practice writing her name and then showing it to me to see if it was satisfactory.

It's sad, in a way that we don't appreciate the wonderful things that our moms do for us until it's too late. (But then again, has it ever been otherwise with youth?) Now when I think about her cooking and all the other wonderful things that she did, it takes me back in time--a time both happily and sadly remembered. Often when I returned home, I would see her bent over working on something as usual. When she saw or heard me coming she would straighten up slowly (I'm sure now that it was from a sore back) and pleasantly greet me. And then In her customary way, she would reach up slowly and brush back a strand of her hair with the back of her hand—a gesture is seems to me that laboring women have done over the ages.

She was a better practical chemist than I was even after I had a Ph.D. Degree in Chemistry. I did learn many things from my mom that were helpful to me, but I didn't realize it until I got a little older and also got more common sense. Of course, my mom knew all the time what was good for me. It didn't come from book learnin' either—it's called a mom's intuition.

One final point adapted from a short story Diane Rooney wrote. My father's occupation was classified as "miner." Our boarders, occupations were also classified a "miners." A miner's helper was listed as a "laborer." My three sisters who worked in the factory were "trimmers." And then there was my poor mom—who could and did outwork them all—her occupation was listed as "none."

My Three Sisters

MY three sisters--Hattie, Mary and Ann.

I was the youngest in a family of four. Whenever I mention that I had three older sisters, people would usually say, "Boy, you sure must have been spoiled." Well, not exactly, but they were pretty nice to me.

Hattie.

My oldest sister, Hattie, had to quit high school in the early 1930s because she had to help support our family. It was sad because she was a good student and especially talented in mathematics. Hattie cried when she had to leave school because she enjoyed learning and was doing so well. However, that's the way it was at that time in Big Mine Run. Getting a job to help out the family took precedent over getting an education.

If she had been given the opportunity to complete high school, Hattie would have been an excellent college student. As she grew older and we got talking about the past, she always regretted that she was not able to finish high school. Then she would mention how she could always add up a column of numbers faster than anyone else could.

Her first job was doing domestic work in various households, including the well-known Pepper family that owned a soft drink bottling business in Ashland. (Everyone agreed that Pepper's ginger ale was the best ginger ale drink ever made---bar none.)

After that, she was able to obtain work at the Shirt and Pajama factory at the bottom of town in Ashland that paid more money. She got a job as a trimmer, which required her to cut or trim off all the small loose threads from the sewn shirts. Trimming shirts required skillful hands because you had to use a pair of scissors to snip off all the loose ends, and you had to do it fast. She enjoyed doing piecework because she got paid according to how much work she did. Since she was faster than the other trimmers, she got paid well. When she got paid, she generally gave me a little change from her pay envelope.

Because she was the first in the family to quit high school in order to help our family, Hattie also learned how to do many other household chores. Even though she had to do housework, she never liked it. On the other hand, she turned out to be a very good cook. In addition, she was an excellent baker and made all sorts of wonderful desserts. She enjoyed making fancy cakes for special occasions for which she got paid. I remember a lamb-shaped white cake she made (from a mold) which was covered with white coconut. She used tiny colored candies for the eyes nose and face and then she tied a small blue ribbon around its neck. It turned out to be an especially nice gift. She also made a similar Santa Claus cake.

Hattie also made tan-colored cookies called "Michigan Rocks." I never did find out why they called them by that name. They contained nuts and dates and everybody liked them. They were about two inches in diameter and about one and one-half inches high with a somewhat rounded but uneven top. She baked them mainly for major holidays like Christmas and Easter; however, she baked so many that we were eating them for a long time after the holidays ended.

Hattie was fairly tall and somewhat self-conscious about being overweight. As a result, she did not have as many boy friends as my other two sisters did. She smoked and played poker for money with the men. I did not appreciate the fact that she enjoyed gambling with men in our own home. The card players often used colorful language and I found it embarrassing. I never lingered or watched them gamble very long, I would always leave the house. Hattie knew I was upset by her behavior, but I felt she thought I wasn't just grown up enough to understand.

Mary age nine.

My sister Mary was the next oldest child in our family. Everyone called her Mamie; that's because the name Mamie is derived from Mary. She also quit high school to go to work. However, she was only an average student and did not mind going to work rather than continuing on in high school.

Even though she was rather young, she left Big Mine Run in the mid-1930s to seek employment.

For a time she did housework in both Philadelphia and New York City. The salary she received was not very much, but at that time it was about the only work a girl could get if she did not have a high school education. She also contributed financially to the upkeep of our family.

After about a year, Mamie left the city and returned home. Then she got a job in the same factory where my sister Hattie worked. She was also a trimmer, but she was not as fast as Hattie was at that kind of work. At times, Hattie would help Mamie to meet her quota of shirts for the day. Even

Mary and Ann.

though they would argue and fight with each other as family members often do, it was nice to see my one sister helping out another.

Mamie was attractive, medium in height, and had the usual number of boy friends. She liked to dance and looked forward to dancing events on weekends. She had a pleasant disposition and everyone liked her. She was the most easy-going of all my sisters and had a good sense of humor. Mamie loved to chew gum. When she was told to get rid of the chewing gum in her mouth while at the kitchen table, she would always stick the chewing gum underneath the edge of the table. One day we looked under the table and found that it was lined with hardened old gum from one end to the other.

Sometime in the 1930s she participated in a roller skating marathon. It was a very popular event that was held in Marion Heights, about eight miles from Big Mine Run. About thirty couples participated in the contest and each man had a woman skating partner. The couples had to skate together around the clock in an indoor roller rink with only short breaks or rest periods. The event had strict rules and couples who failed to meet them were eliminated from the contest. In some cases, one member of a couple would be so exhausted that other partner had to hold up the person to continue skating. If anyone fell to the floor or could not continue skating according to the rules, the couple was dropped from the contest.

In many ways it was a difficult and grueling event, but the young couples were more than willing to accept the challenge. It was an entertaining event and drew huge crowds since the winning couple was awarded a substantial cash prize for that time. I remember our family attending to see how well my sister was doing. Mamie and her partner dropped out of the contest with only a few couples remaining so she did not win anything. I remember that she was so tired when she came home, that all she wanted to do was sleep. Mamie had three children— Diane, Gail and Mark.

Ann age eight.   Ann age 18.

Mt youngest sister was named Ann. For some reason everyone called her "hunya." I had more in common with her than my two older sisters since we went to school together. My older sisters were working in the factory at the time, so I did not see them as much during the day. I remember coming home for lunch with Ann while we were both in grade school. We would come home to an empty house since my mom was also generally working somewhere. Ann and I would have a spiced ham or minced ham sandwich, and then we shared a small pie for dessert with a glass of milk.

Ann was tall, thin, and attractive and the boys liked her. She always fixed her hair and dressed well before going to school. In fact, she spent an inordinate amount of time attempting to look her best. She was a good student and graduated from

Ashland High School with excellent grades. Ann was a good dancer and often attended weekend dances with Mamie. She had a pleasant personality and liked to sing. She was popular and got along very well with everyone.

After graduating from high school there was some discussion about what she might do. Some thought was given to her becoming a nurse. The truth of the matter is that she would have done well in college. However, there was no money for further education so her opportunities were also limited. She also got a job at the same factory where Hattie and Mamie worked in Ashland. Since World War II provided many job opportunities with good pay, she then went to work in a shipyard in Chester, Pennsylvania. It was too bad because both Hattie and Ann should have gone to college.

Ann had good common sense and always seemed to do the right thing, even when she was a youngster. She was especially devoted to my mother and had a good relationship with her. While all my sisters were hard working individuals, Ann was the most energetic worker of the three; it was a trait she got from my mom. Ann had two children, Marsha and Jimmy.

I always got along well with three sisters. Since I was the only little brother they had, I felt that needed to look after me. Indeed they did, and they had a positive influence on me during my formative years.

My Uncle Bill & Aunt Mary

My Uncle Bill, Aunt Mary and Harry.

William Kuschick (my Uncle Bill) was a young man when he came to America from Russia. His schooling was equivalent to about the fifth grade in our public school system. While he attempted to seek employment in various industries in different places in the country, he ended up as a coal miner in the anthracite region.

Bill lived in Frackville most of his life and had steady employment for many years at the Repellier Colliery in Saint Clair. I recall that he always came home from work in clean clothes, since the Repellier Colliery had a wash house, however not all collieries had one. A wash house was a small building where the miners could undress after working, take a shower and put on clean clothes. Their clothes were placed in a wire basket or simply gathered and secured together and raised to the ceiling with a simple pulley and rope system. It was a good use of space since they did not need lockers for their clothing. If you glanced up to the ceiling of a typical wash house, you would see wire baskets full of clothes or miners' clothing just gathered together hanging from the ceiling.

Since my Uncle Bill has steady employment, he and my Aunt Mary were well off financially compared to the average miner and his family. They always purchased brand names of articles of clothing. Whenever an occasion arose, they would quickly remind everyone that they bought items with labels that everyone knew were expensive such as "Jantzen" bathing suits, "Florsheim" shoes and so on.

In the fall of 1935, Bill purchased a brand new Chevrolet Coupe that cost $650.00. When you bought a car at that time, you had to drive it at a fairly low speed for several hundred miles to "break it in." I remember that he had a small fan installed on the dashboard to keep the windshield clear since new cars at that time did not have built-in defogging or air conditioning in them. It was exciting looking over the new car and riding in it, since not many coal miners were buying new cars in the mid-1930s.

As a youngster I spent many summers and weekends with Bill and Mary. They never had any children until very late in life when they had a boy, named Serge. Bill liked sports and always took me with him to all kinds of events. At the time, Shenandoah had a professional football team called the Shenandoah Presidents and he took me to see them play. He also took me to professional baseball and basketball games in which Frackville competed. I recall seeing Ron Northey play baseball in high school in Frackville, before he went to play for the Phillies in the major leagues. We also went to see boxing matches. I remember watching Al Etorre fight in Mahanoy city. Etorre once fought Joe Louis for the heavyweight title. He even took me along when he went to a poolroom; he took me everywhere.

Most Sundays during the summer, we went to Paradise Park in Lavelle. The park had a nice swimming pool with several concession stands and a large grass area off to one side of the pool. It was a rather quiet place because it was small and did not have the usual games or rides for kids that some other parks had. We always got there early on a Sunday morning. Most of the time we were the first ones at the park, because Mary wanted to get the picnic table and fireplace just below the pool. It was the best location, since Bill could park his car right next to the table and fireplace and we did not have to carry our food very far to heat it. You may be surprised, but Mary cooked a full dinner on Saturday night, so we only had to heat our food when we got to the park. Sometimes my own family or other friends would also join us at the park. We swam, ate, lay out in the sun and just relaxed for the day and did not leave until it was getting dark.

My Aunt Mary had a vegetable garden and she also raised chickens and ducks. It was a good thing she was an excellent cook, because Bill loved to eat. She always purchased quality cuts of meat as well as top brands of other food products. One of Bill's favorite meals was roast duck with buckwheat (kasha) filling. But most of all he enjoyed simple boiled potatoes which he sprinkled with a lot of salt. Bill would eat all his potatoes first, and then he proceeded with the rest of the meal.

One day while I was watching my aunt Mary peel potatoes, I noticed that she was using a knife rather than a potato peeler like my mother used. As a result, Mary seemed to waste a lot of the potato. She would start with a fairly large potato and when she got through slicing off the peeling, she would only have a small potato left. I told her that my Mom just skimmed off the potato peel and therefore did not waste any potato. Mary laughed, she did not say anything and just kept on slicing away.

Since my parents were Catholic, we never ate meat on Friday. So I never ate meat on Friday when I stayed with my Uncle Bill and Aunt Mary. Bill was an atheist and would always tell me that you don't eat meat on Friday when you can't afford it. Mary would always tell him not to say anything to me about that, and if I did not want to eat meat on Friday it was all right.

Bill never really made an issue of it and he never tried to change my religious beliefs.

Sometimes on a Friday when Mary worked at the Russian church bazaar in Frackville, she would bring home deep-fried perogies (pyrohys). It was the first time I ate deep-fried ones and they were good. When my Uncle Bill got paid, he always brought home a container of vanilla ice cream with cherries; it was a day that I always looked forward to.

Mary also raised canaries. She had birdcages in every room and about 30 canaries in one upstairs room alone. It was my job to see that all the birds had enough seed and fresh water. During the summer I gave them lettuce from Mary's garden. I would place the lettuce between the wires of the cage and the canaries would pick on it until they pulled it into the cage. I also had to clean the damn cages and that was one dirty job I hated to do. Sometimes a canary would escape from one of the cages and it was always difficult getting it back in its cage. Most of the time I would need my Aunt Mary's help in capturing the little bird.

I enjoyed taking a bath at my Aunt Mary's house because she had a bathroom. However, the water in Frackville was very hard and it was difficult to make many suds. One day when I stepped out of the tub to towel off, Mary noticed some undissolved soapsuds still on my body. She immediately told me to go back in the tub and wash off properly. For a while, it seemed that the same thing happened every time I took a bath. However, after a while I got wise and rinsed off very good before stepping out of the tub.

When Mary sent me to the store for a loaf of bread, she always checked it to see if it was soft when I returned. If the bread wasn't soft enough to suit her, she would make me return it. I never liked to return the bread to the store. After a while, I learned to squeeze the bread many times on my way back from the store; it seemed to work.

When she sent me to the grocery store, I always had to walk past a small candy store. One day some of the other kids in the neighborhood said that Mrs. Donnelly, who owned the candy store, could cast an evil spell on you if she caught you looking directly into her eyes. After that, I always ran or walked swiftly past her store. Yet it seemed that I was always drawn to at least glancing into the store as I went by, and I can't tell you why. In any event, I was always afraid that the evil eye was going to get me.

One day when I was about twelve years old Mary asked me to kill one of her chickens. My Uncle Bill wasn't home, so she gave me his hatchet and at the same time handed me a flapping chicken. I felt terrible, since I had never chopped off a chicken's head. I got the feeling the chicken was looking at me and wondering what I was going to do. Mary was strict and if she told me to do something I knew it had to be done. I finally managed to get the chicken's neck on a large block of wood and hacked off its head. Later Mary laughed when she explained to Bill how I went about it; it appears that I also chopped off part of the poor chicken's beak. I never killed another chicken in my life, and I've never been fond of eating chicken ever since that experience.

One day Bill had a terrible thing happen to him at the Repellier Colliery where he worked. He accidentally chopped off his thumb while cutting timber down inside the mine. I remember when my Aunt Mary called, she was so excited that the word "thumb" got garbled and we thought she said, "tongue." Bill was a rugged individual and went back to work in about a month. While he wasn't able to clench his hand together or make a tight closed fist, he managed to do almost everything he did prior to his accident.

Bill was knowledgeable about current events and always listened to the news on the radio. Prior to that I can't recall ever listening to the news very much on the radio at home. He always had his own opinion about world events and shared them with me. He was especially keen on education and I learned a lot from him. At times he would explain to me how politicians operated. However, I was quite young and when I told him that it difficult for me to believe that any politician would be dishonest, he would only laugh at me.

One day several workers were pouring concrete in his basement. He pointed out that the foreman on the job didn't have a high school education but knew how to figure out how many cubic yards of concrete were needed for the basement. Then he asked me if I could do the same calculation. At first

I forgot to do the correct conversion from cubic feet to cubic yards, but after a while I got the correct answer. Bill was a practical man and always looked for results.

My Uncle Bill had a lot of patience and he never scolded me. He did however tease me about Christine Pechansky, the girl next door. When I got annoyed about that (as boys about ten years of age often do) he would often tease me more, but it was always done in a friendly manner. Overall he was a levelheaded guy with good judgment about things in general. I had the good fortune of living with him and my Aunt Mary for many summers as well as many weekends over the years.

As I look back, it was my mom and my Uncle Bill who had the greatest positive impact on my life as far as family members were concerned. They always encouraged me to make something of myself, and that meant getting an education. Some years later when I graduated as valedictorian of my class from Butler Township High School in 1942, Bill and other family members were in attendance. When he heard my name called out, Bill said, "My hair just stood on end." He wasn't surprised—he was shocked.

When I was young I never really told my Uncle Bill how much I appreciated what he did for me. However, when I grew up and had more plain old common sense, I told him how important he was in my life. He was a retired coal miner by that time, and I felt he appreciated what I had to say. I'm glad that I finally got around to telling him before he died.

Our Boarder Mike

Margie Colahan, Mike (our boarder) and Harry.

When I was only about four years old we had a boarder, who was Russian, named Mike Romaskevitz. He boarded with us for a number of years. Mike was a coal miner who did not have any family, and since he was a source of income my mother took him in. He paid a certain sum for his meals and lodging with us. Many coal region families kept boarders, and over the years we had several that I remember as a child.

I was about six years old in the picture above taken in front of our home. Mike is holding our dog, Tiny, and I'm on the right and the little girl next door (Margie) is on the left. I believe that our family car then was a Whippet, probably a model from the mid-1920s.

Mike was a World War I veteran who served in the United States Army. He was a big man who was burned badly while fighting with the American Army in Europe. I can still recall the image of his web-like hands. They were scarred, unsightly and he was unable to squeeze his hands together to make a tight fist.

Mike never married and did not seem to take things seriously. He had a big hearty laugh and never seemed to give anyone any trouble. However, he liked to drink and smoke and did both to excess. He spent most of his time with us, but on occasion he would spend some time at a veteran's home and hospital in Bath, New York. Whenever he came to visit us, he would always hold out some money to give to my mother immediately upon entering our home, and we always laughed about that. As I got older, I wondered about his family background, but I was never able to learn much about that part of his life.

He had a good friend named Brownie McGuire who lost his leg while serving in the United States Army in World War I. Brownie lived with the McGuire family in Big Mine Run. He was a small and slender guy who also smoked and drank too much. When the two of them went walking, Brownie always had difficulty keeping up with Mike. It was a comical scene to see them staggering together, when they had too much to drink.

They would often sit on our front porch drinking and talking about the war and telling tales about all sorts of other things. As kids, we found their stories interesting and fascinating. Brownie would roll up his pants leg and show us his varnished hollow wooden leg. At the time I thought it was the most curious thing I ever saw.

As Mike grew older he spent all his time at the Veteran's Hospital in Bath, New York. One day when I visited him at the hospital,

I realized that his health was seriously deteriorating. Not long after that, I received a letter that he passed away. He was one of many homeless soldiers, I suppose--who just quietly pass away.

"Gike"

Sometime in the 1930s there was a coal mine explosion at the Bast Colliery in Big Mine Run. While it wasn't recorded in the listing of mine accidents in the anthracite region where five or more were killed, it was one I remember when I was about ten years old. This story is about one miner who I knew that was injured in that mine accident.

Gurney Buhl was a young man who lived at number four Woodland Heights, only six houses away from ours. He was a physically fit individual, about thirty years old, and an excellent baseball pitcher. Gurney's nickname was "Gike" and that's all everyone ever called him. It seemed that everyone in Big Mine Run had a nickname, and no one used first names except your own family members.

One summer afternoon in the early 1930s, I heard several sharp horn blasts at the Bast Colliery and I knew that there was an accident. I recall many people running toward the colliery, which was about a quarter-mile away to find out what happened. It was similar to some movie scenes we have all seen where people would rush to the site of a mine disaster.

After a while, we heard that Gike was one of the miners who was injured. Later we found out that his eyes were damaged in the mine explosion and that he was taken to the Wills Eye Hospital in Philadelphia, which had an excellent reputation for treating people with major eye problems. Gike remained in the hospital for an extended period of time.

When he was finally discharged we learned that he not only lost his sight but also lost one arm in the accident. It was damaged so badly that part of the limb had to be amputated above the elbow. I recall that his sleeve was always folded up and pinned to the upper part of his arm just below the shoulder. However, during the summer his stump of his arm was exposed. It was a tragic time for him since he had four young children at the time of the accident.

I often saw Gike walking around the neighborhood and I was surprised how well he managed to find his way about. I had never known a blind person before and for some reason I got interested in how he viewed the world and how he got along. He loved to talk and some people got tired of listening to him because he would often repeat his stories. However, I enjoyed chatting with him, and as a result I listened a lot.

Even though Big Mine Run was only a small patch, George Chuplis operated a gambling place in the basement of his home about a block from Gike's house. The guys would gather there to play cards, drink beer and eat potato chips and pretzels. Poker and pinochle were the favorite card games and throwing darts was also popular. I recall playing poker for pennies with Joe Baldino, John Mikurak, George Mickle, George Chuplis, Nicky Pechansky and Johnny Latsko.

Gike always walked alone to the gambling place, feeling his way by touching the fences and houses along his pathway. He would find a comfortable seat and listen to all the chatter. He was a good talker himself and often joined in the conversations. Most of the time someone would buy him a beer since he did not have much money. I remember paying ten cents for a bottle of beer for him and he would always politely wish me luck. He would say, "Here's to ya, 'Boya,'" that was one of my nicknames.

Sometime after his accident, his wife had a baby girl named Shirley. Well, that was the topic of conversation for quite a while. Gike got razzed about that a lot but he didn't seem to mind. In fact, he seemed to enjoy the attention that he was getting. However, what he really enjoyed (besides his new daughter) was all the free beers everyone was buying him.

Gike preferred drinking beer from a glass. When he poured his beer from the bottle he extended his thumb into the glass; when the liquid touched his thumb it was time to stop pouring. Gike never spilled a drop. When he has a sufficient number of beers, he would stagger back home all by himself without the use of a cane or any sensory device.

One day a group of guys were sitting around and Gike decided to show us how he could tell the different denominations of paper money by gently rubbing his fingers over the numbers. He would say, "This is a two dollar bill. This is a five spot. This one is a dollar bill." He was always right and for some time we marveled at his skill. It turned out that he always performed this feat at a table where he had a confidant seated next to him. While Gike was feeling and rubbing the bill carefully, his confidant would tap his foot on Gike's shoe the number that corresponded to the bill. Gike won many free beers that way. We all had a good laugh, after we learned how he did it.

I often played checkers with him and he always won. He was very good at checkers. The checkerboard had cutouts where the round and square pieces fitted into slots. Gike had a habit of twisting a small curl on top of his head with his finger as he was thinking about his next move. He particularly enjoyed playing for a beer because he rarely lost. That way he felt he earned the beer and that he wasn't just being treated to a free drink; however, he never turned down a free drink.

One summer evening a number of us kids were sitting around looking for something to do. Gike suggested we play some athletic games he played as a youngster in the early part of the 1900s. One game involved throwing a broomstick at a three-pronged wooden object with a one-foot stem that was cut from a small tree. The wooden object was about 30 inches high and was placed in a small circle about thirty feet away from a base line. When someone knocked the object over from the base line, the person who was "it" (the tagger) would pick up the broomstick and try to tag some kid with the broomstick before he could reach the base line from which the stick was thrown. If the tagger was successful, he would exchange places with the person who threw the broomstick. It was a fairly rough game because broomsticks were flying through the air several feet off the ground. When you were actually playing the game, you found yourself ducking all the time.

We were not aware of any of the games that Gike suggested to us; however, we found that they were different, simple and fun to play. He seemed to enjoy sitting around listening to us while we played. Maybe it took him back to another time when he was just a kid playing those same games himself.

Gike was a sports fan and he spent a lot of time listening to his radio on the front porch. He particularly enjoyed listening to the Phillies baseball games. When I was old enough to drive our car I always tapped on my car horn and called out to him when I passed his house; he always hollered back and waved. He would tell me that he always recognized my horn and voice. Sometime later he got interested in CB radio.

After graduating from high school, I left Big Mine Run and worked for a year before I entered the Army in World War II. I lost track of him and never had much contact at all with him from that time on. However, I remember him as one of the more colorful and unforgettable characters I knew at Woodland Heights. The last time I saw Gike was some sixty years ago; however, I learned later that he lived to be in his nineties. I often marveled at his up-beat nature. He seemed to be able to adjust to his handicap and get on with his life. I never saw him in a depressed mood. Perhaps I can best describe Gike as a man who lost his sight, but a man who never lost his vision.

My Friend Nicky

Nicky Pechansky's family was also Ukrainian and we were good friends with them. They only lived two houses away from us, so we saw each other all the time. Nicky Pechansky was the youngest child in the family and the same age as me. He had two older brothers' named Metro and John. Metro, the older of the two, did not seem

Nicky Pechansky (in front),
John Pahira and Harry.

to bother with people very much and I got the impression that he was a loner. However, Johnny was very friendly, popular and everyone enjoyed his company. The Pechansky family also had three older sisters named Anna, the oldest, Mary and Christine, the youngest. As it turned out, Nicky's three sisters were about the same ages as my three older sisters named Hattie, the oldest, Mary and Ann, the youngest.

Mary Pechansky and my sister Mary were close friends and they did many things together. They played with each other as youngsters, picked huckleberries during the summer, and went on dates and dancing together with their boyfriends. Christine and my sister Ann also were good friends and they too did all sorts of things together. Nicky and I played hide and go seek with Christine and Ann, as well as other kids games. My mom and Nicky's mother were also good friends.

Christine Pechanksy.

Christine's son, Peter.

Nicky and I were good buddies, and I guess we knew each other from the time we were about five years of age. He was small and frail for his age, and one leg was very slightly shorter than the other. As a result, he had a very slight limp; however, I never noticed it until we were older.

We played, smoked, went swimming and picked huckleberries; we did many things together. Nicky and I would throw "goonies" (small stones) at bottles to see who would be the first to break one. We also looked for small flat pieces of stone (skippers) and skimmed them across a pond to see how many "skips" it would take before the stone sank or reached the other side. We would count: 6, 7, . . . 10 skips perhaps, before the skipper would sink. If we weren't watching each other too closely, a little bit of cheating would go on.

However, when I wanted to convince him that I was really telling the truth about something, I would look at him straight in the face, hold my right hand in the air and say, "Honest-to-God." Of course, he used that same expression with me.

We simply walked into each other's house all the time; we never bothered to knock on the door. It was just the way things were in Big Mine Run in those days. One day I walked into his home (we were both about nine years old at the time) and I found him getting ready to fry an egg. I was surprised to see him do something like that because I never fried an egg by myself at that age. I watched him put some kind of shortening in the pan, (probably lard) take an egg, crack it and flip it into a small frying pan. He scrambled it like he knew what he was doing, and frankly I was impressed. As he sat down eating the egg, I looked at him thinking he had done something nifty.

One day when we were alone in the house, he motioned me to follow him from the kitchen to the dining room. He walked over to a bureau and pulled out a long barreled revolver. It belonged to his oldest brother Metro. The barrel of the gun had a small cut on the top and it looked to me like someone tried to file off the end of the barrel to make it shorter. We proceeded to take turns holding the gun and pointing it at each other. Then we poked one another in the back with the barrel and called out, "hand's up" just to see what it felt like. I never learned whether the revolver was loaded or not, but at the time we thought we were just having fun and acting grown up.

Front row, left to right: George Horvath, Edward Colahan, Leo Young, Edward Bielarski and Charley Horvath. Second row: Peter Puketza, Louis Young, Edward Colahan, Teddy Bielarski and Nicky Pechansky standing in the truck.

Nicky and I also played poker for pennies with Joe Mickle, George (Baxie) Mickle, George Chuplis and other kids in the neighborhood. When he lost money while playing poker he did not seem to mind. He was a carefree kid and did not worry about anything. When we didn't have any pennies, we played poker for stick matches. In general, kids played cards with kids and grown-up guys played with each other. The older kids always played for small change money.

He bought cigarettes and smoked somewhat regularly even at a young age. In those days you could buy a single cigarette for one cent. Not only did he become a regular smoker early, but even started to drink beer at a relatively early age.

Nicky always spent any money he earned, whereas I tended to save mine. If he had a nickel and wanted an ice cream cone, he would buy one and enjoy it. I would want an ice cream cone, but somehow I wanted to hold on to my nickel more. One day Nicky and I went into the local grocery store, which was only one room in a regular house. As it turned out, the owner of the store didn't always come out to the storeroom right away. Nicky walked over to the ice cream refrigerator and took a popsicle and quickly pulled out the popsicle stick to see if it had "free" written on it. If it didn't read free on the stick, he would put it back and take another popsicle. If it said free, then he pushed the stick back in and bought it when the owner showed up. Then after eating the popsicle, he would turn in the free stick to the storeowner for an another popsicle.

It was not unusual for Nicky to walk to Brown's drug store in Ashland (I think it was located at third and Center Street over a mile away) and later on walk home. One day I went with him to see what he was up to. I was surprised to learn that he enjoyed playing the pinball machine in the drug store. He spent fifteen or twenty cents playing the machine for a half-hour or so and then we walked back. While I watched him play the machine, I kept my fifteen cents in my pocket. However, he did many things alone and seemed to have a personality similar to his oldest brother, Metro.

Nicky seemed to want to do all the things grown-ups do while he was still a kid. As he grew into his teen-age years he did not develop physically along with the other kids. He was somewhat small for his age and always had that "young kid" look about himself. However, he was a popular guy and everyone liked Nicky. Sometimes I got the impression that people also pitied him.

As it turned out, he never did wait to grow into manhood normally. He rushed into adulthood on his own and in his own way. Many years later, I was sorry to learn that he died as a young man. When I heard that he died, my mind went way back in time to when we were very young kids playing together. I could almost hear him say about some small challenge we were facing, "Go ahead an' do it, don't be a 'fraidy-cat,'" and I would say, "I ain't afraid, an' you're a 'faridy cat' yourself."

"Hard Coal Joe"

Sometime in the mid-1930s, when I was about ten years old, Joe Baldino and I were buddies in Big Mine Run (we just said, "the run"). Joe was the youngest in a family of seven brothers and four sisters. His nickname was "Hard Coal Joe" and he was a tough hard-nosed kid even at a young age. Although he was feisty and mischievous, most people seemed to like him. He was the quintessential "Peck's bad boy."

We were an odd couple. He was rebellious about many things and didn't like to go to school, but we still got along with each other. He was an independent kid and somewhat of a loner. While his older brothers were always there to look after him, I don't think he felt that he needed their protection. Joe's trademark was an old knit cap that he wore all the time. It was one of those light woolen caps (no peak) but with side flaps for his ears. However, the side flaps were always folded up and buttoned on top of the old dirty cap. And he always wore a very wide leather belt as you can see in the picture below.

Front row, left to right: Harry, Joe Baldino and John Pahira. Second row, Nicky Pechansky and Teddy Bielarski.

We did some things together that weren't too bad, but they weren't too good either. About that time, the Bast Colliery had just closed down so there was only a very small number of employees remaining at the colliery. However, the coal company still employed cops to patrol the area around the colliery complex. After the cops made their rounds, Joe and I would stroll up to the colliery looking for old pieces of scrap iron, brass and copper that we knew we could sell. Even though they were junk items, we were not allowed to take them—but we did. When we found items like that, we would go back and get our wagon and return to the colliery. After we filled our wagon (sometimes a wheelbarrow) with junk metal, we hauled it to Joe's garage, which was across the street from his house. When the junkman came around, we would sell our booty; however, we always bargained with him for more money than he originally offered us.

Most of the items we took weren't too big, but they were heavy because they we made of iron. Junk iron was the most common metal we found and the junkman paid the least money for it. On the other hand, we were always looking for brass and copper because the junkman paid much more for those items.

One day as we were wandering around the colliery, we found an old electric motor. We got excited and wondered how much money we could get for it. It was very heavy and we didn't stop to think about how difficult it would be to move it. As it turned out, it was so heavy and cumbersome that we were only able to move it a short distance each day. Somehow after many days of struggling with the motor, we finally managed to get it to Joe's garage. When his older brother, Tony, saw what we did he scolded us for taking it. He said, half-jokingly, "You goddamn kids are gonna go to jail one of these days." However, he didn't tell us to return the motor.

As I mentioned in a previous story, we also helped ourselves to coal that was being transported on a Reading Railroad branch that ran directly through Big Mine Run. We would hop up on the coal cars even as the cars were moving and throw off large lumps of coal and then gather it all up later. Sometimes the coal cars were left standing in one place for a while (we were always glad when that happened) and in those cases it was much easier to steal more coal. On one occasion when I was throwing coal off from the top of a coal car, Joe yelled to me, "Ruby! (one of my nicknames) run, run, the cops." I was so absorbed in throwing coal off the coal car that I wasn't paying any attention to the coal cops. To this day, I believe I would have been caught by them if it wasn't for my buddy Joe.

We never considered it outright stealing when we took coal or scrap iron. I think we felt that the coal company had lots of money and we didn't have any. Was it wrong that we took those things? Well, yes. However, we never felt that we were doing something terribly bad.

The picture below of Joe and his brother Leo shows him at about 15 years of age. He just came home from working in a coalhole in Buck's Patch about a quarter of a mile from Big Mine Run. He also had the nickname of "Coal Car Runner" Joe. One day while talking about the past, Joe explained to me how he almost got killed in a rock fall while working in that coahole with his brother Leo.

Leo and "Hard Coal Joe" Baldino.

Sometime afterward, Amil Bielarski took over the ownership of that same coahole that Joe worked in. Amil, my brother-in-law, ran the bootleg operation a number of years before the Centralia fire actually caused him to close down the coalhole.

Fast forward now, from the mid-1930s to 2004—almost seven decades later. Remember now, I had no communication whatsoever with Joe Baldino during all this time. Then early in

2004 I made contact with Diane Rooney who was instrumental in getting me re-acquainted with Joe during one of her many trips to the anthracite region to carry on her research. As it turned out, Joe was residing in a home in Ashland formerly lived in by the Verbish family who was related to Diane.

So one evening late in August, 2004 I telephoned Joe and left a brief message on his voice mail. Later that evening when I called back, a man's voice answered, "hello." I said, "Is that you Joe?" The next voice I heard was, "Holy Christ, Harry Bobonich, I haven't spoken to you in fifty, maybe sixty years." Believe it or not, the very next thing he said was, "Remember the time we stole that electric motor? We had a helluva time lugging it to our garage." That set the tone for our conversation. I said, "Remember the time you warned me about the cops when I was throwing coal off the coal cars?" You hollered, "Ruby! Run, Run, the cops."

Our conversation went back and forth like that; we were reminding each other of the crazy things we did as kids. Maybe in a way, we were those kids again in or own minds—if only for a few moments.

Joe then reminded me that he and Johnny Horvath (another one of my buddies) went to jail for trespassing. Then Joe mentioned that he had been sent to jail three times on minor charges such as trespassing and stealing things. He also told me that he and Stanley (Stiney) Bielarski were sent to a reform school in Phonexville, Pennsylvania for six months for stealing copper wire. Stiney and I were also buddies and were in the same grade in both grade school and high school. After leaving the reform school, Joe was drafted into the United States Army.

Then after a while he started to tell me that most of his family had moved to California many years ago. In fact, he did also, but now he is living in Ashland. He followed up by telling me about people that we both knew who had died. It's something that elderly people seem to do, especially when they haven't seen or talked to each other in some time. I told him that I was writing a book on Big Mine Run and my recollections of the coal region. Joe proceeded to tell me proudly that he was a Coal Region History buff. I told Joe that I was pleased to hear that. Then I suggested that I wanted to visit with him to talk about the "old times" and to include some of our escapades in my book.

In March 2005, Joe Baldino visited me at our home in Shippensburg. I happened to be standing in our driveway when he pulled up to our home. I recognized Hard Coal Joe right away even though I had not seen him in about sixty-five years. As you can imagine, we chatted about all sorts of things we did when we were kids; then we also talked about the other kids we grew up with in Big Mine Run. Joe showed me the medal he won for participating in the Battle of the Bulge in World War II.

It was only a reunion of two—two Big Mine Run kids getting together after so many years. We owe that meeting to Diane Rooney--a "get-together" that never would have happened without her. And when Joe and I were kids growing up in Big Mine Run, Diane's cousins of yesteryear were also kids growing up in Gilberton or some nearby patch in the coal region.

Our Neighbor Anna

Anna Colahan was our wonderful next-door neighbor at 15 Woodland Heights in Big Mine Run. Her maiden name was Rosti and she lived in Ashland before marrying Edward Colahan our neighbor. She was a simple, honest person and never pretended to be anything she was not. Anna enjoyed talking with people and made friends easily. It seemed she always knew the latest news and gossip and was eager to share it with others. Nevertheless, she was a good person who could be relied on if you needed her assistance, and our family liked her. She had a habit of using certain expressions like, "Bejabbers, I never thought she would do that." Or, "Bejesus, my husband is coming home late again."

Anna had a habit of simply walking into our home anytime she chose and would sit down and start talking. She never knocked; she just walked in through our parlor, into the dining room and then to our kitchen. We didn't think anything about it; we just accepted it as a normal thing to do.

Even after I was married and visited my mother with my wife Gloria and our two children, Anna would always come over to see us. If she happened to see my car pulling up to my mother's house, she would often walk into my mother's house at the same time we did. She would always ask Gloria if she could hold our two children, Chris and Greg when they were babies.

Anna, who was overweight, liked to eat and she was especially fond of my mother's good cooking. Who wasn't? She liked perogies (pyrohy), potato pancakes (bleenies), homemade sausage—well, she liked everything my mother made. If she happened to stop in while we were eating, she would simply sit down and start a conversation. My mother always served her a portion of what we were eating on a small dish, and Anna would eat it like she was a member of the family.

Anna had one of the few telephones in the neighborhood and for years she generously allowed us to make and receive calls. She also has hot running water with a shower in the basement, which I used frequently since we did not have hot running water in our home.

I was grateful that Anna lived next door because she would check on my mother several times a day when my mother was older and lived by herself for a period of time. Anna was very patient and would help my mother in any way she could. While she never had very much money, she never complained. Anna was a good person and a wonderful neighbor and a true friend to my mother. She had two very nice children, Edward and Lorraine. I was surprised and saddened when I learned one day that Anna passed away at a relatively early age.

My Most Memorable Teacher

Joseph Wolfgang, William O'Donnell and Daniel Helwig.

It seems that we all had that one special teacher we remember from our school days. You know, the one teacher that we felt made a difference in our life. In my case, it was Mr. Daniel Helwig, who was my teacher in grades six through eight in a one-room schoolhouse. Mr. Helwig had a very positive impact on my life. He is pictured in the photo above on the right. Mr. O'Donnell was my mathematics teacher and principal and Mr. Wolfgang was my basketball coach. Both of them were also excellent high school teachers.

Grades one through five were taught in one building in Big Min Run, Catherine Dougherty taught grades one through three in one room while Mary MacDonald taught grades four and five in an adjacent room. They both were my teachers through the fifth grade. It was always considered a big change and a little scary to go from fifth to sixth grade because you had to change buildings, and besides, the teacher in the new building was a man.

When I started sixth grade, Mr. Daniel Helwig was hired as a new teacher to teach grades six through eight in Big Mine Run. (Several years later, he was also my teacher at Butler Township High School.) I recall that he purchased a brand new 1936 Plymouth and had to drive about eight miles daily from Lavelle where he lived.

Mr. Helwig had a lot of patience and he always encouraged us to learn. He would take us on hikes into the woods and would point out the names of different flowers, birds and trees. He seemed to know everything. I was always pleased when he chose me along with another student to go out into the woods and chop down an evergreen tree for the classroom at Christmas time.

He would also read stories like Tom Sawyer, Huckleberry Finn and others to us in class. He chose interesting books to read and would laugh out loud at humorous incidents in the book to share his feelings with us. I looked forward to his readings and consequently became interested in reading more books.

Mr. Helwig also taught us to do various crafts. It was the first time I ever did anything like making small craft items all by myself. It was a broadening experience and also a rewarding one.

One day he appointed me as class librarian. I had never been in a regular library so I didn't know how to sign out books and other matters like that. Of course, Mr. Helwig taught me what to do. Since we didn't have a library, we used the closet at the rear of the room. It was my job to sign out books and keep the library records in order. It was just small things like that, which made a difference.

He used his broad knowledge in different subjects to encourage us to learn. I believe that it was during his classes and teaching that I came to understand the value of how important it was to get an education. Mr. Helwig's successful teaching was all the more noteworthy when you consider that the kids in Big Mine Run at that time were somewhat difficult to deal with. In other words, he had his hands full as we used to say.

He earned a master's degree from Bucknell University, and many years later, I too, earned a master's degree in chemistry from the same institution. In his own special way, he made me feel that if I didn't always try to do my best, I was not only letting him down, but more important—I was letting myself down. So I pay tribute to Mr. Daniel Helwig, an outstanding teacher, who made a difference. As you can see, I still remember him fondly—some seven decades later.

Chapter 6

STORIES ABOUT BIG DAYS

Celebrating More Than One Christmas

For a number of years our family celebrated Christmas twice. It may seem a little strange at first, but it was true. We celebrated Christmas on December 25, but then about two weeks later; we also celebrated Christmas on January 7. Here's the story of how it happened.

When I was a kid, our family as well as the other Ukrainian families celebrated Christmas on January 7 which followed the old Julian Calendar. It was an important religious holiday and celebrated as such with various customs. The entire holiday was steeped in religious tradition. When anyone entered another Ukrainian household at Christmas time they always said in Ukrainian, "Chrystos Rodyvsya" or Christ is born. The person greeting the visitor would then say, "Slavite Yoho" or Let us Glorify Him.

My mother prepared a huge meal for Christmas Eve with twelve separate non-meat food dishes, which had a religious significance. The Christmas Eve Supper or Holy Supper was called (sviata vecheria). Each dish was dedicated to one of the twelve Apostles. The different food dishes included: borsch, boiled eggs, potato, cabbage and prune perogies (pyrohy), stuffed cabbage (holubtsi), herring, homemade cheese with the sign of the cross on top, butter with the sign of the crucifix also on top, mushrooms (hryby) and gravy, assorted vegetables, and horseradish.

She also made platted bread with raisins as well as cheese, nut and poppy seed rolls. My mom also baked donuts, which we called "pam puh heh" (pampushky) for Christmas that resembled jelly donuts; however, they didn't have any jelly in them. I always enjoyed eating some while they were still warm, because they were coated with powdered sugar and almost melted in my mouth. We made a lot of donuts and ate them for a long time after Christmas. We also dipped them in our coffee like all dunking donut people do.

My mom also prepared a special sweet dish made with boiled wheat, poppy seed, honey, chopped nuts and sugar which was called "pshenytsia." I was often given the job of mashing down the poppy seeds with a wooden mallet until they were milky. I also had to use the same wooden mallet in mashing down the wheat, which was in a small sack. It took quite a while to finally get the poppy seed and wheat ready to mix with the honey.

At the beginning of the meal, my father would take a very small portion of the (pshenytsia) in a teaspoon and toss it up to the ceiling. If some of the mixture stuck to the ceiling, it was considered good luck and that our family would prosper in the New Year. As a small child, I would glance up at our living room ceiling and see the small light yellow stains from previous years.

At the Christmas Eve Supper my mother always set a place at the table with an empty chair; it was to honor our ancestors. Sometimes a neighborhood bachelor would be invited and he would also share in the festivities, just as if he were a member of the family.

During the Yuletide and New Year holidays, we always made a popular alcoholic drink called "boilo." The ingredients included orange and lemon juice, honey, caraway seeds, cloves and a lot of whiskey. We heated the entire mixture, without the whiskey, on the stove in a small pink teapot. The whiskey was added while the mixture was cooking. You had to be careful at this point because the whiskey could easily catch on fire. After it was finished, we kept the teapot on our coal stove but off to the side where it was kept warm. The boilo was always served warm or hot. It was the mother of all hot toddy drinks.

Sometime during the holiday season, a small group of singers (koliadnyky) visited each Ukrainian home and sang Christmas carols in Ukrainian. They were usually a little "tipsy" by the time they reached our home (their last stop) since they got a free drink at the various other places they visited. Their caroling was loud and enthusiastic and the singers stomped their feet on the floor so hard that at times I thought they were going to go through the floor and land in the cellar. Our entire family joined in the caroling. Sometimes my sisters and I would giggle at some of the singers' antics. I still remember some of the words of one Christmas carol we sang called, "Boh Predvichny" (God Eternal).

It seemed to us kids that it always snowed on the sixth or seventh of January and that made it seem more like Christmas. Some Ukrainian families only celebrated Christmas on the seventh of January. For those families, Christmas trees were free several days after December 25 because nobody was selling Christmas trees then. In addition, they had the benefit of many Christmas sales after December 25.

Since we celebrated Christmas two weeks after December 25, others often poked fun at us "greenhorns" or "hunkies." However, while our family celebrated Christmas as a serious religious holiday on January seventh, my three older sisters and myself were permitted to also celebrate Christmas on December 25. As a child, there were times when I felt somewhat awkward celebrating Christmas at two different times.

As my sisters and I grew older there was a gradual shift from the January Christmas to the more traditional December Christmas. This occurred because the older traditional people were not only dying off, but they recognized that their children preferred the December 25th date. As a result, the Ukrainian church, which was located in Centralia, had fewer church residents and it became less influential in the lives of the younger people outside of Centralia.

Since our family was quite poor, like many others, we didn't get many bought presents. We would get fruit and even some lumps of coal in our stocking. The presents that we got were always placed under the tree for December 25. The January Christmas was mainly a religious celebration.

As I reflect back to the time when I was a kid, I now think it was nice of my parents to try to teach us something about our heritage. It was a time when ethnic groups held more closely to their older ways and beliefs, but that is no longer the case. However, time changes many things and so the January Christmas, like many older traditions, has all but faded away.

Easter Time

Since there were two different calendars in use at the time, we also celebrated Easter on two different dates, just as we did Christmas. However, the Easter Bunny could not compete with good old jolly Santa Claus. So the two Easter dates were mainly celebrated as religious days.

My mom prepared many foods for Easter including fresh and smoked ham, pork, sausage (kielbasa), hard boiled eggs, fish, homemade baked cheese, beet relish, horseradish and a variety of vegetables.

She also baked wonderful large round bread called paska. Before baking the paska, she would coat (using a brush made of feathers) the top of the loaf with a mixture of the yolk of an egg and water so that after it was baked in the oven it would have a shiny brown crust on top. When the paska was being baked in the oven, no one was allowed to make any noise near the stove for fear that it would collapse in the oven. When the bread was done, it had a nice dark yellow color because a large number of eggs were use in baking it. The paska bread also had raisins in it. I always liked to cut off the first slice from a large loaf and eat it with margarine or sometimes with margarine and jelly.

Since the paska was an Easter ritual bread and taken to the church to be blessed, everyone tried hard to bake a successful paska. We were always happy when my mom's paska turned out well. The paska we baked was about a foot in diameter and a foot high. However a friend of mine named Olga Gadomski, said that some of the paskas they baked were as large as two feet in diameter.

My mom also baked another kind of bread similar to the paska bread, except that it was platted and longitudinal in shape. It also had a yellowish color and shiny appearance when it came out of the oven. I can still remember the wonderful, intoxicating smell of freshly baked bread when my mom lifted the loaves out of the oven,

Whenever a Ukrainian family visited us on Easter they would always greet us by saying in Ukrainian, "Chrystos Voskres" or Christ has Risen. Then we would say, "Vo Istinu Voskres" or Indeed He is Risen. In turn, we would use the same expressions when we visited other Ukrainian families.

Most of those traditions have faded away and we now seem to be a much more homogenized society.

At Easter time we got a basket with some of our own colored eggs, some homemade Easter eggs, jellybeans and one bought milk chocolate figure. My chocolate piece was a male figure like "Popeye" while my sisters' chocolate pieces were small girl figures.

Of course we colored eggs with dye colors like most other people. We would start with about six glasses, which were filled with warm water. Then we placed one small dye colored pill into each glass. After the pill dissolved, we would take a hard-boiled egg and place it on a spoon and then put it into one of the glasses to get colored. We competed with each other to see who could make the best-looking colored egg.

While we were coloring the eggs, we would play the game of cracking each other's egg. I would hold an egg in my hand with only the tip of the egg shown. Then my sister, Mary, would take her egg and try to crack mine by striking the tip of her egg into mine. The person who ended up with the egg cracked was considered the loser. However, we were discouraged from playing the game while we were still coloring eggs. And we always had to eat the cracked eggs first and let the other colored ones in the bowl because they looked prettier.

After all the eggs were colored, we would visit our neighbors and play the "egg cracking game." I had a purple colored wooden egg but they soon got wise to me. Some of our neighbors had colored glass eggs and we looked out for those.

Another method of coloring eggs, which was elegant, involved a procedure where the eggs were marked with a stylus filled with hot bee's wax. These highly decorated eggs were called "pysanky" and required a skillful hand. The Ukrainian tradition of pysanka writing goes back over a thousand years. Here's a general description of how they were made.

You start by taking a fresh egg and then wash and dry it carefully. Now you draw faint pencil lines or patterns on the egg depending on what design you want. For example, you can draw a light pencil line around the equator of the egg. Then you could draw about three longitudinal (top to bottom) pencil lines on the egg. These markings are used as guidelines and can vary depending on the person coloring the eggs.

Now you take a stylus filled with hot bee's wax, which is heated with a candle, and cover over the pencil lines with wax. The egg is then placed in a light color dye such as yellow. After the egg is colored, it's removed and dried. Using the stylus, wax is now applied to some areas of the yellow colored egg depending on the design you wanted. After that, the egg in then placed in a slightly darker color dye like green. This process of applying wax and then using other darker colors is continued with the darkest color being applied last.

Finally, the wax is removed which shows the colors that were covered up at each stage in the process. If you do it right, you end up with a remarkably elegant multi-colored pattern on the egg. We were not very good at making pysanky eggs, but we enjoyed trying to make them. John Pechansky, who lived two doors away from us, made very nice pysanky eggs.

I have some beautiful ones that were made over seventy years ago and they still look great. They are a fine expression of Ukrainian folk art. I wonder how many people are still making pysanky eggs today?

The Wedding Day

Weddings in Big Mine Run were no small affairs--they often lasted several days. There was always plenty to eat and drink (especially beer and whiskey) and the musicians kept things lively. It seemed that everyone looked forward to a good wedding.

When a young couple decided to get married, they soon learned that planning for the wedding was a big job. Setting the date and location came first. Then the couple had to decide on who was going to be the bridesmaid and the best man, as well as the rest of the wedding party. The list of names of those invited to the wedding was a problem because the list always seemed to grow longer. The conversation would go, "We have to invite Mary if were going to invite Pauline and so it went." Arrangements for the church ceremony and the practicing sessions in church all had to be attended to. The big problem of preparing food for everyone had to have the cooperation of a number of people; no one in Big Mine Run ever hired a caterer in those days. Even though some of the planning got hectic, everything seemed to work out by the day of the wedding.

The first day of the wedding was highlighted by the church ceremony. Those participating in the formal wedding party always looked stunning and they got a lot of attention. Of course, the bride in white was the most beautiful of all and everyone wanted to wish her well. There was a groom, of course, but nobody paid much attention to him. The ladies gowns were all pretty—red, blue, green and yellow were popular colors. The men were dressed in tuxedos and they also looked nice. They almost looked like different people in their formal attire. Indeed it was a time when everyone attending the wedding got dressed up, especially the ladies.

The automobiles of the wedding party were decorated with colored streamers and ribbons. The people that decorated the cars always took time to make sure all the vehicles in the wedding party looked attractive. The decorations on the cars had to be taped securely so they not only looked nice, but that the decorations stayed on as the cars drove away.

After the church ceremony, the wedding party went to the photographer to have their pictures taken. Everyone then went to the home of the bride where the wedding celebration usually took place. A formal dining table was set for the bride and groom, their parents, the wedding party and close relatives.

The bride and groom are usually so busy talking to people and being congratulated that they don't have time to eat. I suppose though, that they are so excited that they aren't that hungry anyhow.

Large dining tables were also set for other relatives and friends. Many others ate informally by filling up their plates and eating from a small table, counter or from their lap.

Typical things to eat included: ham, chicken, cold cuts, cheese, potato salad, mashed potatoes, carrots, peas, corn, bread, rolls, pies and cakes. There was coffee of course, soda, beer (a lot of beer), and liquor to drink. Family members and close friends usually did the cooking. Everyone knew who the best cooks were and in general those were the ones that did the cooking.

The wedding cake was always large, white and decorated with a miniature bride and groom at the top. At some point the newlyweds made the first cut in the cake and each took a bite of cake from each other. Then one of the cooks would cut small pieces of the cake, which were placed on a napkin and handed to selected guests.

One custom that everyone enjoyed was the time when it came to dance with the bride. It was one of the highlights of the wedding since every wanted a chance to dance with her. Some lady was always in charge of that event and she just knew how to handle things. Each person who wanted to participate had to make a donation (about a dollar) before being allowed to dance. Another woman would stand right next to the dance floor holding out her apron from her body and the dollar donations were tossed into her apron. The length of time each one danced with the bride was short in order to get everyone involved and also to collect as much money as possible for the newlyweds. It was physically demanding for the bride, because the dancing went on for quite a while.

Another popular event was the occasion when the bride tossed her bouquet to all the young unmarried ladies. According to custom, it was believed that the one who caught it would soon be married herself. Sometimes there was a little bit of pushing and shoving to get the bouquet, but that was all right. There was always that one favorite girl in the group that most people wanted to see catch the bouquet. However, as it turned out, she was usually the one that didn't make the catch.

All in all, the wedding was an exciting event and everyone was in good spirits. It was a time when people seemed to forget their troubles if only for a day or so. Often people who had not been speaking to each other would "make up" at a wedding. It was a time when people liked to do a lot of talking and gossiping. A familiar topic was trying to guess who was going to get married next.

The elderly particularly, seemed to enjoy the wedding festival, maybe it reminded them of happier times. Older women danced more than men did and that's because they danced with each other. I was somewhat surprised how light they were on their feet and how well they danced. I chuckled when I saw my mom dancing with other women. It was one of the few occasions when they could socialize with each other and they took advantage of it. The music was also to their liking. The musicians played many lively polkas, and other enjoyable music.

Little girls danced more than boys of their same age. When I was in college and served as the best man in the wedding party for my sister Ann, the younger girls (about ten to twelve) all wanted to dance with me. I guess I looked pretty good in my tuxedo.

The bride and groom usually departed in the early evening of the first day after saying goodbye to their families and friends. Of course, everyone, especially the ladies, enjoyed showering the couple with rice as they were leaving. After that things settled down just a bit. However, people went on dancing, eating and especially drinking beer. Many others just sat around and talked with friends and relatives that they had not seen in some time. The celebration continued well into the night.

However there were always a few guys that drank too much and arguments and small fights would break out. Sometimes they started when someone insulted another person, but more often they started over jealousies of former lovers who were now married to someone else. While they did occur, other more levelheaded people quickly stepped in and quieted down the scuffles in order not to spoil the wedding.

The second day was not as hectic and lively as the first, but the wedding still went on. It consisted mainly of family members, close relatives and friends. There were no musicians, but recorded music was provided and everyone was still in a relaxed and lively mood. There was a lot of cleaning up to be done and that got started late in the afternoon of the second day. Usually the poor cooks also were the ones who took care of that chore.

So it was another wedding day, a time when we would all remember. A new family was united and everyone wished them well. Two young people starting off on the greatest journey and adventure of their life. And young people hardly in their teens taking everything in and wanting to be grown up too—little did they know how fast that time would come.

The Big Parade—ABA Night

The Annual Labor Day homecoming celebration in Ashland was always one of the big events of the year for us kids. It was the Mummer's Day Parade and was sponsored by The Ashland Boys Association (ABA). We always called it the Labor Day Parade. It's one of the oldest and most successful large parades held in the coal region, with numerous cash prizes for the winners. Marching firemen, high school bands, drum and bugle groups, floats, clowns, and many other groups came from quite a distance to participate. It was not unusual to have over 60 organizations and individual performers take part in the parade.

It was a huge event and it always attracted many people. There were vendors stationed at every street corner peddling typical parade items, especially balloons. There were always some balloons flying high in the air that got away from some kiddies that weren't holding on to the string very tight. Some mothers would scold the crying youngster and others would try to console their child. Some kids held on to their balloon, but suddenly there was "pop" and the balloon had burst. Now there was more crying, because the child was only holding a string in its hand.

The parade groups would line up near the bottom of town prior to the start of the big event. I recall for years that a dapper sort of guy with the nickname of "Sheiky" would always lead off the parade. They would then proceed to march up Center Street, which was rather flat for about seven blocks. The judges sat on a flat truck near the Hotel Loeper. This was the most exciting part of the parade since the various bands and groups performed their best in front of the judges. From then on, the parade continued to march up Center Street, which was rather steep for the next twelve blocks. So you can see that the participants in the parade had a long way to march. By the time some of the parade groups reached the upper part of town and completely away from the judges stand, some marchers would be so tired that they would sit down on the street when the parade came to one of its many stops. On such occasions, some of the male marchers at the end of a group would quickly run over to a saloon for a quick beer and the catch up with their group later on.

Big Mine Run always had its one lone performer in the parade. His name was Brooks Wolfgang and he was about twenty-one years old. He had a reputation of always dressing up in a very fancy woman's outfit for the occasion. He would dance, prance and kick his heels high, especially at the judges' stand. He was actually quite graceful and apparently has some acting ability because he always won a prize. The kids from Big Mine Run would always look for him in the parade. When we spotted him we would say, "There goes Brooksie" and then we would giggle and laugh.

Several kids from Oakland always pulled a small wagon loaded with a bag of coal. Their official entry name was called "Oakland Anthracite Boys." The kids had a sign they carried that read, "The Oakland Miners," and each youngster wore a miner's cap with a lit carbide lamp. The Oakland Miners always got a prize and everyone looked for them each year. As I remember, they always received a nice round of applause from the crowd.

The Ashland High School Band, of course, participated and they were always greeted with a lot of loud shouting and clapping. I believe they were exempt from receiving any cash award. However, there was a substantial amount of money awarded to all the other participants each year, so there was a keen sense of competition to win prize money.

The day of the parade was an especially exciting time for us kids. We would walk from Big Mine Run to Ashland and then walk up to the top of town, a distance of about two miles. Then we would continue walk around while the parade was going on. The sidewalks were always crowded and it was difficult for families to move around, so they generally stayed in one place to watch the parade. However, most of the kids just squeezed through the crowds with ease and went from one location to another to get a better view. Then sometime around midnight we would walk home slowly, quite tired and ready to go to bed.

Maybe it was only an ordinary parade, but for us kids, the Labor Day Parade was really something; it was our own special Mardi Gras. While many other things have vanished from the coal region, the wonderful ABA Parade continues on to this day.

Building a Bonfire

About two weeks before the Fourth of July, about five or six of us kids would start to build a huge tepee-shaped wooden structure to make a bonfire. Charles "Gyppo" Young was the guy who usually got it all started, so he sort of ran the operation. It was always built in the same location, right next to a crick (creek to you) that flowed from Homesville through Big Mine Run towrd Ashland.

The crick had a dark (almost black) color and all kinds of waste and sewerage emptied into it. Nevertheless, several of us would take off our sneakers and socks and step into the crick. We would wade up the crick toward the patch of Homesville looking for old logs and boards that we would throw into the water. Others near the bonfire site would be waiting in the crick to catch the logs and boards that came floating down. We pulled anything out of the water and dragged it to the bonfire site that would burn and help make our Fourth of July fire bigger. Sometimes we had to wrestle an old railroad sill out of the crick and it took several of us to do that. Old tires were always a good find, because we would place them on the very top of the bonfire structure.

On the average, the crick was only about one and one-half feet deep. However, there were times when you would accidentally step into a hole and you would get soaked up to your crotch. We waded around for hours in the filthy germ-laden dirty polluted water. We never thought about the possibility that we might catch some disease. That didn't matter, working on the bonfire was a big deal and everybody involved felt that they were doing something important.

After several weeks of work, we would finally complete our bon-fire structure several days before the Fourth of July. Then close to midnight on July the Fourth, we would throw gasoline on it and torch it. It made a huge fire and got everyone's attention. A lot of people in the patch always looked at the bonfire from a distance and a number of cars also stopped since the highway ran close to the crick. We, of course, would stand fairly close to the huge bonfire, proudly looking at our achievement and setting off firecrackers. Most of us stayed for hours and didn't go home until very late. The fire blazed brightly for many hours and continued burning until about noon the next day.

One time several wise guys pulled a dirty trick on us. They waited until about midnight on July the third and soaked our unguarded bonfire structure with gasoline and torched it. Our beautiful bonfire burning brightly (they told us) but we weren't there to see it at the beginning. However, we soon got word of what happened and we all dashed to our bonfire site and just sadly watched it burn. We were all mad as hell. After that, we always guarded our bonfire several nights before the big event. We wanted to be sure that we got the pleasure of torching it ourselves—after all it was our bonfire.

The Fourth of July

It was a lot of fun for a kid to have a small hand held cap gun on the Fourth of July. You could buy a small paper roll of red caps with about 30 red dots in it, which were used as bullets for you gun. You just torn off one red paper dot and placed it in your cap gun. Then you pulled back the hammer and pressed on the trigger. The tiny paper bullet went off with a "bang" along with a small puff of smoke. The roll of bullets only cost a few pennies and you could go around shooting off your cap gun all day.

If you didn't have a cap gun, you took one of the paper dots and exploded it by placing it on a rock and then hitting it with a small stone you held in your hand. It didn't hurt, but the cap exploded with the same bang as it did in a cap gun.

There was another type of pistol called the Dick Tracy gun, which held an entire roll of 30 caps. It looked exactly like the one Dick Tracy had in the comics. We called it an automatic gun. The big advantage of the Dick Tracy gun was that you could keep on shooting until the entire roll of caps was used up. Sometimes one of the caps wouldn't explode, but you just kept pulling the trigger and you would hear--bang, bang, bang.

All the kids in the neighborhood would be setting off red-colored fireworks all day. The most common firecracker we exploded was about two inches long and about as round as an ordinary pencil. They weren't very powerful, but they did go off with a loud bang. Sometimes we would place a firecracker under a tin can and watch the can fly into the air when the firecracker exploded. If a more powerful firecracker was ignited under a can, it would not only send it up high into the air but would blow it apart.

Sometimes one of the older guys would light a small firecracker and throw it into a group of us kids that were just standing around. If we saw it coming, we would run like hell. On a few occasions, we were not aware of the lighted firecracker until it exploded near our feet. There would be a lot of shouting, cursing, and we would be damn mad. I recall one time when that happened, my hearing was affected for a few minutes.

The most powerful firecrackers we had were called "cherry bombs." They were bright red (as all firecrackers were) and about the size of a large cherry. They exploded with a very loud band and were dangerous. Some kids in Big Mine Run would throw a lit cherry bomb from an overhead bridge onto an open truck passing by on the highway below. When the firecracker exploded, the driver would become frightened and stop his vehicle. When he got out of his truck, and realized what happened, he would be very mad. He would shake his fist and shout all kinds of profanity. All the kids in the area would run away.

There were other safe fireworks that were also set off, which were nice to look at. Small children were given a "sparkler." It was a slender rigid wire about 16 inches long, which they held in their hand. The other end of the sparker was coated with a chemical and sparkled when ignited. Children generally turned the ignited sparkler in a circle as it gave off bright flashing sparks.

Roman candles, which were about the size of an ordinary thick, candle were fun to watch. When ignited, a Roman candle shot out a ball of sparks about 30 feet and then a few seconds later another ball shot out about the same distance. Each

Roman candle contained about five or six balls of fiery sparks. Sometimes kids would aim them at each other.

Flowerpots were also nice for children to look at. The pots were shaped like a regular ice cream cones only somewhat larger. When they were placed on the ground and ignited, they shot out colored sparks straight up into the air. They were popular because they lasted for several minutes.

Skyrockets were the most exciting fireworks to watch. A rocket was always ignited from its stationary position on the ground. The rocket firework could be directed to shoot straight up into the air or at an angle. As the rocket ascended into the air, it left a trail of sparks behind. After the rocket reached its maximum height, which usually was quite high, it exploded. After the explosion, there was a brilliant display of sparks of varying colors.

The highlight of the Fourth of July was the large fireworks display that different towns put on each year. Frackville always had a huge fireworks display on the Fourth of July, and my Aunt Mary and Uncle Bill invited me to spend the holiday with them to watch the fireworks. Just as it was getting dark, a very high exploding firecracker bomb went off high overhead. After that, there was a continuous display of starbursts and every other type of design possible going off overhead. The sky was lit up with all kind of colored displays, and the show went on for quite some time. The night air was filled with gunpowder smoke, but nobody seemed to mind.

At the end of the fireworks show (the finale) a large number of fireworks and bomb-exploding devices were sent into the air at the same time. The entire sky was lit up with multi-colored designs of fireworks mixed in with very loud explosions. It was one continuous explosion after another and the sky itself was all lit up. Many folks and even some kids closed their ears because the noise was so loud. Then suddenly, the night sky was dark and everything seemed so quiet. It was the end of another wonderful Fourth of July!

When the Carnival Came To Town

We all looked forward to the time when the carnival came to town. The carnival always made a visit to Girardville and stayed for about a week. It was a traveling amusement show that was very popular and attracted large crowds of people.

There were a variety of games that you could play where you tossed balls, hoops, darts, or pennies at objects to try and win a prize. Shooting games were especially popular with adults. They would should a BB gun at balloons or other objects to try and win a prize. There were many fancy and desirable prizes on exhibit that you could win. However, even those who were good shooters and who could toss things well generally only won a minor prize.

The carnival had different rides that were popular with kids. Although I didn't go on many rides, it was fun to watch the merry-go-round with the loud music. The large Ferris wheel was one of the big attractions. On one occasion I recall being stopped at the very top, because someone was getting on at the bottom or ground level. It was a little scary because you were up so high and not moving, but at the same time it was exciting. You could see all the rooftops of the houses in Girardville.

Vendors sold hot dogs, hamburgers, French fries, soda and of course cotton candy. It was fun to watch the man turn the small paper cone around in a circle and make it into a large fluffy pink cotton candy cone. It looked like you got a lot for a nickel, but as soon as you tried to take a bite, it melted in your mouth. Many kids bought one, including me, because it not only looked good, but it had a nice flavor and sweet taste.

Gambling games were particularly popular with adults. The barker was the man who solicited customers with a loud and colorful sales talk

Indicating how you could double or triple your money by just stepping up and playing the game. Of course, you had to place your bet and select a number where you thought the Wheel of Fortune would stop. Even though most people knew that the games of chance were manipulated dishonestly by the carnival, they still played because it looked like a "good deal," and they felt that they might win.

The most popular event of all at the carnival were the "side shows." Performers would come out on a small temporary stage and put on a short free show. The barker would talk up the show "big time" on how much more you would see on the inside of the tent for a small fee. One side show would feature scantiy clad dancing girls. We would look at them and then bump each other as 10 or 12-year-old kids tend to do--meaning–look at that! Another side show would bring out fire-eaters and sword swallowers. Other shows would feature grotesque figures like (a) the tattooed lady, (b) the world's strongest man, (c) the snake man, (d) the smallest person in the world, (e) the tallest man, (f) the palace of illusions and other unusual sights. Even though the barker always exaggerated on what you would see on the inside, people didn't seem to mind too much if they were fooled a bit. The carnival was not only entertaining but something different and everyone seemed to have a good time.

For the most part, we just walked around all evening looking at everything that was free. It was a fun night because everything was different and entertaining. About 10 p.m. it was time for us to think about going home. We had a two-mile walk from Girardville to Big MIne Run and during all that time we chatted about all the things we saw. And sometimes we talked about what it would be like to be a member of a traveling carnival show.

The Circus Is Coming

The circus, like the carnival, was a traveling entertainment show for the public. The circus team always set its huge tent in a large open field at the bottom of town in Ashland. It was always an exciting time, because several days before the circus arrived, signs would be posted letting everyone know that the circus was coming to town.

I usually visited the circus grounds when the caravan of trucks, wagons and circus people first arrived. I enjoyed watching the men getting the animals out of the cages and also setting up their tents. One time I carried water in a bucket for the elephants to drink, and I was given a free pass. Frankly, I would have carried the water for nothing just to see the elephants up close.

The biggest attraction at the circus was the big tent or "Big Top." It was a huge tent and the place where all the action took place. The circus featured clowns, acrobats (including trapeze acts), and trained animals (elephants, lions, tigers and dogs). There was always something going on inside the tent, it was one performance after another. Parents generally took their kids to the circus, because the show focused on entertaining children.

My parents never went to the circus. I just walked to Ashland to see the clowns and elephants by myself. I rarely had a pass, so I would peek under the big tent to see what was going on. The men on the inside who watched out for us kids trying to sneak in were never nasty. Sometimes they would let us watch for a few minutes and then tell us to move on. I wonder if they thought about the time, when they too, were just kids?

Chapter 7

STORIES ABOUT OLD RADIO PROGRAMS

Remember radio? I was about twelve years old when we bought our first radio in the mid-1930s. It was a floor model about four feet high with a highly varnished wood-simulated finish and a large round-lighted dial. Since it was an attractive piece, we put it in our parlor where we had our "best-looking" furniture.

Some of my most entertaining and exciting times go back to that Golden Age of Radio. What fun it was to lie on the floor and listen to those wonderful, realistic radio programs; I was listening to radio in color! I could use my imagination to "see" what I wanted to see. What's more, I was a participant.

Most of the time, my sisters and I would gather in front of the radio and listen to the same programs. It was all so new and exciting; everything on radio seemed entertaining. Most of the time we didn't turn on the overhead light to save on the electrical bill. However, we didn't mind since there was some light from the large lighted radio dial. We also felt that some programs like Gang Busters, The Shadow and Inner Sanctum Mysteries were better to listen to in a dimly lit room. We always listened to our favorite programs while sitting or lying on the floor; we never sat in a chair or on the couch.

Return with me now to those thrilling days of yesteryear recalling those wonderful radio hours with our own radio heroes. This is how it was—the programs that I remember the best.

Gang Busters

I always looked forward to listening to Gang Busters; it was one of my favorite programs. The opening sound effects were loud, realistic and so riveting that you never wanted to miss the beginning of the show. The sirens going off, the rattle of submachine guns, and the sound of marching convicts headed off to jail—that's how Gang Busters came on the air.

Gang Busters.

It was an exciting show that dramatized real-life stories in which cops tracked down and captured notorious criminals. Just hearing the name "Machine Gun Kelly" and the rat-a-tat-tat of the machine gun sent shivers up my spine. The program described in vivid detail how John Dillinger, "Baby Face" Nelson, Willie Sutton and other well-known criminals met their fate. The message was clear; crime does not pay.

A special feature of the show was called Gang Busters Clues and it came on at the end of the program. The announcer provided detailed information about actual criminals wanted by the FBI and police. Immediately after that, they made the following announcement: "If you have seen this man, notify the FBI or your local law enforcement agency, or Gang Busters . . . at once." Wow, I thought—what if I saw somebody that fitted that description? It turned out to be a successful element to the show and helped capture over 100 wanted men.

The show was sponsored by The Colgate Palmolive Company and was so realistic that the term "Coming on like Gang Busters" has become part of our everyday vocabulary.

The Lone Ranger

I inched closer to the radio when I heard the announcer saying:

With his faithful Indian companion, Tonto, the daring and resourceful Masked Rider of the Plains led the fight for law and order in the early western United States. Nowhere in the pages of history can one find a greater champion of justice. Return with us now to those thrilling days of

The Lone Ranger.

yesteryear. From out of the past, come the thundering hoofbeats of the great horse, Silver! The Lone Ranger rides again!

I felt that by moving right next to the radio, I would be closer to the action. Everyone who ever listened to The Lone Ranger remembers the exciting music. I didn't know that it came from the "William Tell Overture." To me, it originated on The Lone Ranger Program—it was The Lone Ranger music. Yeah!

Silvercup Bread sponsored the program. It was a wonderful and exciting classic western for young kids. The Lone Ranger wore a black mask and used silver bullets in his six-gun. My heart pounded a little faster when I heard the Masked Man shout, "Hi-Yo, Silver, Awa-a-ay !" Wow—that was good stuff!

Tonto, his Indian companion, always called the Lone Ranger kemo sabe, which means "faithful friend." Together they rode the Wild West tracking down lawbreakers and turning them over to the law to be tried for their crimes.

At times I imagined what it would be like to ride along with my two heroes. I could feel my hair tingle when I heard the following, "A fiery horse with the speed of light, a cloud of dust and a hearty Hi-Yo Silver! The Lone Ranger rides again."

For years, radio buffs tried to determine the origin of kemo sabe without success. As it turned out, James Jewell, who was the director of the program for a time, admitted that he simply came up with the name after a camp called Ke-Mo-Sah-Bee in upper Michigan.

The Lone Ranger never objected when he was temporarily mistaken for an outlaw by other lawmen. A sheriff, after admitting his mistake would say, "Why if it hadn't been for the masked man here . . . look, he's gone! . . . say who was that masked man?" Then came the closing—"Why, sheriff, don't you know? He's The Lone Ranger!" Then I heard the riveting music coming on and far off in the distance, I could hear, "Hi-Yo, silver, Away!"

The Shadow

The Shadow began with that familiar opening:

The Shadow.

Who knows what evil lurks in the hearts of men? The Shadow knows--and now, a thrilling adventure of The Shadow, and his relentless fight against the forces of evil, demonstrating to young men that crime does not pay. The Shadow, mysterious character who aids the forces of law and order, is in reality Lamont Cranston, wealthy young man about town. Years ago in the Orient he learned a strange and mysterious secret—the hypnotic power to cloud mens' minds so they could not see him. His friend and companion, the lovely Margo Lane, is the only person who knew who the invisible Shadow was.

The sinister voice of The Shadow made criminals cringe. They would say, "Where's that voice coming from? Who are you?" Then I would hear Lamont Cranston say, "I am The Shadow." The criminals never saw him, but they eventually did hear his gripping, haunting laughter—and then it was too late. The invisible Shadow was here, there and everywhere. The

Shadow, which was sponsored by Blue Coal, was one of radios' most famous fictitious crime fighter programs of all time.

The captured villains were sent to jail and in some cases to the Death House itself. At the end of the program I heard, "The weed of crime bears bitter fruit. Crime does not pay. The Shadow knows . . . Hehehehaha!" Afterward, when I calmed down I would think of how nice it would be to be able to make myself invisible.

Very early radio listeners may remember that for a time Orson Welles played the role of The Shadow in the show's early years. His deep, rich voice made a convincing and believable Shadow. During that time Agnes Moorehead, the actress, played Margo Lane, The Shadow's companion.

Inner Sanctum Mysteries

Inner Sanctum Mysteries started with somber organ music and was soon followed by a slowly opening creaking door. Then, this is what I heard, "Good evening friends. This is your host, inviting you through the gory portals of the squeaking door . . . 'eerie laughter.' And now, if your scalpels are sharpened and ready, we'll proceed with the business of the evening."

It was a suspense show and full of horror. I didn't listen to it regularly because scary shows like that did not appeal to me. However, I had to listen to it once in a while because I heard so many others talking about it. Besides, I just had to listen and actually get scared to see what it was like. Like everyone else, I still remember that awful squeaking door.

As the mystery show ended, I heard the announcer saying,

"Everybody died but the cat, and we only overlooked him because we couldn't find him . . . 'more eerie laughter.' And now it's time to close the squeaking door. . . Good niii—iiight. . . Pleasant dreeeaaammmss . . ."

The squee-eeking door would slowly close, and then shut with a—KER—THUNK! After listening to one of these horror programs, I would always look under the bed and checkout the bedroom closet before climbing into bed. In those days, there was no night light left on, and that only made matters worse.

By the way, Edgar Allan Poe wrote some of the scripts for the Inner Sanctum Mysteries show.

Mr. Keen, Tracer of Lost Persons

Mr. Keen, Tracer of Lost Persons was one of radios' longest winning detective programs and was sponsored by Bisodol. Mr. Keen was a kindly old detective who investigated and tracked down missing persons. Unfortunately the missing persons often turned out to be murdered persons.

Mr. Keen's partner, Mike Clancy, wasn't too bright. When Clancy wanted something clarified, Keen would patiently explain the circumstance; the radio listeners of course would have figured it out for themselves before Clancy got the message.

Keen and Clancy did not have any official position but they did have arrest powers. Mr. Keen used his charm and persuasive powers in his work and he was often able to enter homes without a search warrant. Clancy, who was always at Mr. Keen's side, was fond of supporting Mr. Keen and would often say, "We usually work along with the police, Ma'am."

Clancy was fond of using Irish cliches and his favorite one was, "Saints preserve us Mr. Keen." A typical conversation between the two went something like this.

Clancy: Sakes alive, Mr. Keen, it's another dead body. And saints preserve us, Boss, it don't have no head.

Keen: Yes, Clancy, this dead body has been murdered.

Clancy: You don't mean it, Mr. Keen.

Keen: I'm afraid I do, Clancy. This doesn't look at all good for our client.

Clancy: But how could the po-lice think our client had anything to do this murdered body?

Mr. Keen: The phone call I received Clancy, Headquarters said our client was released from custody six hours ago.

Clancy: Saints preserve us, Mr. Keen.

The similarity between Mr. Keen and Mike Clancy has often been compared to that of Sherlock Holmes and Dr. Watson. In the tradition of Holmes who always outwitted his adversaries, Mr. Keen lived up to his name and always "tracked down" the missing person he was after.

Major Bowes' Original Amateur Hour

Major Bowes' Original Amateur Hour showcasing new talent was a favorite of many people. Major Bowes' opened his show by saying, "Around and around she goes, and where she stops nobody knows." It was his way of referring to the "Wheel of Fortune" that might provide an opportunity for some entertainer to hit the big time.

Sometimes I wished that someone I knew would be on the program, but that never happened. The amateurs who did perform had to rely on radio listeners who voted for their favorite entertainer by phone or mail. Major Bowes' didn't mind using his gong to stop a performer if it did not go well.

Over the years, thousands of contestants appeared on the show, but only one became a superstar. Do you remember who that superstar was? Well, it was none other than the skinny singer from Hoboken, New Jersey who appeared as a member of a pop quartet in 1937. It was ol' blue eyes himself—Frank Sinatra.

Frank Sinatra.

After Major Bowes' died, Ted Mack another well-known name associated with The Original Amateur Hour took over. However, it was Major Bowes' soft and cheerful voice that I remember most of all about the amateur hour when he said, "Around and around it goes . . .

The Jack Benny Program

Jack Benny.

The Jack Benny Program, which was sponsored by Jell-0, was a very popular comedy show for the entire family. Benny had the ability to shift the focus of his program away from himself to his cast who got laughs by deflating his own ego. It turned out to be a very successful tactic. While Jack played the role of the fall guy, he was a superb comedian with a great sense of timing for delivering lines. He also wanted to give the impression that he was miserly, cheap and that he was the stingiest man on radio. His feud with

260

Fred Allen (a comedian on another radio program) was only a publicity stunt to attract more listeners to both programs.

Jack had a black valet and chauffeur named Rochester. When Jack wanted his old Maxwell car, he would call out, "Oh Rochester." And Rochester would always answer in his gravel-voice by saying, "Yes, Mr. Benny" or "Yes, Boss." Jack always instructed his chauffeur to only put one gallon of gas in his car at a time; he went to extreme measures to convey the idea that he was stingy. When Rochester went to start up the Maxwell, all you could hear was a sickening chugging, and sputtering noise that gave you the impression that the car would never get underway.

Several of the many memorable lines from the show were: Mel Blanc shouting out, "Train now loading on track three—all aboard for Anaheim, Azusa and Cuc—amonga." It was also Mel Blanc's voice doing Benny's sputtering, coughing antique car. Another line was Jack's delayed response when he said the single word, "Well." Then there was his well-known phrase, "Now cut that out." Perhaps Jack's most memorable line was the one in which he received one of the longest laughs in radio history. Here's the scene: A robber says, "Your money or your life," holding up Jack at gunpoint. There was a very long pause and no answer from Jack. The gunman repeated his words, "Your money or your life." Again, there was a very long pause. Finally, the exasperated robber in a much louder voice called out, "I said, your money or your life." It was then that Jack said his famous line, "I'M THINKING . . . . . I'M THINKING."

Here's one humorous episode involving Jack meeting the Little Mexican at the train station. The Mexican only spoke one word at a time.

Benny: Are you waiting for the train?

Mexican: Si.

Benny: Are you meeting someone?

Mexican: Si.

Benny: A relative?

Mexican: Si.

Benny: What's your name?

Mexican: Sy.

Benny: Sy?

Mexican: Si.

Benny: This relative you're waiting for—is it a woman?

Mexican: Si

Benny: What's her name?

Mexican: Sue.

Benny: Sue?

Mexican: Si.

Benny: Does she work?

Mexican: Si

Benny: What does she do?

Mexican: Sew.

Benny: Sew?

Mexican: Si.

There was always a question about Benny's violin playing. While he could play the violin quite well, he could not make a living as a professional violin player. Jack's violin was only a prop for his comedy routine on the show.

Other performers on his show were: Mary Livingston, his wife; Dennis Day, his Irish tenor singer; Phil Harris, the bandleader, who always greeted Jack with, "Hiya Jackson" and Don Wilson, the announcer.

The Charlie McCarthy Show

Charlie McCarthy.

The Charlie McCarthy Show was funny and very popular. Nobody thought that ventriloquism would be successful on radio, but Edgar Bergen somehow made it work. Bergen's dummy, Charlie McCarthy, was like a real person to radio listeners. Charlie all by himself (in a way) was the hero of the show. He would always flirt with glamorous Hollywood

Charlie McCarthy

female stars who were guests on the program. Charlie was radios' lovable bad boy.

He carried on a feud on the program with W. C. Fields who had a big red nose and also loved to drink. One of Charlie's great lines from his feud with W.C. Fields, was, "Pink elephants take aspirin to get rid of W.C. fields." Not surprisingly, it was Charlie who got all the big laughs.

Bergen often portrayed himself as the father figure to Charlie, who often needed talking to, because of his mischievous behavior. Here's a typical example of how their conversation went about a particular situation.

Bergen: Don't you know, young man, that alcohol is a slow poison?

Charley: Is what?

Bergen: It's a slow poison.

Charley: Is that so?

Bergen: Yes.

Charley: Slow poison.

Bergen: That's what it is.

Charley: Slow poison, eh?

Bergen: Yes.

Charley: Well, I'm in no hurry.

Bergen also used several other dummies on his show, including Mortimer Snerd, who were also successful. But Charlie with his brashness and rascality was the top dummy and was loved by everyone. When I saw a picture of Charlie, I was surprised to see that he wore a monocle. The large royalties from the sale of Charlie mementos, which included everything from dolls to mugs, was further evidence of his popularity.

The Amos n' Andy Show

Amos 'n' Andy were the owners of the Fresh Air Taxi Cab Company. It got that name because the only cab they owned was a dilapidated old taxi without a windshield. Their show was a situation comedy and one of the funniest ever on radio. While Amos 'n' Andy were black, the actors that portrayed them were white. The program was sponsored by Pepsodent and then later by Campbell's Soups.

Amos was the hard working sensible half of the partnership and tried to do the right thing. Andy, on the other hand, was just the opposite. He wasn't too bright, never worked and always chased women.

Andy was always being sold a "bill of goods" by George Stevens, the "Kingfish" of the "Mystic Knights of the Sea" lodge hall. Even though you knew poor Andy was going to be ripped off, it was still very funny. The Kingfish was so slick that Huey P. Long, Louisiana's famous politician was named after him.

The show also had several other well-known performers. Ruby was Amos' fine church-going wife. However, the Kingfish's wife Sapphire, was a domineering, sharp-tempered person. Sapphire's Mama, Randolph, was even more aggressive. Amos 'n' Andy had a lawyer with the interesting name of Stonewall whom they would consult on legal matters.

It's been said that The Amos 'n' Andy Show changed the format of radio comedy. Almost everyone listened to the show including presidents Calvin Coolidge, Herbert Hoover and Franklin Delano Roosevelt. When George Bernard Shaw, the Irish novelist, visited America, he said, "There are three things I'll never forget about America—The Rocky Mountains, Niagara Falls and The Amos 'n' Andy Show."

Fibber McGee and Molly

Fibber McGee and Molly, which was sponsored by Johnson's Wax, were a married couple who played in a situation comedy show. The clever opening of the cluttered closet by Fibber was well known and always got a big laugh. The audience always imagined poor Fibber being buried underneath all that junk that came tumbling out of the famous closet. Anyone who ever listened to the show remembers Fibber's marvelous line when he said, "Gotta clean out that closet one of these days."

Fibber, who always exaggerated everything, was an incurable windbag. However, Molly would always put him in his place by saying, "T'aint funny McGee." However, Fibber's tall tales were always part of the show but it only took Molly's reprimand of "McGee" to bring him back to reality.

Gildersleeve was Fibber's bothersome next-door neighbor. They were constantly engaged in back-fence quarrels and liked to play tricks on one another. After Gildersleeve lost an argument with Fibber, he would end up saying, "You're a ha-a-a-rd man McGee." Here's one exchange between Fibber and Gildersleeve that was interrupted by Molly.

Molly: Please, gentlemen . . . Please. . . . This is no way for good neighbors to talk.

Fibber: We ain't good neighbors . . . we're enemies.

Gildersleeve: Yes we are . . . the best of enemies. You think I'm a stuffed shirt and I think you're a gabby little good for nothing runt.

Fibber: There . . . ye see, Molly? You don't find me and Gildersleeve indulgin' in sentimental, hands-across-the-fence drivel.

Molly always ended the show with a simple, "Goodnight, all."

The Aldrich Family

The Aldrich Family was a situation comedy program that had one of those memorable openings. All listeners remember Henry's mother calling out, "Hen-Reee! Henry Aldrich!" Then Henry, with his sqweaky voice, answering, "Coming, Moth—er!"

The format of the show focused on Henry's adolescence, his teenage love problems and the generation gap. It turned out that the teenage themes were very successful.

Henry's adventurous spirit always got him into difficulty each week. It seemed that he could make a crisis out of just any simple matter. Henry's best friend and companion in mischief was Homer Brown. Most listeners of the show will remember some of Henry's favorite expressions such as: "Jeepers!" " "Yikes!" "Gee Whiz!" and "Golly-Jeepers!"

The Aldrich Family was one of the best-remembered radio comedy family programs of all time. It was so successful, that other shows tried to copy its format.

Grand Ole Opry

On Saturday nights we tuned in to listen to the Grand Ole Opry show. I recall George Hay, the master of ceremonies, coming on the air saying, "This is station WSN from Nashville, Tennessee, let 'er go boys." Then the fiddles and banjos would start playing with a lot of enthusiasm. The program, which was sponsored by The Prince Albert Tobacco Company, was broadcast from a powerful radio station that could be heard in about 30 states.

In the beginning the music came mainly from the hills and the churches. It was actually billed as a big-time hillbilly music and variety show. As we all know now, it's what we call country music today and very popular.

My father turned up the sound on the radio so loud that you could hear the music all over the house. I thought it was sort of funny the very first time I heard it, because it was different from popular music that I normally heard on the radio.

The name Grand Ole Opry came about in the following manner. One day Dr. Walter Damrosch, the conductor of the National Symphony Orchestra, made a remark that there was no place for realism in the classics. George Hay, whose show immediately followed Damrosch's grand opera program, said, "From here on out folks, it will be nothing but realism of the realist kind. You've been up in the clouds with grand opera; now get down to earth with us in a shindig of grand ole opry!" The name stuck and history was made.

Anyone who ever listened to the Grand Ole Opry remembers Cousin Minnie Pearl. Minnie was actually an educated person but played the role of an ordinary country girl. She told stories of the simple life in Grinders Switch, Tennessee and she was very popular with her down-home humor. Of course, everyone recalls her famous hat that she always wore with the price tag still dangling off to the side.

Bill Monroe (the Father of Blue Grass Music), Hank Williams (the Father of Country Music), Red Foley, Ernest Tubb, Eddy Arnold, and Roy Acuff and his Smoky Mountain Boys were some of the other star performers on the show.

Your Hit Parade

On Saturday nights we listened to Your Hit Parade, which was sponsored by Lucky Strike Cigarettes, and the band itself was labeled the Lucky Strike Orchestra. Most people familiar with the show will remember the tobacco auctioneer calling out tobacco prices at rapid-fire speed, and always ending with "Sooold to American!"

Since my three older sisters listened to the program regularly, I also joined in and listened to it. I think the reason I liked the program was because they enjoyed it so much. I recall my sisters buying song sheets so they could learn the words to the music.

Each week, well-known vocalists would sing the top ten most popular songs of the week. The show was structured in such a manner as to keep everyone in suspense by keeping the top three songs until the end of the program. The other songs and musical numbers were presented randomly with some "Lucky Strike" extras thrown in.

It was always a big moment to find out which song was the number one tune of the week. Listeners would debate which tune should be the one to be selected. Of course, everyone would root for his or her favorite song to be the number one hit. Then the time came to play the third most popular song and then the second and finally the most popular song of the week would come on—it was the highlight of the show.

If you tune in yesterday, here's a list of some of the most popular songs I remember from Your Hit Parade: "I'll Be Seeing You," "Now Is the Hour," "Tangerine," "You'll Never Know," "As Time Goes By," "Long Ago and Far Away," "Till the End of Time," "Sentimental Journey," "White Christmas," "Chattanooga Choo Choo," "I'll Walk Alone," "South of the Border," "Marie Elena," "White Cliffs of Dover," "Over the Rainbow," "Don't Fence Me In," "I'll Never Smile Again," "Coming In On a Wing and a Prayer," "My Sisters and I," "There I Go," "Blueberry Hill," "Pennies From Heaven," "A-Tisket-a-Tasket," "You Must Have Been a Beautiful Baby," and "Lullaby of Broadway."

And Your Hit Parade ended with:

So long for a while . . .

That's all the songs, for a while . . .

So long to Your Hit Parade . . .

And the tunes that you picked to be played . . .

So long . . .

The Kate Smith Hour

Kate Smith.

Kate always opened her show with her usual friendly greeting by saying, "Hello, everybody, this is Kate Smith." The theme song for the show was, "When the Moon Comes over the Mountain"—a song that everyone identified with her. She was a spirited woman with a strong, booming voice and everybody liked her.

She was overweight and used to laugh at various comments about her size. She once remarked, "I'm big and I'm fat, but I have a voice, and when I sing—boy, I sing all over."

In 1938 on Armistice Day she introduced Irving Berlin's song "God Bless America." She managed to get the exclusive rights to the song, which became so popular, that there was consideration of making it the national anthem. Even up to the present time, it is considered to be "her song," and nobody could sing it like her.

Now seven decades later, the song had enjoyed renewed popularity due to the tragic events of "911." When I hear others singing it today, I always think of Kate Smith's wonderful voice booming out the words, "God Bless America."

She was a simple, unpretentious woman from Virginia who talked to people as if she knew them all her life. Kate became "the songbird of the south" and was considered to be "the first lady of radio." Kate always ended her program with, "Thanks for listenin' and good night folks."

Walter Winchell's Journal

Walter Winchell, the news reporter, opened his program by tapping his telegraph keys and at the same time bellowing out, "Good evening Mr. and Mrs. North and South America and all ships at sea, let's go to press—FLASH."

Walter Winchell.

He spoke in a rapid-fire style and covered the news as well as gossip about well-known people. While he was an important and powerful reporter, he was also a showman and entertainer. I enjoyed listening to his staccato style voice delivering his opinions, one-liners and his anecdotes.

During his 15-minute show, Winchell often tapped on his telegraph key giving his presentation a "news room" sound that made him believable. I recall one picture of him broadcasting his show when he looked like a typical reporter. He was in shirtsleeves with his hat pushed back on his head and tapping on his keys as he read his script.

He viewed himself as a reporter for the common man. Winchell, who was sponsored by Jergen's Lotion, had no fear and took on everybody. He developed a powerful network of sources that kept him abreast of all sorts of news and made him a hit for many years. He was probably the most popular commentator in the history of radio.

He once sponsored a contest for some worthwhile cause (I forget what it was) whereby participants had to send in a dollar to submit a slogan. As a youngster a dollar was a lot to me; however, I sent in my dollar because I believed in him and the cause he was supporting.

Even though he was one of the most powerful radio broadcasters of his time, his career plummeted rapidly. His fame and notoriety also went downhill fast. When he died, it was reported that there was "no one" at his funeral.

The Colgate Sport's Newsreel

Colgate Shave Cream sponsored The Colgate Sport's Newsreel featuring Bill Stern. His program opened with the announcer spelling out loudly:

"C-0-L-G-A-T-E ! Colgate presents Bill Stern."

His manner of presenting stories about sports legends was very exciting and I enjoyed listening to his program. He was also a teller of tall tales and even reminded his audience that some of his stories were legend. He would then say, "but they're all so interesting that we'd like to pass them along to you." It was said that Stern never let the facts get in his way of telling a good story. Nevertheless, he was quite popular and had a wide listening audience.

I especially enjoyed his stories about some legends like "the Gipper" from Notre Dame or Babe Ruth who were already my heroes. Even though I had read about these heroes, Bill Stern had his own special way of making them bigger than life itself, and that was fine with me.

He would tell several stories and refer to them as Reel One, Reel Two and so on. He would close each story with the line, "Portrait . . . of a hero!" Then he would close his show by saying, "That's the three—o mark for tonight." It was a reference to the traditional reporter's "30" for ending a story.

News Broadcasters

News broadcasters in the 1930s were a new phenomena. However, after a while, people began to have favorite news commentators and would listen to them regularly. Here are some of the names of reporters that I recall listening to.

Lowell Thomas was one that I especially liked. In the beginning of hie career, he believed that his popularity as a news reporter was due to the fact that his program preceded Amos 'n' Andy which was a very popular radio comedy show. Lowell Thomas however, had a pleasant way of reporting the news and in time became very popular on his own. He always started his program with, "Good evening, everybody."

Lowell Thomas, who was sponsored by Sun Oil Company, held the record for the longest daily news broadcaster of all time. He always ended his program by saying, "So long until tomorrow."

Gabriel Heatter, who had a rather somber speaking voice, was another reporter we listened to. He was one of the few successful commentators who did not have any newspaper experience. There was one sentence he was fond of using when it was appropriate to do so. In the early days of World War II, it was always a good feeling when he would say, "Ah, there's good news tonight."

On occasion we listened to H. V. (Hans von) Kaltenborn. I recall Kaltenborn's scholarly voice when reporting the news, and he always sounded professional to me. Kaltenborn was outspoken on various issues and his liberal politics often got him into trouble.

The Night the Martians Landed In New Jersey

It was October 30, 1938 and I was 14 years old. It was the evening and I was listening to the radio alone. I happened to be listening to The Mercury Theater on the Air. Suddenly I heard the announcer saying:

Ladies and gentlemen, we interrupt our program of dance music to bring you a special bulletin from the Intercontinental Radio News. After checking on several earlier news bulletins, it has now been confirmed by the authorities that strange cylindrical objects from outer space have landed in central New Jersey. Investigators at the scene at Grover's Mill in New Jersey, where one of the cylindrical objects landed, reported that the space ship hit the earth with a terrific force.

At first, I was both curious and anxious. Then I became frightened, because a very excited news reporter at the scene started shouting that the round top of one of the cylinders was slowly opening. Something or somebody was preparing to come out. The reporter's voice, even more alarming now, began to describe a strange alien figure coming out of the top of the space ship. At this point I began to get more frightened.

Further announcements were even more frantic. Something inside the spacecraft was shooting deadly rays at soldiers who were attempting to secure the area and setting them on fire. Within a few minutes the powerful heat rays were turning everything they hit into flames, and fires were spreading everywhere. I was glued to the radio. My God, I thought, monsters are actually invading us. Now I really became scared.

My older sister, Mary, was working in Philadelphia at the time and I kept thinking about her. I tried to tell my family what was going on, but as I recall they didn't take me seriously. They didn't even bother to listen to the radio broadcast I was trying to describe to them.

News bulletins told of more spaceships landing in other areas, and that the invaders were monsters from Mars. More reports now coming out stated that the Martians had taken control of a large part of New Jersey. I wondered how all this could be happening. Additional bulletins reported that people who were fleeing the area blocked emergency workers trying to reach the scene and bridges and highways were all clogged with traffic. Police enforcement agencies and the Army Reserves were unable to control the panic. All hell broke loose. By this time, the unbelievable news had spread quickly and people all over the northeast were in fear. Rumors were spreading like wildfire.

More and more people were learning about the Martian invasion. The horrible news spread into the south and even across the nation. People were fantasizing all sorts of terrible things and acting irrationality. Some people standing on rooftops in New England imagined that they could see a red glow in the evening sky, which indicated to them that New York City was burning. A sudden, overpowering terror was affecting many people at once.

Can you imagine how I felt when I heard the last surviving news reporter at the scene describing how a poisonous black smoke was spreading across New York City? Now the reporter began coughing and choking—he couldn't catch his breath. His last words were, "I can't . . . I can't."

After what seemed like a long time to me, an announcer finally said, "You are listening to a CBS presentation of Orson

Welles and The Mercury Theater on the Air, in an original dramatization of The War of the Worlds by H. G. Wells." Ironically the same announcement was made in the beginning of the program; however, most people (including me) never heard it or paid any attention because the program then went directly to an orchestra playing dance band music.

A little later Orson Welles, after recognizing the panic situation he created, closed the show by stating that "The War of the Worlds had no further significance than as the holiday offering it was intended to be—the Mercury Theater's own radio program version of dressing up in a sheet and jumping out of a bush and saying boo."

Orson Welles.

Here are two headlines about the panic broadcast from several New York newspapers the following day: "FAKE RADIO

'WAR' STIRS TERROR THROUGH U.S." from the New York Daily News, October 31, 1938. And "RADIO LISTENERS IN PANIC, TAKING WAR DRAMA AS FACT," from The New York Times, October 31, 1938.

The Halloween trick Orson Welles played on American radio listeners won him fame and notoriety. It was done in a newscast format and therefore believable. It is still talked about today.

It was a night that the world came to an end—well, almost. WOW! What a scary night! It turned out to be the most famous single radio program of all time—and I was "there."

Dunning, John. Tune in Yesterday. Englewood Cliffs, New Jersey: Prentice-Hall, Inc. 1976.

Harmon, Jim. The Great Radio Heroes. New York, New York: Ace Books, Inc. 1967.

MacDonald, Fred J. Don't Touch That Dial. Chicago, Illinois: Nelson/Hall Inc. 1979.

Wertheim, Arthur Frank. Radio Comedy. New York: Oxford University Press, 1979.

Chapter 8

STORIES ABOUT PEOPLE THAT MADE THE HEADLINES

The Angel of Mercy

Dr. Robert Spencer. Courtesy of Attorney Harry Strouse.

I grew up in Big Mine Run, a patch of only a few hundred people. However, I always considered Ashland as my hometown, since it was only one mile away. When I was about twelve years of age, it seemed to me that people who did extraordinary things always lived somewhere else. However, I soon learned that Dr. Robert Spencer, an Ashland physician, did an unbelievable thing.

I was quite familiar with the location of Dr. Spencer's Office and Clinic. I recall that when I was just a kid I would always stare at Dr. Spencer's office when I walked by, because I had heard about "things that went on" in there. Later when I really understood what was going on in the clinic, I still glanced discreetly at his office as I walked by.

What was this remarkable thing that Dr. Spencer did? Genovese, in his excellent book, pointed out that Dr. Robert Spencer performed 100,000 illegal abortions from 1919 to 1969. The New York Times also reported that Dr. Spencer performed more than 100,00 illegal abortions. The Los Angles Times stated that he performed at least 30,00 abortions and a film documentary on Dr. Spencer stated that he performed more than 40,000 abortions.

In an interview with Paul Krassner in 1962, Dr. Spencer admitted that over a period of 30 to 40 years he performed 27,006 abortions. By that time Spencer was quite old and his health was deteriorating; however, he did continue to do some abortions over the next seven years. With a little extrapolating, it is my view that Dr. Spencer performed approximately 30,000 abortions over his lifetime.

In any event, 30,000 illegal abortions is still an unbelievably very large number. How did all this happen? Where were the authorities? Why did he spend his entire life doing that?

Robert Spencer was born on March 16, 1889 in Kansas City, Missouri. His father, who was an attorney, moved to

Williamsport, Pennsylvania when Robert was only several years old. Robert liked the outdoor life and enjoyed growing up in north central Pennsylvania.

After finishing high school, he enrolled at Penn State University where he majored in biology. In 1911 he graduated from Penn State with honors and was accepted for admission to the University of Pennsylvania Medical School. While he was in medical school he planned to marry Jule Butler, his first cousin. However, both families were opposed to the marriage but Robert was not to be deterred. He proceeded to get married and then graduated from medical school in 1915. He interned at the Philadelphia General followed by a period of study at the Rockefeller Institute. After that, he served in the Army Medical Corp from 1917-18. When Dr. Spencer left the Army he returned to private practice in Williamsport.

In 1919 Dr. Spencer moved to Hazleton, Pennsylvania. During this time, his wife Jule made an unusual request of her husband. Jule asked him to perform an abortion on a friend of hers who came from a well-known Williamsport family. The young unwed woman had become pregnant, and if something weren't done, the scandal would have caused havoc in her family. Dr. Spencer realized that the only way to solve the problem was to terminate the pregnancy. He quietly and efficiently performed his first abortion.

Dr. Robert Spencer.

The following year he accepted the position as chief pathologist at the Ashland Miners' Hospital in Ashland. After five years as chief resident pathologist at the Ashland Hospital, Dr. Spencer went back to full-time private practice at 531 Center Street in Ashland.

It may surprise many people to learn that Dr. Spencer was a fine doctor and an excellent diagnostician. He was well read and contributed to medical journals. He also kept current on new medical procedures as well as new developments in technology. Spencer was especially interested in scientific instruments that might help him in his work. He even designed some special equipment for his own medical practice. Dr. Spencer also took a course under Dr. Chevalier Jackson at Philadelphia, the developer of the bronchoscope, and was the first physician in the region to do bronchoscopic work.

Harry Strouse, an Ashland attorney, said, "I read in the paper that he removed an open safety pin from a girl's esophagus. So from then on, Dr. Spencer was something a little different. He was out of the ordinary run of doctors." Whenever anyone swallowed some foreign object, It was always Dr. Spencer that was called upon to use his skill with his bronchoscope to retrieve it.

A young woman once told me that Dr. Spencer removed a sliver of metal from her grandfather's eye. She stated that the successful operation saved her grandfather's sight.

Joe Baldino, a childhood buddy of mine, went to Dr. Spencer a number of times for medical treatment. Joe said the Dr. Spencer was the only doctor who was able to cure his very bad case of poison ivy. Although he did mention that the "goddamned salve" that Dr. Spencer used burned like hell, but it took care of the poison ivy. Joe, who had served in the army also, told me that Dr. Spencer cured a terrible skin rash he had contracted after being discharged from the army. That was the typical pattern with patients that went to Dr. Spencer, he always seemed to be able to solve the problem; his patients had confidence in him and they trusted him.

Emil Ermert, a retired mining engineer, pointed out that the coal miners and their families' felt that they had a friend in Dr. Spencer. It wasn't unusual for him to rush to the scene of a mine accident to treat the injured, rather than treat them after they arrived at the hospital. At times he even went into the mines to treat injuries.

Dr. Spencer became an expert on miners' black lung disease, more commonly called miners' asthma. His pioneering work in the treatment of black lung disease was greatly appreciated by those who got miners' asthma, but sadly there was no cure for the disease. The condition resulted from coal dust accumulating in the miners' lungs after years of working, making it difficult for them to breathe. I recall my father, later in his life, gasping for breath because his lungs weren't functioning normally due to miners' asthma. It was a terrible disease and most miners eventually ended up with it.

Shortly after opening his clinic in Ashland, he did not charge for any abortions that he performed. In the beginning it was the wives of miners and farmers who came for abortions.

The following message was attached to the wall in his clinic so all his women patients who wanted an abortion could read it.

I will help you, if you agree to the following:

Do not consider this operation if you are not convinced it is for your own good.

If you think it is a sin, do not have the operation.

Dr. Spencer decorated the walls of his office with various other signs and plaques that he collected from souvenir shops while traveling around the world. One sign in particular was fastened on the ceiling over his operating table where his patients clearly could see it. The sign read, "Keep calm."

A film by Danielle Renfrew and Beth Seltzer titled, "Dear Dr. Spencer" states that he performed his first abortion in 1923 for a poor widowed woman with too many children. He had compassion and somehow could share the deep feeling of suffering she had; he could not turn her down. (Although his first wife, Jule, mentioned that he performed his first abortion in 1919.) Shortly thereafter young unmarried women started to come to him in larger numbers. Then married women who were pregnant started to come regularly. So it wasn't only the poor and the middle class who came, but well-known wealthy people also sought his services.

Unfortunately some desperate women at that time attempted to abort themselves, often resulting in permanent injury. Others women who were pregnant went to non-professional people who often "botched" the pregnancy, which also ended in permanent injury and at times even death. However, the women who came to Dr. Spencer for abortions did not have clandestine appointments in shabby apartments or sleazy motel rooms. He operated an eleven-room fully equipped hygienic medical center. The women were treated with respect and received excellent medical care.

Dr. Spencer's name and his work soon spread during the 1930s and 40s. Pregnant women from all over the state came to him. The demand for his services became so great that he had to begin charging for abortions that he performed, but even then his fees were modest. His wife Jule became very annoyed that he did not charge higher fees, because it seemed they were always having financial problems. She had been reared in a well-to-do family, and wanted to maintain her previous life style.

Dr. Spencer and his wife had two children. Their first child, a son, and later a daughter were both born with disabilities. Mrs. Spencer, who was distraught about her childrens' problems, thought that their close cousin relationship might have been a contributing factor. Dr. Spencer told his wife that their close kinship had nothing to do with it. However, their marriage was also further weakened by the long hours Dr. Spencer spent in his office, it seemed to her that he was always working.

After 30 years of marriage, on May 16, 1945 Dr. Spencer's divorce from Jule became final. In September of that same year he married Eleanor Becker. Eleanor was an elementary school teacher for 17 years in Mt. Carmel, just several miles away.

As the news continued to spread about Dr. Spencer in the 1950s, he found that women were not only coming from surrounding states but also from all over the country. So it was not unusual to see automobiles with out-of-state license plates parked in the vicinity of his office. Also, the number of women who registered as one-night guests at Hotel Loeper was greater than you would normally expect. Some women even came from foreign countries! He would only perform an abortion when the fetus was no more than eight weeks old. On rare occasions, he would extend it to ten weeks, but no longer.

Business was booming; however, he was never interested in making a huge profit so he continued to keep his fees quite reasonable. Eleanor Spencer said, "Sometimes there would be somebody who came in that didn't have the fare to go back. [Dr. Spencer] would give it to them and he would even buy them a dinner. They were that poor."

Michael Kaufman, New York Times reporter and biographer of Dr. Robert Spencer, stated, "In college we all kept Dr. Spencer's name in our wallets—as sort of a talisman in case of an emergency." When I read Michael Kaufman's comment, it reminded me of a personal incident I had when I was in college in the 1950s, I gave a friend of mine Dr. Spencer's address since he requested that information from me.

On January 4, 1954 a warrant was issued for Dr. Spencer's arrest. It was based on a complaint from Mrs. Lillian Frie of Pottsville who had an abortion in his office. He was shocked that she would do such a thing after coming to him for help. However, Dr. Spencer continued to carry on his medical practice. The trial was finally held some twelve months later, on January 12, 1955. Many people felt that his medical career would come to an end; surprisingly, the jury found him not guilty.

Just because he was acquitted, Spencer did not feel that he got a "good break" and that he should now mend his ways. I think he felt that perhaps some people were now beginning to see his point of view. Following the trial, he felt vindicated and sought support for his stance on abortion. However, the community did not openly agree with him and they did not come over to his side. While he was still alone on his views of abortion, he was not to be denied. He wrote to a number of organizations soliciting support for his views. He even wrote the governor and other legislators trying to get them to understand that the abortion laws needed to be changed.

One year later, December 9, 1956, Mary Davies, a twenty-six year old single woman died on the operating table in Dr. Spencer's office while undergoing an abortion. Shortly after he started the abortion procedure, his patient ran into difficulty and despite everything he tried to do to save her life, he was not successful. Dr. Spencer reported the death to the county coroner and also called the district attorney.

Several months later, on February 21, 1957 a warrant was again issued for his arrest. However, the trial didn't begin for about two years. This time the prosecution was determined to win the case against Dr. Spencer; after all, a woman had died in his office while he was performing an abortion on her. The prosecution brought in Dr. Milton Helfern, Chief Pathologist and Medical Examiner for New York City and Dr. Alexander

Goettler, the well-known toxicologist who was called to testify in the famous Lindberg baby kidnaping case in the 1930s.

Genovese writes the following:

My interview with Mrs. Lulu Anns was very revealing. The Protestant housewife from Minersville noted that the jury members were all older, married people, somewhat sympathetic to a young woman's plight. It could very well have been their own daughter. She knew Dr. Spencer but said nothing about this when being selected. She had a chronic skin condition on her legs and found Spencer's homemade salve the only relief for it. She told me she must have bought a hundred jars of it over the years. . . .

It was her opinion (and that of most of the jurors) that Mary Davies tried, through some inept person, to have an abortion before she came to Ashland. The "bad job" wasn't working and out of desperation she went to Dr. Spencer who was merely trying to help.

A documentary film produced in 1998 by Renfrew and Seltzer titled, "Dear Dr. Spencer" pointed out that:

Pauline Wasser, a juror on the case, stated that she knew Dr. Spencer performed abortions; however, she did not believe in abortions because she was a Christian. She added, "The girl from New York [Mary Davies] that had died in his office had a lot of other medication in her purse and we felt that she must have had other medical problems other than being there for an abortion."

The prosecution team felt they had a strong case against Dr. Spencer. However, on January 15, 1959 a jury of seven men and five women on their third vote found Dr. Spencer not guilty. The headline on the front page of the Ashland Daily News on Friday, January 16, 1959 read: "Dr. R. D. Spencer Acquitted by Jury on Both Charges." In essence, the jury contended that the Commonwealth failed to prove its chares of (1) abortion and (2) death by abortion.

It is interesting to note that the predominately conservative catholic juries acquitted Dr. Spencer each time he was brought to trial for illegal abortions. Dr. Spencer never worried too much about the authorities. Paul Reidler, an Ashland resident, said, "When he was to be raided by the state police, the county police gave him word of what was going on. [Then] he would get rid of his patients in the office, and when they came there was nobody there that he was doing abortions on." Sometimes he was told by the county police that it might be a good idea to close down the clinic for a short time because the state police were planning a surveillance of his office. He would go on vacation and then return to business as usual. However, he never paid off the police to be allowed to conduct his medical practice. Also, some of his friends would inform him of possible police activity.

In short, the community protected him because they liked him. Harry Strouse said, "The town's people in effect built an invisible shield; that is, as far as possible the town's people would protect the doctor even though . . . a lot of them personally did not approve of abortion." Bracey Elwood, Ashland pharmacist, stated, "People just went to him and depended on his sympathy to perform an abortion, It wasn't advertised, it wasn't talked about. No one criticized it; it was just a necessary service."

It would be fair to say that there was a "live and let live attitude" in the town. One woman in Ashland stated it well when she said, "Judge not and ye shall not be judged."

For the next seven years he conducted his clinic business as usual. However, it turned out to be a difficult time for Dr. Spencer because his regular technician of many years was not available to help him. Spencer was growing older and had difficulty keeping up with all the patients coming to his office.

Harry Mace, a con man, saw an opportunity to make money and talked Dr. Spencer into an arrangement where he could be helpful to him. Harry suggested a plan whereby he could serve as a "go-between" in helping women who were seeking an abortion. He would set up transportation for them to get to Spencer's Office as well as assist them whey they left the Spencer Clinic. He even talked Spencer into letting him collect the fees, thus allowing Spencer to concentrate on providing medical care and not having to deal with administrative matters.

As it turned out Mace was charging patients $600, even though Spencer's fee was only $100; Harry kept the balance of the money for himself. Harry started to provide so many patients that Spencer could not handle the increased traffic. The situation was clearly out of hand. Spencer was so engrossed in what he was doing that he didn't comprehend the mess Harry had got him into. Further, he was not aware that Harry was overcharging his patients and keeping the extra money.

During all this time, the police were observing closely what was going on at Spencer's Clinic. The authorities clearly saw the increase in the number of (a) patients visiting his Clinic, (b) out-of-state cars parked in the vicinity of his office, and (c) women staying at Hotel Loeper for a one-night visit--and that's all they needed to see. They decided that it was time to move and take action against Dr. Spencer, and indeed they did.

The district attorney's office now felt that they had sufficient evidence to convict Dr. Spencer, who was now referred to as "The King of the Abortionists." On February 23, 1966 the Schuylkill County District Attorney addressed the court to issue a search warrant to search Dr. Spencer's Clinic. The prosecution charged Dr. Spencer with abortion and conspiracy to do an unlawful act. Corporal Charles Skurkis, a member of the Pennsylvania State Police at the Mahanoy City barracks, swore to the affidavit. The prosecution attempted to prove that Dr. Spencer performed an abortion on Miss Lucille Kingman of Buffalo, New York in his clinic during the period of time from

January 3-5 when she visited his office. This was the third time Dr. Spencer was arrested and charged with performing an illegal abortion. Paul Reidler said, "The people that arrested Dr. Spencer didn't do it willingly, they did it unwillingly. And they cut it as short as they knew how to do it."

Did Dr. Spencer feel that Harry Mace was a friend who not only supported abortion, but also came just at the right time when he needed help? Was Harry's proposal to raise funds for a new Spencer Clinic a factor that resulted in Spencer not checking on Harry more closely? While Spencer was swindled and fooled by Mace (and perhaps not thinking as clearly as he should), he still bears responsibility for becoming involved with a con man like Harry.

As I was doing research on this article, I was surprised to learn that Corporal Charles Skurkis was the state policeman that swore to the affidavit in Dr. Spencer's case. At the time Charles Skurkis swore to the affidavit, our oldest son, Greg, was 15 years of age. Five years later, he married Charles Skurkis' only daughter, Arlene who is now a physician.

By the time of his third arrest, Dr. Spencer was in his late 70s and in poor health. For the next several years he tried to continue his practice but was unable to work full time. His physical condition continued to get worse and finally his wife Eleanor persuaded him to have an operation for his double hernia. Dr. Spencer was 79 years old when he consented to have Dr. Romualdo Schicatano operate on him. Genovese in his fine book, The Angel of Ashland wrote:

Spencer: [talking to Dr. Schicatano] All right. I want you to take care of it for me. I know that murder is a mortal sin in the eyes of the Catholic Church so I figure I stand the best chance of surviving with a good Catholic like you behind the knife. I don't trust the other witch doctors and they don't like me anyway.

Over the years Spencer and Schicatano would argue about abortion. Spencer tried to convince his friend to see his side favoring abortion, while Schicatano would strongly take the opposite view. However, they were friends and they respected each other. Dr. Schicatano was a fine surgeon but was somewhat concerned about operating on a friend who was not only 79 years old, but also had other health problems.

Nevertheless, he operated on Dr. Spencer in early January 1969 and he seemed to be recovering normally. However, several days later, Dr. Spencer suddenly began coughing. The coughing spell became worse and within minutes Dr. Spencer fell to the floor. Upon examination, they found that his death was caused by a blood clot. Since Dr. Spencer died, his case was never brought to trial. Would he have been convicted? We'll never know.

His death was reported by a number of leading newspapers around the country including The New York Times and the Los Angeles Times. Several leading magazines such as Time and

Newsweek also covered the story. Spencer's death was also the lead story on the Huntley-Brinkley National TV evening news report, the best-known news team of that period.

There was just a handful of people at Dr. Spencer's funeral. He was an atheist and didn't want any religious service. The minister read the 23rd Psalm and said a few words. It took about three minutes. Thus ended the short eulogy of Dr. Robert Spencer—Ashland's most famous resident. "There was nothing that would have offended him," said Mrs. Spencer.

Understandably, there were no women there who had visited his clinic for an abortion. However, hundreds of cards and letters arrived at his office for his wife Eleanor. What about the thousands of others who had come to him at one time in their life, desperate for his professional help and received it? Perhaps it is safe to say that many of them, when they heard of his death took a moment alone to remember his kindness to them in a time of need. I don't doubt that many of them said a prayer for him. Although Dr. Spencer was an atheist, I betting that he would have said, "That's all right." He left a collection of over 30,000 letters from women who had written him over four decades asking him for his help. All the letters began with the following words, "Dear Dr. Spencer, I . . ."

Finally, I would like to comment again on his superb diagnostic ability. It was rather common for doctors in other towns to send their referrals to him for his opinion. Dr. Spencer did not hesitate in sending his patients on occasion to specialists in some of the best hospitals in the northeastern part of the country. Not surprisingly, his diagnoses were invariably confirmed.

Genovesee wrote:

A few days after his funeral, Eleanor was going through some of her husband's personal effects. She came across a medical diary that he began when his health started to fail him. In it she discovered his description of the hernia operation as it was to be done by Dr. Schicatano. He had written down a list of all the possible complications that could arise. The last one on the list was embolism. It was the only one underlined and he had two questions marks after it. Did Dr. Robert Spencer actually predict his own death? I, for one, am inclined to believe that he played the consummate diagnostician right up to the very end—his own.

It may surprise many people to learn that Dr. Spencer also had a strong interest in science. He was provocatively scientific and his curiosity was endless. He was interested in everything in nature. If he didn't become a doctor, he would have made a superb medical researcher.

Without question, Spencer was an abortionist—but was he "just an abortionist?" Was he a "saintly abortionist?" Throughout history there have been many courageous people who had to withstand criticism and risked their reputation for something they strongly believed in. They were individuals who stayed the course—they were ahead of their time. Many people now feel that Dr. Spencer was one of them.

Harry M. Bobonich, Ph.D.

A Closer Look at Dr. Robert Spencer

After reading about Dr. Spencer and writing a short story about him I became more interested in trying to understand what really went on inside his mind. The big question—why? Why? Why did he do what he did? What drove him to perform about 30,000 illegal abortions during his lifetime?

To begin with, Dr. Spencer was a very competent doctor. He could have made much more money and worked fewer hours by carrying out his regular medical practice. However, he chose to do otherwise—he chose to do abortions. While he was an intelligent person, he was at the same time a complex individual.

Let's look at several incidents that happened in his early childhood as pointed out by Vincent Genovese. When Robert was about five years of age his parents bought him some baby ducks. He playfully guided them around the garden holding a small stick. One day he accidentally killed a duckling by hitting it on the head. Robert felt that he was responsible and promised never to mistreat another animal.

When he was about six years old, his eight-year old brother contracted diphtheria. It was a contagious disease and very little could be done to cure it. As a precautionary measure, Robert was moved from his home out into the barn. He was afraid to be alone, but did what he was told to do, including praying for his brother. That night a strong thunderstorm hit and Robert felt even more frightened and alone. Later in the night his father visited Robert and told him that his brother had died.

Did these experiences Robert had in his early childhood affect him in some way? Did they sow the seeds of compassion in him from even that early age?

In 1962 Paul Krassner, interviewed Dr. Spencer with the understanding that he would go to prison rather than reveal [Dr.] Spencer's identity. Krassner asks Dr. Spencer a key question.

Paul Krassner: How did you come to start doing abortions?

Robert Spencer: Well, I'll never forget the case that first came to my mind—this was when I was going to high school. My father was the district attorney, and he had an interesting case brought to him by one of the leading ministers, in which this minister said, "Look at these letters that my daughter's getting—I can't make any sense out of them, they're all sorts of, well, sometimes threatening letters, and they're so bizarre that I can't make anything out of them."

So my father says, "Supposes you get some of her handwriting"—and when they compared, they find that she's written these letters to herself. And when the investigation came on, by golly, she's illegitimately pregnant—she's just gambling around trying to find something, I guess, to help her out, and when the father knew that, darned if he didn't blow his brains out. The minister killed himself.

And I thought, "Good gracious, to think a person being that way, and a few little cells removed at a time like that—look what that could've saved." It could've saved, certainly, the life of the father; whatever became of the girl after that, I don't know. Whether she became a hysterical wreck or not, I don't know. It just shows how those things go—and you go to work, and you just think, "Well, here's our country, why, they wouldn't even permit a thing like that if it was rape."

So even at that early age in high school, Robert felt that an abortion could have prevented the tragedy that occurred in that family.

When he was an upperclassman at Pennsylvania State University, he spent one summer with a medical doctor who was a friend of the family. Robert was very impressed by the "caring attitude" the doctor had for his patients. It turned out that the summer experience had influenced him in becoming a doctor. So, was this latent feeling of compassion growing and strengthening in Robert? Did he envision himself one day to be in a position to be helpful as the doctor?

His decision to marry his cousin, Jule, while in medical school was an indication of his persistence and independence since both families were opposed to the marriage. Robert was strong-minded and once he made up his mind about something it was virtually impossible to change it. This was a trait he carried with him throughout his life.

After completing his medical studies, he served in the U.S. Army for several years during the great flu epidemic in the United States 1918-19, which killed about a half million people. While in the Army, he wrote to the Surgeon General's Office recommending a new sanitary procedure that should be followed to reduce the spread of the disease. Dr. Spencer's diagnosis and recommendation turned out to be correct. Here we see Spencer becoming much more confident not only in his abilities, but also in his willingness to express his views on more worldly matters.

After leaving the Army, he set up practice in Hazleton, where an unusual thing happened. His wife, Jule, requested that he perform an abortion on a young unmarried friend of Jule's family. Dr. Spencer went ahead and performed his fist abortion, even though it was illegal to do so.

Was this first abortion to be a rare operation for him—or would it lead to others? I think it is fair to say that he must have begun to think more about abortions and that there would be an increasing demand for them. He very likely thought about what role he might play in this contentious issue.

Sometime in the mid-1920s, Spencer set up his private medical practice in Ashland. I believe that by this time he had made up his mind about abortion, and felt that a woman had a right to choose and decide for herself if she wanted to terminate her pregnancy. He operated a well-equipped and modern clinic and was in a position to provide excellent help to pregnant women who would choose to come to him.

Then one day a poor widowed woman who already had a large family came to him for an abortion. Dr. Spencer felt sorry for her and performed the operation. Pandora's Box was now opened; there was no going back. He started doing abortions openly and regularly even though it was illegal to do so. In the beginning, he didn't even charge to do an abortion. The word soon spread, at first it was mainly local women that came to him and then they start coming from all over.

Dr. Spencer knew that if he did not help these women, they would in many cases attempt to abort themselves or end up having some incompetent person perform the abortion with disastrous results. One young woman tried to use a glass soda straw to terminate her pregnancy prematurely. Eleanor Becker, Dr. Spencer's second wife, said, "And when she came in to see [Dr. Spencer], he worked terribly to save her life."

What a drastic step for him to take! He could easily have been arrested and convicted and put in jail ending his medical career. It was a courageous thing for him to do, and many would obviously say a foolish thing for him to do.

However, Dr. Spencer was a deeply thoughtful man who followed his conscience. He was defiant of the law and publicly argued what he did was correct. He was dedicated to using his knowledge and skill to help people, and he believed he was doing the right thing. In doing so he had to withstand ridicule, blackmail, censure, public arrest and court trials for his commitment to the principle of choice for women. He felt that it was a woman's right to control her reproductive destiny. It wasn't easy for him to take such a strong position on abortion so openly. He was alone (at least publicly) on his view on abortion and he knew it. However, he was tough-minded and didn't waver from his position; he took on anyone in a discussion on abortion.

During the 1930s there was no integration of the races and there were no African Americans living in Ashland. Since there was no lodging available for black women in Ashland, he arranged for overnight accommodations for these women in a facility near his clinic. His services were available to all; he treated everyone equally.

Just think for a moment about the unbelievable decision he chose regarding what he would do with his life. Undoubtedly he would have many, many women seeking his services. He would be facing many long hard hours of work with very little pay; and he would be placing his career and even his life in jeopardy!

His professional colleagues did not approve of what he was doing. Furthermore, they were annoyed and resented the manner in which he persistently argued his views with them. It was clear that they misunderstood his assuredness as arrogance. However, they learned over time that his diagnoses of medical problems were generally correct. I suspect some of his colleagues may have secretly admired him as well as his medical skills but kept it to themselves. Eventually his conduct irritated enough of his professional friends that the local Schuylkill Chapter of the American Medical Association censured him and dismissed him from the Chapter.

Dr. Spencer was not meek about taking a position on global matters if he felt strongly about it. It should not come as a surprise that he felt that the increase in world population was a significant problem, and that very little was being done about it. He took the time to write state and national organizations expressing his views on the matter. Clearly his view on birth control was consistent with his willingness to perform abortions.

In 1998, Danielle Renfrew and Beth Seltzer produced an informative and illuminating documentary film titled, "Dear Dr. Spencer." It is a powerful film that features interviews with Dr. Spencer's second wife, townspeople and particularly women who came to him for an abortion.

The film portrays Dr. Spencer as a compassionate man dedicated to helping people who were suffering. He was a skilled physician who wanted to help those who came to him for any kind of medical help, and that certainly included doing abortions. He particularly cared for women who were pregnant, but did not wish to be. Dr. Spencer was not only available to patients, but more importantly, they trusted him.

In the film, three of Dr. Spencer's abortion patients courageously described their experience in his clinic when they were there some years ago. Three women (Hettie Jones, Anna Columbo and Lynn -----) all felt that at the time they were in a desperate situation and were grateful that Dr. Spencer was able to help them. In a sense, he gave them a new lease on life. He was only one of a handful of competent physicians in the country who was willing to perform an abortion for a nominal fee.

Dr. Spencer was a short man with a happy face; however, he was feisty, independent and a free thinker. For example, he did not think it was wrong for married people to have more freedom in sexual relationships. He felt that it was a natural instinct for men and women to have polygamous relationships. In spite of his beliefs, he was well liked and respected, not only in Ashland, but also throughout the area.

Even though he was well known, his manner of dress made him more conspicuous. He always wore a beret and a bow tie. Can you imagine wearing a beret in Ashland in the 1930s? People always commented on his "funny looking hat." They also made other snide remarks. But that was Dr. Spencer—he was a "free spirit."

In the film "Dear Dr. Spencer" I saw him operating an "aqua car" which he purchased in his late 70s. The aqua car, which could travel on land and water, was similar to the Army duck in World War II. I chuckled when I saw Dr. Spencer operating his car on a lake and waving to the crowd. Of course, he was wearing his beret and bow tie. Why did I laugh, well, as a young soldier some three decades earlier I also operated an Army duck in the Amphibian Engineers.

He was such a controversial figure, that people would often glance at him discreetly or even stare at him indiscreetly if they happened to see him in town. It was not unusual for a grown-up woman to say in a low voice to her daughter or another younger girl, " See that man across the street—that's Dr. Spencer—you will hear more about him when you grow up."

During the five decades of his work his office was raided five times; however, the authorities never found any incriminating evidence against him. He was also arrested three times but never convicted. During all those fifty years, he went on performing illegal abortions, often as many as ten in one day. When Eleanor Becker was asked about the abortions that her husband was performing, she replied, " I worried about it. I didn't want anything to happen to him. You never knew what could."

Even though he worked long hours, it is still incredible that he was able to accomplish all that he did. Dr. Spencer performed all the abortions in the small town of Ashland in the anthracite region, and not in a major city as you might expect. He made a rather remarkable impact not only on Ashland, but also on the larger community he served.

Sometime late in his life Dr. Spencer's physical condition deteriorated to a point where he had to be taken to The Geisinger Medical Clinic in Danville. He required extensive medical treatment in order to save his life. When he left the hospital, he thought that perhaps he should no longer do abortions. Of course, others close to him strongly suggested the same thing. But then, it was back to the same old routine, some desperate pregnant woman would visit him and he could not turn her away. Again, his compassion and determination to help seemed to be more important than any concern for himself. Throughout his life, he believed that alleviating suffering and saving lives was his purpose for living.

Dr. Spencer thought that it was just a matter of time before abortions would become legal. In his heart, he felt it would happen in his lifetime, but it didn't. However in 1973, the Roe v. Wade decision legalized abortion in the United States, just four years after he died. If he had lived to hear the decision, he would have glowed. Dr. Robert Spencer, the small town doctor from Ashland, lived and died believing he was right.

In a small town like Ashland, it is common that people have a regular doctor that they see from time to time. Dr. Spencer never saw the thousands and thousands of abortion patients that he treated once they left his office—they were one-time visitors.

He was a small man and for many, many years he lifted and carried women from one location to another in his office.

In doing so, he strained his stomach muscles to the point where he had to have a double hernia operation late in life. He died suddenly a short time after the operation. In a way, his death was directly related to doing abortions. I'm sure if he were somehow asked if he would do it all over again, he would say, "YES!"

He was not one of the giants of the passing parade in the history of the proud town of Ashland. He was "the giant"— much taller than his height of five feet and five inches. In Dr. Spencer's mind, he had no choice. I think that Dr. Spencer felt he was destined to do what he did—and he was glad to lead the way.

Dougherty, Richard. "Accepted as Abortionist." Los Angeles Times, 17 March,1969, p.1.

"Dr. Robert Spencer, 79, Dies; Performed 100,000 Abortions." New York Times, 22 January, 1969.

"Dr. R. D. Spencer Acquitted by Jury On both Charges." Ashland Daily, 16 January, 1959.

Genovese, Vincent. The Angel of Ashland. Amherst, New York: Prometheus Books, 2000.

"King of the Abortionists." Newsweek, 17 February, 1969, p. 92.

Krassner, Paul. Impolite Interviews. New York, N.Y. Seven Stories Press,1999.

"R. D. Spencer Dies a Ashland," Pottsville Republican, 22 January, 1969.

Renfrew, Daniellle and Beth Seltzer. A film titled, "Dear Dr. Spencer: Abortion in a Small Town." 1998. First Run/Icarus Films, 153 Waverly Place, New York, N.Y.

The Valley of Terror

Living in the lower anthracite region of Pennsylvania during the latter part of the 19th century was not for the faint hearted. A series of violent crimes plagued the area. Schuylkill County in particular and some regions in Carbon, Columbia and Northumberland counties were also places of danger, violence and killings; it was a valley of fear. "During the thirteen years between 1862 and 1875, there were 142 unsolved homicides and 212 felonious assaults in Schuylkill County alone," according to Arthur H. Lewis.

Who was responsible for all the violence? What was the cause of all the lawlessness? How did it all end?

Let's go back to an earlier time in Ireland where an organization known as the "Molly Maguires" had its origin. One story (of several) tells of an elderly woman named Mollie Maguire who was being cruelly evicted from her home by a mean landlord. Some outraged neighborly Irish peasants rallied around Molly to support and protect her. After the confrontation with the land agent, a small group of peasants decided to ban together to fight other landlords who were exploiting and oppressing them. The newly formed group became known as the Molly Maguires, a name that soon caught on. Later when the Irish immigrant miners settled in the anthracite region of Pennsylvania, they brought their "habit" of protest with them.

Bimba described the behavior of the American miners of Irish descent this way:

When Irish immigrants and miners of Irish descent in the anthracite [region] entered into a life and death struggle they found that they were in conflict with coal corporations in which British capital was heavily invested. The age-old struggle between English landlords and capitalists and Irish workers and peasants, to a degree, reflected, under new conditions and changed circumstances, in the struggle in the coal fields . . . . Centuries of history through which the Irish masses, battered by oppression and scourged by famine, had struggled, formed a background of stubborn resistance and determined struggle for the Irish miners in the anthracite [region].

When the Irish miners settled in the anthracite region, they found the working conditions deplorable. The superintendents and mine foremen, who were the bosses, represented the mine owners. These bosses were mainly concerned with making profits for their absentee employers at the miners' expense. The coal miners at that time not only worked long hours, but for very low wages. In 1840, a miner was paid one dollar a day and a laborer only received eighty cents. By 1848 a miner received $1.25 a day and a laborer was paid eighty-three cents daily. The miners' wages were subject to frequent changes because the price of coal often changed. In 1869 the miners received $3.03 a day, but in 1871 the daily wage dropped to $2.75. However, after the long strike in 1875 there was a series of decreases in pay. By 1877, the miners were only receiving a daily wage of about $1.65. In many cases the miners had to purchase their food and supplies from company stores that were owned and operated by the mine owners. Since these stores controlled the prices of their goods, the workers were often overcharged for items they bought. In most cases there was little left in their paychecks after the company stores were paid.

Furthermore, the miners worked under very harsh conditions; the coal mines in many cases were unsafe and actually dangerous. Reporters who visited these mines labeled them as death traps. According to Bimba, "In Schuylkill County 566 miners were killed and 1,665 maimed in seven years; in 1871 alone, 112 were killed and 339 permanently injured."

In the 1870s, P. F. M'Andrew a clerk of the mining district of Schuylkill wrote:

The employees in coal mines are handled so as their labor shall realize the largest amount of profit to the employer, and this at the risk of life and limb, consequent upon diversity of their labor, besides the danger to be encountered in working in deep mines that are so often idle that, from standing gas, decay of timber, the absence of ventilation, and standing water, not only makes the mines unsafe but virtually dangerous. The miners' occupation in some cases is but little better than semi-slavery.

The lack of concern by the coal mine owners for the safety and welfare of the miners was a crucial factor in the trouble that developed. The mine owners showed no interest in improving the difficult working conditions of the miners, and in fact opposed legislation to improve them. The bitterness and resentment of the workers increased to the point where the foremen and superintendents of the collieries were subjected to threats and violence. Fires were set and other damage was also done to equipment and buildings of the owners. Eventually the anger of the miners led to more serious threats, injuries and even killings. The coal operators felt that the unreasonable demands of the miners as well as all the violence originated with the militant Irish miners and referred to them as the Molly Maguires. Not surprisingly, the Molly Maguires were labeled hoodlums, gangsters and murderers who took the law into their own hands.

It was Benjamin Bannan, editor of the Schuylkill County Miners Journal, in 1857 who introduced the name "Molly Maguires" to the American public. He used the term for his anti-Irish bias for all the aspects of the Irish character he found unsavory and objectionable. The coal owners soon picked up this term and used it to their advantage.

Many of the victims who incurred the wrath of a Molly or a friend of a Molly would receive a threat notice. The threat would come in the form of a crude anonymously served warning or "coffin notice" such as the following.

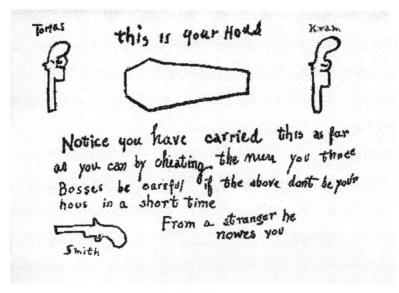

Coffin Notice

Listed below are some other representative Molly Notices I have read:

Now men I have warented ye before and I willnt warind you no mor -but I will gwrintee yo the will be the report of the revolver.

The following notice was nailed to the desk of Editor Foster of the Shenandoah Herald.

Mr Edtore wie wil give ye 24 hurse to go to the divil out ye son of A Bitch R we wil send ye After gomer Ja mes and Mr.----and some more Big Bug with ye F molley we aint done Shooting yet.

This is to give you the Gap men a cliar understanding that if you don't quit work after this NOTICE you may prper for your DETH. You are the damdest turncoats in the State—there is no ples fit for you bute Hell and will soone be there. Molly Sind by the real boys this time-so you better loocke oute.

Schuylkill County was the stronghold of the Molly Maguires and it was here that they were most active. Kenny described this region this way:

The area in question was a triangle of land stretching from Shamokin (in Northumberland County) northeastward as far as Hazleton (in lower Luzerne County) and eastward through Ashland, Shenandoah, Mahanoy City, Tuscarora, and Tamaqua (all in Schuylkill County) as far as Mauch Chunk, the seat of Carbon County.

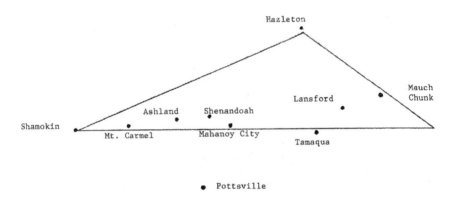

Molly Maguire Territory.

The infamous social turmoil of the anthracite region, in short, was to be found primarily in its wilder, less settled areas, and in particular the area under consideration. It was here that immigrants from north-central and northwestern Ireland tended to settle. All but two of the twenty Molly Maguires who were hanged lived in this territory. And thirteen of the sixteen Molly Maguire assassinations, including all the killings after 1868, occurred in the triangle of land in question.

Most of the writings about the violence and killings in the lower anthracite region pointed to the Mollies as terrorists. This biased view of the Mollies came from the coal mine owners and many in the press who supported them. The Miners' Journal published a list of fifty-one murders that were committed in Schuylkill County between January 1, 1863 and March 30, 1867. While the authorities felt that the Mollies were mainly to blame for practically all the trouble, it turned out that the number of killings attributed to the Molly Maguires during this period was four.

By 1873 Franklin B. Gowen, President of the Philadelphia and Reading Coal and Iron Company, had built up a powerful cartel in an attempt to control the railroads and mine owners. It was the first major industry-wide cartel in the country. (And for all you who have played the well-known board game Monopoly, you now know where the name of the square on the board game named "Reading Railroad" came from.)

Gowen was a powerful leader of the movement to control the miners. He used ruthless tactics against the unions and was known as a union-buster, a reputation well deserved. It was Gowen who was largely responsible for the notoriety of the Molly Maguires. He once said, "The name of a Molly Maguire being attached to a man's name is sufficient to hang him."

The miners, who were exploited by the coal companies, lashed out in return in the only way they knew to get even. The rebellious Irish miners fought their bosses and the coal companies at every turn. While no one condones violence or murder, the Mollies saw no other way to improve their lot. In the conflict between the mine owners and the Mollies, both were to blame and both resorted to guerilla warfare.

At this point, the coal authorities decided that some bold initiative had to be taken since matters were getting out of hand. In 1873 Gowen sought the help of the Pinkerton Detective Agency in Philadelphia. Gowen explained to Allan Pinkerton, President of the Pinkerton Detective Agency, the problem he was facing dealing with the Molly Maguires in the anthracite region.

After further discussion, Pinkerton agreed to take on the case against the Mollies. He looked over a list of people available to him and after some time chose the best man for the job he had in mind. Pinkerton then explained his strategy to Gowen. He would hire a bold, tough detective from Chicago named James McParlan to be an undercover agent. McParlan, who was born in Ireland, would change his name to James McKenna. He would pretend to be a miner from Colorado who was seeking employment in the coal region.

James McParlan.

More recently though, he would indicate that he was running from the law after a killing in Buffalo, New York. His mission as a spy was to join the Molly Maguires organization, find out who the leaders were and expose them for their wrongdoings.

Inthefallof1873McKennaleftPhiladelphiaandtraveledbytrain to Port Clinton in Schuylkill County. It turned out to be a two-and-a-half-year dangerous assignment, one he would never forget.

Broehl tells the following story:

Arthur Conan Doyle creates appropriate atmosphere for this day in his Sherlock Holmes novel, The Valley of Fear. Doyle met William Pinkerton during a transatlantic crossing shortly after the turn of the century, became intrigued with Allan Pinkerton's account of the Mollies, and constructed the American portion of Valley of Fear as almost a paraphrase of the actual story. "Jack McMurdo"--Doyle's name for James McKenna--is staring moodily out of the train window.

Through the growing gloom there pulsed the red glow of furnaces on the sides of the hills. Great heaps of slag and dumps of cinders loomed up on each side, with the high shafts of the collieries towering above them. Huddled groups of mean, wooden houses, the windows of which were beginning to outline themselves in light, were scattered here and there along the line, and the frequent halting places were crowded with their swarthy inhabitants . . . The young traveller gazed out into this dismal country with a face of mingled repulsion and interest . . .

James McKenna also looked out of the window before getting off the train and got his first view of the coalfields, little did he know what lay ahead of him. After leaving Port Clinton, he traveled from town to town becoming familiar with the entire Schuylkill County region. McKenna then began to concentrate on getting to know important Mollies in key towns. Mahanoy City was one of the places he paid attention to because the Mollies were active in that vicinity. He also focused on Pottsville and Shenandoah where the Molly Maguire organizations were strong. After a while he realized he needed to establish a base of operations, so he set up headquarters at different times in Pottsville and Shenandoah. As McKenna became better known, he gradually became more trusted and gained the confidence of the Mollies. His acceptance allowed him to obtain valuable information, which he was able to send back to the Pinkerton Agency.

Since the miners were unable to negotiate any improvement in their working conditions, they went on strike for six months. It became known as the long strike of 1875 and was a difficult time for the miners. In fact, it turned out to be a disaster, since the coal operators had the upper hand and would not concede anything. In the end, the miners were forced to return to work on company terms. This harsh action by the coal mine owners only led to more hatred and violence. The coal mine owners were in control and could have dealt with the situation in a more reasonable and humane manner, but they chose otherwise.

During all this time, McKenna was continually infiltrating the Molly Maguire organization. Early in 1874, he traveled to Shenandoah to meet Michael "Muff" Lawler, the body-master of the Molly Maguires there. It was at Shenandoah that McKenna became a member of the Mollies. About this time, an incident occurred in Big Mine Run where McKenna confronted a thug who had intended to shoot Lawler, possibly saving Lawler's life. That event and other similar incidents continued to increase McKenna's reputation with the Mollies. He was not only successful in joining the Molly Maguires, but was now in a position to find out what they were planning to do. While he had many close calls, he always seemed to be one step ahead of the Mollies.

In the spring of 1875, Robert J. Linden a Pinkerton assistant superintendent began operating as McKenna's contact person in the coalfields. During this time, Linden was a captain in the Coal and Iron Police. According to J. Walter Coleman, the Coal and Iron Police was a private police force employed by the coal mining companies and controlled by Gowen. Its purpose was to protect the property of the mining companies, but then later was used as a weapon for the coercion of striking workers. So Linden was in a position to take action on information from McKenna in many cases before the Mollies could carry out their plans.

McKenna's undercover work was so successful that the Mollies seemed to be constantly on the defensive. The Mollies felt they were losing their fight with the coal authorities and began to suspect that someone may be leaking information to them. At the same time McKenna suspected the Mollies were becoming suspicious of him, but he never learned why or who may have tipped them off. By the spring of 1876, McKenna felt his luck running out so he left the anthracite region in a hurry. By this time he had provided the authorities with enough information that they were able to bring a significant number of Mollies to trial.

The trials for the Mollies, which were mainly held in Pottsville and Mauch Chunk, started in early 1876 and concluded late in 1878. The authorities conducted many trials staged with glamour and sensationalism. James McParlan's (alias James McKenna) appearance as a chief witness for the prosecution created quite a stir in the courtroom. His testimony at the different trials was detailed, extensive and damaging. As a result, his comments and revelations made good copy for the press. Since the mine owners had the support of the press, it was generally viewed that the law was bringing terrorists to justice for their crimes.

In general, the trials were very similar and ended with the same verdict, "guilty as indicted." During the trials, the Molly Maguires were implicated in sixteen killings with most of them taking place in Schuylkill County. In 1876 the march of the Mollies to the courtroom began. The roundup by the authorities was completed; however, the worst was yet to come for the Molly Maguires.

In June 1877, ten Mollies were hung in one day, six in Pottsville and four in Mauch Chunk (now Jim Thorpe). This bizarre event became known as the "Day of the Rope" or Black Thursday. It was the largest hanging in one day handed down by a court in the history of the state of Pennsylvania. In 1878-79 there was an additional ten Molly Maguires hung—three each in Pottsville, Mauch Chunk, and Bloomsburg and one in Sunbury.

A listing of the Molly Maquires that were hung;

Name	Date	Location
Bergin, Martin	1879	Pottsville
Boyle, James	1877	Pottsville
Campbell, Alexander	1877	Mauch Chunk
Carroll, James	1877	Pottsville
Donahue, John	1877	Mauch Chunk
Donnelly, Dennis	1878	Pottsville
Doyle, Michael	1877	Mauch Chunk
Duffy, Thomas	1877	Pottsville
Fisher, Thomas	1878	Mauch Chunk
Hester, Patrick	1878	Bloomsburg
Kehoe, John	1878	Pottsville
Kelly, Edward	1877	Mauch Chunk
McDonnell, James	1879	Mauch Chunk
McGehan, Hugh	1877	Pottsville
McHugh, Peter	1878	Bloomsburg
McNamus, Peter	1879	Sunbury
Munley, Thomas	1877	Pottsville
Roarity, James	1877	Pottsville
Sharpe, Charles	1879	Mauch Chunk
Tully, Patrick	1878	Bloomsburg

To die for faction is a common evil

But to be hanged for nonsense is the devil.

John Dryden

Another forty-five Mollies were identified and charged, but only thirty-three were rounded up since twelve escaped. Twenty-four Mollies received jail sentences. Nine ended up in one of the following categories: (a) convicted, not sentenced; (b) charged, never tried; (c) pardoned and (d) tried and acquitted.

One of those sentenced was Patrick Dolan Sr. who was the Ancient Order of Hibernians (AOH) bodymaster at Big Mine Run, Schuylkill County. Dolan was convicted of conspiracy to reward Thomas Hurley for the murder of Gomer James and sentenced to eighteen months in prison.

Most of the members of the AOH were miners, and Irish miners who were Molly Maguires were also members. It was a semi-secret fraternal society that originated in Ireland. According to Broehl, it was "by the 1870s the most benevolent and immigrant-aid lodge in the country." However the national AOH organization disapproved of the activities and conduct of the Schuylkill County AOH chapters. Barney Dolan was also an A0H member who lived in Big Mine Run and was the County delegate for Schuylkill County prior to John Kehoe.

I recall that there was a Dolan family still living in Big Mine Run where I lived for the first eighteen years of my life. As a kid I remember talking to a man named Joe Dolan on several occasions. His grandfather was one of the Mollies. The Dolan residence, a red-roofed building, is still standing in Big Mine Run.

The Pinkerton Agency and mine owners planned well. Their aim was to select the most militant of the Molly Maguires and get them convicted in court. The executions of the Mollies would then serve as an example to frighten others into submission.

Press reports on the executions were in agreement with the court's decision. Here are some examples:

The Chicago Tribune in its issue of June 22, 1877 carried an editorial headed. "A Triumph of Law and Justice."

"Justice At Last," was the headline at the Philadelphia Times of June 22, 1877.

On June 22, 1877 The Philadelphia Public Ledger article read:

The doomed men behaved with decorum, and generally with a humility remarkable to men of their coarse natures and wicked lives . . . None of them indulged in bravado; and none of them professed that loud and boisterous piety and ostentatious confidence of forgiveness and blissful immortality . . . law and justice has been vindicated.

On June 22, 1877 the New York World, which was unfriendly to the miners' cause, wrote the following about the executions of Charles Sharpe and James McDonald:

The double execution at Mauch Chunk yesterday is a disgrace to public justice in the state of Pennsylvania. The demeanor of the men on the scaffold, their resolute and yet quiet protestations of innocence of this crime . . . were things to stagger one's belief in their guilt . . . They were "Mollie Maguires," they were arrested and arraigned at a time of great popular excitement, and they were condemned and hanged "on general principles." . . . The official explanation which is sent from Harrisburg of the delay [of the reprieve] we are sorry to say is rather worse than no explanation at all . . . What more plausible explanation do the facts themselves suggest than the Governor of Pennsylvania was willing in deference to one class of his constituents to see the men hanged, while in deference to another class, if for no other reason, he was willing to make pretense of saving them.

On June 22, 1877 a New York Times article read: The Molly Maguires were duly hanged in Pennsylvania yesterday. No one will question the justice of inflicting the extreme penalty of the law on their crimes, which were revolting. But we do not think the way in which the hanging was conducted will tend to make capital punishment regarded as the proper means of repressing murder.

There were large crowds to witness the executions. The prisoners were paraded, as usual, on the scaffold. They were allowed to show such indifference to punishment as they could forgiveness of everyone; to protest their innocence in more or less braggadocio fashion, and generally to do everything to make their killing partake of the character of a cheap tragic show rather than a solemn scene of retributive justice.

We venture to say that a very small part of the great numbers who saw the hanging have any deepened sense of the terrors of the law, while by many, the most hardened of the condemned murderers will be remembered as heroes not without a slight halo of religious sentiment about them.

In his publication Hard Coal Dockets in 1994, Carbon County Judge John P. Lavelle (my former high school teacher at Butler Township) wrote:

Historians feel the Molly Maguire trials were a surrender of state sovereignty. A private corporation initiated the investigation through a private detective agency. A private police force arrested the alleged defenders, and private attorneys for the coal companies prosecuted them. The state provided only the courtroom and the gallows.

If you visit Pottsville you can see a plaque on the wall of the main entrance to the county prison. It reads:

Here in this Schuylkill County prison yard on June 21, 1877 the largest mass execution in Pennsylvania took place with the hanging of six alleged "Molly Maguire" leaders. That same day, four other alleged "Mollies" were hanged at Mauch Chunk in Carbon County. Between 1877 and 1879, twenty alleged "Mollies" were hanged in Bloomsburg, Columbia County, Mauch Chunk, Carbon County, Pottsville, Schuylkill County, [and Sunbury, Northumberland County]. One hundred and one years following the hanging execution of Jack Kehoe, December 18, 1878, in this Schuylkill County Prison, the Commonwealth of Pennsylvania granted posthumous pardon to Kehoe, reflecting the judgment of many historians that the trials and executions were part of a repression directed against the fledgling mineworkers' union of that historic period.

If you tour the Old Jail Museum in Jim Thorpe, you can see the cell of the prisoner who left his "hand on the wall." J. Walter Coleman told this great story about Alexander Campbell who strongly protested his innocence to the last. Coleman Wrote:

A curious legend or superstition has developed about the death of Alexander Campbell, who is said to have stated to his jailers, that he was innocent, and to prove it he would place his hand on the wall of his cell [17] on the way to his execution. The imprint of his hand, he declared, would always remain there. The rather accurate imprint of a human hand was still to be seen on the wall of Campbell's cell as late as 1931 in spite of much washing and repainting, and was pointed out to scores of curious visitors. It is understood that the design has since been obliterated by replastering.

In 1979, Milton Shapp Governor of Pennsylvania officially pardoned John Kehoe 101 years after his hanging. Kehoe's granddaughter, Mrs. John Wayne, and his great grandson, Joseph Wayne, as well as the Pennsylvania Labor History Society were instrumental in obtaining his official pardon. Alexander Campbell received a posthumous trial at Jim Thorpe where a jury acquitted him 116 years after his hanging.

We will never know how many innocent men went to the gallows. Of the twenty-four Mollies that were sent to prison, no one can say with certainty that all those sent to prison were guilty of the crimes they were alleged to have carried out.

There is some question about how much James McParlan knew about some killings before the actual murders took place. Did he allow them to just happen? Were they beyond his control? Was he personally involved in any killings? My guess is that he had his orders and was told not to intervene, even when he knew a killing was going to take place. We'll never know the full story.

After the trials, James McParlan went on to become superintendent for the Pinkerton Detective agency's office in Denver, Colorado. The sensational trial of "Big Bill" Haywood in Idaho in June 1907 had a striking similarity to the Molly Maguire case. The Haywood trial ranks as one of the most fascinating criminal trials in history. William E. Borah of Idaho, who was about to begin his long career in the United States Senate, led the prosecution while Clarence Darrow led the defense.

An older James McParland.

McParland (who now added a "d" to his name) and the Pinkerton Agency worked on behalf of the prosecution, but they were no match for Darrow. McParland attempted to use his conspiratorial tactics against unions in this case as he did with the Mollies, but it didn't work.

Darrow, the great lawyer, gave a brilliant eleven-hour summation. He delivered a scathing attack on McParland and proceeded to tear the prosecution story to shreds. His superb defense was one of his most famous speeches. However, according to Lukas, Darrow also employed some questionable tactics that apparently were important in winning his case. While there was no proof of any illegality, it was alleged that the defense team: (a) coerced key witnesses, (b) tampered with the jury, and (c) even attempted outright bribery. McParland and the Pinkerton Agency were devastated by the verdict, which went against them.

In his later years, McParland became overweight and still continued to drink heavily. He suffered from consumption, rheumatism and his health continued to deteriorate. One winter day he became frostbitten and part of his foot also had to be amputated. He became increasingly more paranoid about his safety and kept pet bulldogs guarding his residence. How many times at night did he hear a strange noise and suddenly feel his heart beat faster? How many times did he look over his shoulder wondering if some descendants of the Molly Maguires might still be planning to assassinate him? Alone and paranoid to the end, McParland died in Mercy Hospital in Denver in 1918.

Franklin B. Gowen, the powerful Reading Railroad Magnate who engineered the plan with the Pinkerton Agency to crush the

Molly Maguires, was removed from the Presidency of the Reading Railroad after it went into receivership in 1880. J. Pierpont Morgan was appointed to reorganize the Reading Railroad after Gowen was dismissed. Gowen returned to practicing law, a broken and disillusioned man. In 1889, in a hotel room in Washington, D.C. he supposedly committed suicide by placing a revolver to his head and pulling the trigger. There were wild rumors that the Molly Maguires finally got even. Did they or didn't they?

In retrospect, the Molly Maguires lacked a unified organizational structure, a broad social perspective and a well thought out plan of labor relations. Kenny pointed out:

. . . the trade union and the Molly Maguires were clearly very different models of labor organization. The Mollys differed sharply from the trade union in their cultured origins, their inchoate organization, and their strategy of direct violent action. They fought for justice on the individual and local level and did not apparently see their struggle as part of a wider regional or national conflict between social classes. Some of them wanted to settle strictly personal grievances, but most were engaged in a sporadic battle to defend a specific vision of what was fair and just in social relations.

As it turned out the Molly activities did not have any short term beneficial effect on working conditions for the miners in the anthracite region. While they strongly supported unions for miners, who coincided with the labor movement in the United States, it is generally agreed that they did not begin the labor movement in this country.

However, the Molly events were one of the early large movements by the workers themselves. Eventually there was a rebirth of unions in the coal mining region, and trade unions did form and were the precursors that paved the way for the United Mine Workers of America. However, Gowen did such a thorough job on the Mollies and the unions that it wasn't until the end of the century that the United Mine Workers succeeded in organized the anthracite miners.

The Molly Maguire story wasn't just a simple story. It had it own peculiar complexity. Broehl wrote:

The "Molly Maguire" story is at the same time labor history, business history, and social history. It relates deeply to the general histories of both Ireland and the United States. Its enigmas cannot be answered by economic analysis alone; the cultural dimensions—ethnic, religious, nationalistic—are decisively influential.

So the reign of the Molly Maguires is over. There are still unanswered questions and secrets that will never be revealed. There are no more Mollies; they are extinct as the dinosaurs, but they live forever in Sherlock Holmes. They were the last of their kind. It was some story. Just think, all that violent history of the Pennsylvania anthracite region happened—right in my own back yard!

Extreme justice is extreme injustice.
Marcus Tullis Cicero

When the wind blows wild at night

past the breaker melancholy,

If you stand in the dark,

with your ears to the wind

you can hear the sons of Molly.

Deep in the dark of the old mine shaft

you can smell the smoke and fire,

and the whisper low, in the mine below,

is the ghost of Molly Maguire.

The Sons of Molly Maguire, written by Chuck Rogers

Miners' Memorial, between Minersville and Pottsville.
Bronze statue created by James Pontner, Pottsville native.

Aurand, Monroe A. Jr.The Mollie Maguires. Harrisburg, PA. Aurand Press, 1940.

Bimba, Anthony.The Molly Maguires. New York: International Publishers Co. Inc., 1932.

Broehl, Wayne G. Jr. The Molly Maguires. Cambridge, MA. Harvard University Press, 1964.

Campbell, Patrick. A Molly Maguire Story. Jersey City, New Jersey: Templecrone Press, 1992.

Coleman, Walter J. The Molly Maguire Riots. New York: Arno and the New York Times, 1969.

Crown, H. T. and Mark T. Major. A Guide to the Molly Maguires. Printed in the USA, 1995.

Kenny, Kevin. Making Sense of the Molly Maguires. New York: Oxford Univerisity Press, 1998.

Lukad, Anthony J. Big Trouble. New York, New York: Simon Schuster, 1997.

Minersville and the United States Supreme Court

It was 1935 and I was 11 years old. I was in sixth grade in a one-room school building in Big Mine Run. Since I lived in Woodland Heights, I walked to school (along with other kids) down the hill to Big Mine Run. Then I walked along the railroad tracks and down a cinder bank to the school. We would play for a little while in the schoolyard, and when the school bell rang we all went inside and took our seats. The teacher got our attention by asking for silence and then motioned for all of us to rise. We all stood (including the teacher) and we recited the Pledge of Allegiance and saluted the flag. That's how I remember starting every day in grade school.

In that same year in 1935, on what seemed like an ordinary school day of that year, Lillian Gobitas (age 12) and her brother William (age 10) went to school in Minersville (about 15 miles from Big Mine Run) as they always had in the past. But on this day, an extraordinary thing happened. Lillian and William were the children of Mr. and Mrs. Walter Gobitas who were Jehovah's Witnesses. The Gobitas' also had four other younger children. On that fateful day, October 22, 1935 William refused to recite the Pledge of Allegiance and salute the flag. The next day, Lillian also refused to pledge and salute the flag.

The Minersville school board did not have a formal school regulation requiring students to recite the pledge and salute the flag. However, it was generally considered that the informal policy the school board had would be sufficient and not be disobeyed.

The event created quite a stir. Many people in Minersville felt the rebellious action of the children to be un-American, and so the Gobitas family felt the anger of the town.

Walter Gobitas and his family lived in an apartment above their self-service food market (the Minersville Economy Store) at 15 Sunbury Street. One night Mr. Gobitas received an anonymous telephone call warning him that his store would be vandalized by a group of men the next day. As it turned out, the police provided protection for the family and nothing further occurred regarding that particular matter.

Mr. Gobitas, who was a hard-working son of Lithuanian immigrants, treated his customers fairly. At that time in Minersville, many residents were out of work (as was true throughout the coal region) and Walter often allowed his customers to purchase groceries on credit. Walter enjoyed involving his customers in discussions on all sorts of topics. He was well read, inquisitive and loved to talk. The people of Minersville understood Walter's fondness for bantering with them and that he wasn't doing it just for business purposes.

So why did the two Gobitas children not comply with school policy? Jehovah Witnesses strongly believe in the Old Testament's prohibition against graven images and idolatry. The Gobitas parents allowed their children to decide for themselves whether they would comply with school regulations.

Lillian and William (Billy) each wrote a letter to the Minersville school board. Lillian wrote:

"1. The Lord clearly says in Exodus 20: 3, 5, that you should have no gods besides Him and that we should serve Him.

2. The constitution of the United States is based upon religious freedom. According to the dictates of my conscience,

based on the bible, I must give my full allegiance to Jehovah God.

3. Jehovah is my god and the bible is my creed. I try my best to obey the Creator."

Billy's letter was dated November 5, 1935. It reads in part: "I do not salute the flag because I have promised to do the will of God. This means that I must not worship anything out of harmony with God's law. In the twentieth chapter of Exodus, it is stated 'Thou shalt not make unto thee any graven image nor bow down to them nor serve them.' I do not salute the flag not because I do not love my country. I love my country. I love God more and I must obey his commandments. Signed, Your pupil, Billy Gobitas."

The school board felt that the Gobitas children were insubordinate. Further, the board determined that it was their duty to enforce the Pledge of Allegiance and flag salute as part of the daily exercises of the school. The school board wanted to show that teaching civics and loyalty to the government was important. Then the board unanimously formalized a flag-salute policy requiring all teachers and students in the Minersville schools to salute the flag as part of the daily exercises.

After a standoff of two weeks, the school board invited the Gobitas family to its school board meeting. The meeting did not settle anything. The Gobitas children were expelled on November 6, 1935 and told not to return to school.

William, Walter and Lillian Gobitas shortly after his children were expelled from school. Copyright Watch Tower Bible and Tract Society of Pennsylvania.

Despite the anger of the town of Minersville and the difficulty in obtaining a lawyer to represent him, Walter Gobitas decided to sue the school board in federal court requesting that their children be reinstated in school. However, it took a year before Mr. Gobitas received assistance in the Jehovah's Witnesses legal department. While the court case moved forward slowly in Philadelphia, the family had to endure various forms of harassment and persecution.

Meanwhile, the Gobitas family had the problem of where their children would go to school. Fortunately for them, in December of 1935 the Jehovah's Witnesses started its own school in a farmhouse near the small town of Andreas, about 40 miles east of Minersville. The Gobitas children, as well as other students expelled from other school districts, now attended their own church school in Andreas. It was too far to return to Minersville daily, so the Gobitas children stayed with Jehovah Witness friends in order to continue their education. Mr. Gobitas picked his children up on Friday after school so they could spend their weekends at home. On some occasions, he drove Witness children back and forth each day.

In 1937, legal counsel for Mr. Gobitas submitted a bill of complaint against the Minersville School District in the United States District Court in Philadelphia. The Minersvile School District then filed a motion with Judge Albert Maris to dismiss it. The following year, Judge Maris (who was a Quaker) denied the Minersville school board's motion.

In the summer of 1938, federal judge Albert Maris ruled in favor of the Gobitas children. He wrote, "While the salute to our national flag has no religious significance to me and while I find it difficult to understand the plaintiffs' point of view, I am nevertheless entirely satisfied that they sincerely believe that the act does have a deep religious meaning and is an act of worship which they can conscientiously render to God alone."

It was at this point that the court misspelled the Gobitas name and the case henceforth became known as Gobitis v. Minersville School District. Major newspapers in Philadelphia such as the Inquirer and Bulletin reacted favorably to Judge Maris's decision.

The Minersville School Board rejected the ruling. In November 1939, the Third Circuit Court of Appeals unanimously agreed with Maris's ruling. The school board now appealed the decision to the United States Supreme Court testing compulsory patriotism. The die was cast.

Two years later in 1940, World War II was well underway in Europe. With patriotism on the increase in the United States, the Supreme Court overturned the decision of Federal Judge Maris, and ruled in favor of the Minersville School Board. Justice Felix Frankfurter, who wrote the decision, ruled that the Pledge of Allegiance helps "to evoke that unifying element without which there can ultimately be no liberties, civil or religious." He added, "Exempting the Gobitas children make others less loyal to the country."

The Supreme Court in its eight-to-one decision stated that religious scruples did not constitute reason for school children to refuse to make the pledge. Most newspapers across the country did not agree with the majority decision. Incidentally, this Supreme Court is generally considered to be one of the great courts of all time. There was only one dissenting vote and that came from Justice Harlan Fisk Stone. Stone said, "The Constitution may well elicit expressions of loyalty it and the government which created it, but it does not command such expressions." Justice Stone's dissent is considered to be one of the great dissenting opinions in America legal history.

The Supreme Court ruling had a dramatic effect. Public violence directed against Jehovah's Witnesses occurred nationwide. Many of their children were expelled from public schools around the country. Mob violence directed against them was recorded in all but four of the then 48 states. The harassment and persecution continued for three years.

In 1942 in West Virginia, the State Board of Education adopted a flag-salute requirement for all school children. Shortly thereafter, a number of Jehovah Witness children were expelled for not complying with school policy. Parents of the children requested the Supreme Court of the state of West Virginia from enforcing the flag-salute policy. After the court refused the parents' request, the families of the children (one being named Barnette) brought a suit against the school board in the Federal District Court for the Southern District in West Virginia. When the District Court did not rule in favor of the school board (and the Witness children started to return to school), the State Board of Education appealed to the United States Supreme Court.

So in 1943, the United States Supreme Court took on another flag-salute the case known as West Virginia State Board of Education v. Barnette. In many ways, the case was a replay of the Gobitis flag-salute case. In a landmark decision, the Supreme Court by a six to three vote reversed its decision (which it rarely does) of three years ago in the Gobitas case.

Justice Robert H. Jackson wrote "Those who begin coercive elimination of dissent soon find themselves exterminating dissenters. Compulsory unification of opinion achieves only the unanimity of the graveyard." Jackson further wrote, " If there is any fixed star in our constitutional constellation, it is that no official, high or petty, can prescribe what shall be orthodox in politics, nationalism, religion or other matters of opinion, or force citizens to confess by word or act their faith therein."

The court ruled that regulations requiring a student to give the oath of allegiance violated the constitution's guarantee of free speech and worship. The court ruling was handed down on June 14, Flag Day.

Again, Justice Frankfurter ruled in favor of the Board of Education, but now he was in the minority. His opinion was criticized by civil libertarians because Frankfurter was often sensitive to the rights of minorities. Frankfurter (who was Jewish) came to this country as a youngster from Vienna, Austria. It was a very difficult decision for Frankfurter, who wrote:

One who belongs to the most vilified and persecuted minority in history is not likely to be insensible to the freedoms guaranteed by our Constitution. Were my purely personal attitude relevant, I should wholeheartedly associate myself with the general libertarian views in the court's opinion, representing, as they do, the thought and action of a lifetime. But as judges, we are neither Jew nor Gentile, neither Catholic nor agnostic. We owe equal attachment to the Constitution, and are equally bound by or judicial obligations whether we our citizenship from the earliest or the latest immigrants to these shores.

Following the 1943 Supreme Court decision, the Minersville school board invited the Gobitas children to school. The letter from the school did not include an apology. By this time, Lillian was 20 years of age and William was 18 and they were both working at the family store. It was too late for them to complete their public education and so they never received a high school diploma. However the invitation from the school board did benefit the younger Gobitas children. In addition, many other Jehovah's Witnesses children were now able to return to public school and they were no longer required to neither recite the Pledge of Allegiance nor salute the flag.

In 1945 William Gobitas left Minersville and for the next ten years did missionary work with the Jehovah's Witnesses. After that, he worked for the Maryland Casualty Company in Milwaukee and retired as personnel manager in 1976. William also was a piano tuner for a number of years in Wisconsin. He died in 1989 at the age of 64.

Lillian also left Minersville in that same year and worked for seven years at the World Headquarters of Jehovah's Witnesses in Brooklyn. While attending a religion ceremony in Germany in 1952, she met Erwin Klose, a German Jehovah Witness, who had been arrested ten times by the Gestapo during World

War II. Lillian and Erwin were then married in Vienna in 1954. Later they moved to Atlanta where they reared two children, Stephen and Judith.

In a telephone interview conducted by veteran journalist Ione Geier of Frackville, Schuylkill County, in 1988, Mrs. Klose said, "Erwin, who is ten years older than I am and also a Jehovah Witness, refused to serve in the German Army because of his religious beliefs. It's always been interesting to me that at the same time I was being expelled for refusing to salute the flag, he was in a concentration camp for refusing to 'Heil Hitler.'"

During her interview with Mrs. Klose, Geier pointed out that Mr. Gobitas sold his store in 1946 when he and his wife moved to Pottsville. Later they moved to Arizona where his wife died in 1962. By 1988, Walter remarried and was living in Gaston, South Carolina. Geier added that the four younger Gobitas children also left Pennsylvania: Paul residing in Miami, Florida; Joy Yubeta, in Sylmar, California; Jeanne Fry, St. Petersburg, Florida; and Grace Reinisch, Riverdale, Georgia.

Lillian Gobitas Klose, now living in Georgia, has recently celebrated here 79th birthday. In the photo below, she is looking at memorabilia and reminiscing about that time in Minersville so long ago. For Lillian Klose, the trauma and the persecution were worth it, according to L. Stuart Ditzen, Inquirer staff writer. When Ditzen asked if she would go through it again, Lillian responded instantly, "Oh, yes."

Lillian Gobitas, 2003. Photo by John Amis.

Ditzen, I. Stuart (Inquirer Staff Writer). "Defying flag salute tests freedom of faith." Internet note posted, Sunday, June 29, 2003.

Geier, Ione (Special correspondent to the Pottsville Republican and Evening Herald). "Eight by Ione. Minersville case made legal history." Internet note, September 22, 1988.

Labre, Jill .R. (Senior editorial writer and columnist for the Forth Worth Star Telegraph). "Pledge of Allegiance beautiful, if voluntary." Internet note, November 2, 2001.

Peters, Shawn Francis. Judging Jehovah's Witnesses. Lawrence, Kansas: University Press of Kansas, 2000.

Chapter 9

STORIES ABOUT DISASTERS

The Baffling Airliner Crash

"A plane crashed. A big plane crashed near Mount Carmel." It was June 17, 1948 and that was what a young man yelled as he ran past my home. I was washing my car, so I quickly turned on the car radio and picked up the news. A four-engine United Airliner DC-6 had crashed on a sparsely wooded hillside three miles northeast of Mount Carmel, Pennsylvania, killing all 43 aboard.

I jumped into my 1938 Plymouth and headed for the crash site only four miles away. As I approached the scene of the accident, I found that the authorities had roped-off the disaster area blocking automobiles and sightseers from entering the area. Thousands of people came, parking their cars on both sides of the road for miles. Also, many small planes as well as larger ones were flying over the scene of the disaster.

I heard on the car radio that the ill-fated airliner had been losing altitude for some time and was attempting an emergency landing. When the plane was only about 100 feet from the ground, it struck an electric switching structure and burst into flame just prior to crashing. An electric clock in an office at the Midvalley Coal Company determined the exact time of the disaster. When the airliner crashed, it cut off the power to the colliery—the clock stopped at 1:41 p.m. (EST). The plane was only 19 minutes from its destination at LaGuardia Field in New York where it was scheduled to land at 2:00 p.m.

Just prior to the crash, the airliner radioed LaGuardia Field that it was preparing an emergency descent. The radio conversation was also heard by another United Airlines plane that happened to be in the vicinity. At 1:33 p.m. the pilot heard this message from the stricken plane: "New York, New York, this is an emergency descent." LaGuardia Field asked for the message to be repeated, but there was no reply. Later, the pilot who heard the radio message flew over the site and saw that the plane had crashed.

After the plane hit the electrical works, it continued climbing up the mountainside destroying everything in its path. Even though I heard what happened, I was still amazed to see the large hillside area completely burned to the ground for about 600 feet. Everything seemed to disintegrate in the explosion that followed the crash, and the mountainside was charred beyond recognition by the devastating flames. It looked like some giant had taken a huge blowtorch and scorched the earth. The plane was completely demolished except for the four battered engines. One reporter said, "There was little to photograph."

I stepped over the roped-off area, and since no one stopped me I kept on walking. In a number of places, small fires still burned and I could feel the heat from the ground under my feet. At one point I picked up a packet of smoldering letters, glanced at them, and placed them back on the ground. I saw a single shoe, but for the most part everything was shredded and burned beyond recognition. I continued to look about and then realized that I did not want to stay any longer. In fact, I wondered why I came in the first place.

Newspapers reported that among the victims were: Earl Carroll, theatrical producer; Beryl Wallace, television and nightclub entertainer and Mrs. Venita Varden Oake, former wife of movie Jack Oakie. In addition, two six-month old infants were among the fatalities. Within a very short time, the tragic story became a major news event and was reported nationwide on radio and in many major newspapers including The Philadelphia Inquirer and The New York Times.

Several days after the crash, newspaper articles reported that a pouch containing a total of 182 diamonds that were aboard the DC-6 luxury airliner had been recovered from the debris. In addition a valuable brooch, which belonged to a passenger, was found. While almost everything was destroyed, the authorities were able to recover approximately 175 pounds of damaged mail and securities. There were a number of rumors that substantial amounts of money had also been found.

A week later, The New York Times reported on the front page that the airline authorities were searching for a package containing $250,000 in cash. The authorities believe it was jettisoned from the United Airliner a short time before the crash. A postal spokesperson said the package weighed 240 pounds and contained one, five and ten dollar bills--an amount equal to over

$3 million today. (It was significantly more in today's currency than the $200,000 D. B. Cooper took with him in a highjacking caper when he parachuted from a Boeing 727 at 10,000 feet in 1971.)

Recovery of some objects from the United Airliner some distance from the scene of the crash indicated that part of the plane's cargo might have been jettisoned to reduce its weight. The container with the money was never recovered. It's still possible that some day a hunter or hiker will accidentally stumble over the moneybox and wonder how all that cash ever happened to be there.

There were other disasters in the coal region that took more lives, however this plane crash was the largest air disaster to befall the region. While there were several theories on what caused the crash, there was never any conclusive proof of what did cause it. For that reason, it has gone down in the annals of aviation history as a "mystery forever."

Corddry, Charles. "Air Liner Baffles Solution." Mount Carmel Item, 19 June, 1948.

"Earl Carroll Among 43 Persons Killed in Airliner Disaster." Mount Carmel Item, 19 June, 1948.

"Forty One Killed in Plane Crash at Midvalley." Mount Carmel Item, 17 June, 1948.

"182 Diamonds Are found in area of Transport Wreck." Mount Carmel Item, 22 June, 1948, p.1.

"$250,000 is Hunted in Wreck of Plane." New York Times, 26 June, 1948, p.1.

Harry M. Bobonich, Ph.D.

Postscript

I had completely forgotten about the plane crash and the lost moneybox. Then one day in the late 1990's while vacationing at Stanford, California, I picked up a large book featuring many years of coverage of sport stories from The New York Times. I unexpectedly came across an article dated June 26, 1948 which read, "$250,000 Is Hunted In Wreck of Plane." It was quite a surprise and I immediately reflected back some five decades earlier when I visited the actual crash site near Mt. Carmel, Pennsylvania. I knew right then that I wanted to write a short story about the plane disaster and the mystery surrounding it.

As I read the article over several times, it took me back in time. I then began to read the other articles on the front page. It was 1948: Governor Earl Warren of California was the unanimous choice to be the Republican candidate for vice president with Governor Thomas E. Dewey of New York the Presidential nominee; President Harry Truman believes the Republicans' nomination of Governor Thomas E. Dewey improved Democratic chances of retaining the Presidency; President Truman reluctantly signs bill admitting 250,000 refugees to the United States citing its injustices; Joe Louis knocked out Jersey Joe Walcott in the eleventh round at Yankee Stadium to retain his world heavyweight title; Soviet Russia blocked all food shipments to over two million people in need of food in Berlin, Germany; and John L. Lewis, head of the United Mine Workers, signs a contract with the Commercial

Coal Operators on the last day of the present working contract. By the way, as I glanced to the upper right hand corner of The New York Times, I noticed that it only cost three cents.

Byrnesville—All Gone

Byrnesville was a very small village in central Pennsylvania situated halfway up a steep hill between Ashland and Centralia. However, you won't find Byrnesville on any current map. There is no sign that reads: "Welcome to Byrnesville." That's because all the houses have been demolished. It once just was a tiny village, but now it no longer exists.

Byrnesville was founded in 1856 and named after the Byrnes' family who were the first settlers. Most of the people who settled there were Irish immigrants who were employed by the nearby coal companies. Through the years, the population varied depending on how well the coal companies did.

The people who lived in Byrnesville were hard working, devout and patriotic. Most of the inhabitants were Irish Catholic who attended St. Ignatius Church in Centralia. They even had an elementary school in Byrnesville, but it was closed in the early 1930s. The children then went to St. Ignatius and Conyngham Township schools. According to Mike Reilley--the Reilley, Byrnes and Gaughen families all operated small grocery stores there at various times. Even though it was only a very small village, another Gaughen family also had a barroom.

In the mid-1930s, my Aunt Pauline and her husband John Skocik moved to Byrnesville. I was about ten years old at the time and remember helping them carry their belongings from a loaded truck into their new home. It was the first home on the left (yellow in color) as you drove up the hill from Ashland to Brynesville. Since Big Mine Run was only about one and a half miles away, I was not only familiar with Byrnesville but also visited there often. Later when I began to drive, I had to pass through Byrnesville, because at that time it was on the main road to other nearby towns such as Centralia and Mt. Carmel. It was the kind of place that people in the coal region called a "patch."

Byrnesville was a place where nothing much ever happened, but one day something big did happen there. It was only about one-half mile from Centralia, and that as it turned out, was fatal. One day in May in 1962 a small garbage dump fire in a mine pit ignited a coal vein at the outskirts of Centralia. Unknowingly, the fire continued to burn beneath the ground and spread to surrounding areas. In the beginning, the heat, smoke and poisonous gases were more of an annoyance than a real threat. However, after some time it became apparent that the underground mine fire constituted a serious health hazard for the people of Byrnesville.

KeKok described the scene this way:

A Byrnesville man discovered flames at the site the night of July 23, [1981]. Blue and orange tongues of fire danced amid the rocks in the rock pile, and some of the stones glowed orange. Although the flame area measured only about ten feet square, its heat was tremendous. A heavy odor of sulfur [sulfur oxides] hung over the site, and DER [Department of Environmental Resources] inspectors found dangerous levels of carbon monoxide near ground level. The fire outbreak caused a sensation, and many people from Centralia came out that night and succeeding nights to gaze in wonder and fascination. Curiosity seekers who braved the heat and odor to climb the rock pile to the cliff would hear a strange sucking sound, apparently caused by the fire drawing air into the mountain.

Dead leaves blew onto the burning rocks and burst into flame. Trees toppled onto the rock pile, their roots burned by the heat. It was an awesome, primeval spectacle, and it gave Centralia residents and government officials alike a hint of the terrible nature of the beast that threatened Centralia itself.

Finally in the 1980s, the federal government relocated the entire population of Byrnesville for health reasons. Just prior to the relocation project, Byrnesville had about 75 people living in 29 homes. Reilley described the exodus this way:

Leaving behind a house they worked for all those years, a house where all their children were born and where their ancestors lived and died was not easy. It was especially hard to see a bulldozer destroy the building that contained all those memories.

In 1996, the last family moved away and shortly thereafter the last house was demolished. The tiny village of Byrnesville did not die with a whimper; it died with a bang and a crunch

Harry M. Bobonich, Ph.D.

from a bulldozer. If you happen to visit the area and position yourself at 40.77 degrees north (latitude) and 76.38 degrees west (longitude) you would be standing where Byrnesville once stood. The only structure remaining there is a shrine. It's a place where a tiny village was wiped off the face of the earth.

DeKok, David. Unseen Dangers. Philadelphia, PA. The University of Pennsylvania Press, 1986.

Reilley, Mike. "Byrnesville: A Short History of the Village," Internet note.

My Last Visit to Centralia

There are a number of towns named Centralia in the United States, but there is only one that looks like a small atomic bomb has been dropped on it. Centralia, in Columbia County in Pennsylvania, is that place. It was a small town in the anthracite region that I visited in the summer of 1991 that is practically no more. Underground mine fires burning out of control for over forty years have created an environmental disaster.

At one time Centralia had approximately 3,000 people, but today there are only a few houses remaining and only a handful of people live there. It is not a dying town or a ghost town; it's just a place that is fading into oblivion. That was the bleak picture I saw of what was Centralia. It was quite a shock since I remembered Centralia as a small friendly town when I last saw it many years earlier.

I was born in Big Mine Run (you won't find in on any map) only one mile from Centralia if you drove the back road through what used to be called Buck's Patch. Since I spent all of my young life in Big Mine Run, I traveled to Centralia thousands of times and was as familiar with it as the "patch" where I was born.

So when I drove through what was the town of Centralia in the early 1990s, I was very surprised that I was not aware of just where I was in the town itself. I stopped to ask some highway workers where the center of town was and they said, "Right her 'butt', just where you are." It was a strange feeling, since practically all the houses had been demolished and carted away, so everything simply looked different.

As I looked about, I saw hazardous grayish smoke (it looks bluish purple at sunrise) venting through many large vertical pipes extending about six feet above the ground. The same deadly gases were flowing up through large cracks in the ground all over the place. Roadways were seriously buckled and the ground was broken just as it is after an earthquake.

I looked about and tried to visualize what different parts of the town looked like years ago when we visited friends and relatives there. My Aunt Frances and her husband Nick Puketza lived on North Street. My Aunt Pauline and her husband John Skocik lived on Center Street, Joseph Seder, my early violin teacher, on Locust Street, and the Hryhori Bazan family near the Railroad Station—now everything was gone. Even though

I became better oriented after a while, it was still unsettling to look at the bizarre and lifeless environment all around me.

Then I paused for a moment and thought of the many times my parents visited the Hryhori Bazan family who lived close to the railroad station. These social visits always involved having a drink or two (or more) of whiskey. Mrs. Bazan who was a friendly person always asked me if I wanted a drink of temperance. At first I didn't know what she meant, but I soon understood when I saw her holding a large bottle of soda in her hand. Apparently it was a carry-over term from the prohibition days referring to a total abstinence from alcoholic liquors. The Bazans' had two children. Nicholas was the oldest, and his younger sister Anna who married my violin teacher Joseph Seder, who also lived in Centralia.

St. Mary's Greek Catholic Church, where I attended services as a youngster, was one of the few buildings standing near the top of the hill to the north. I recall visiting the cemetery behind the church where our family went on certain holidays to tidy up the cemetery lot of family members buried there. I also remember going to many church picnics over the years where the most favorite product consumed was beer.

The center of town was at the bottom of the hill, but there was nothing there. The hill to the south was also completely bare, it was the former location of the St. Ignatius Roman Catholic Church. "So this is Centralia, no, this was Centralia," I said unbelievingly.

What happened here? How did all this come about? Why wasn't anything done? Well, let's go back to an earlier time. Centralia was a typical small coal mining town that was founded in 1866. The economy of the town centered on the mining and processing of anthracite coal. The entire anthracite region was fairly prosperous during the latter part of the 19th century and for several decades into the 20th century. However, there was a general decline in the anthracite industry from about the time of World War I on. As a result, there was a decrease in population in the anthracite region as a whole. By 1950, Centralia's population had dropped significantly. Those who remained behind were mostly older people, since the younger ones simply moved to other places looking for jobs.

Centralia in the 1960s. Looking north down Locust Street toward the center of town. Note St. Mary's Church in the upper right. Photo by Robert Evans.

In May 1962, a seemingly insignificant thing happened that triggered the disaster of the entire town. Someone noticed a small fire burning in an old mining pit and notified the fire department.

Pretty soon the fire station's siren was heard all over town. At first the shrill warning got the attention of the town's residents because it wasn't a common thing to hear the fire siren in the middle of the day. It soon became clear that the fire was not in Centralia itself, but somewhere just beyond the edge of town. It was reported that someone set a garbage dump on fire in a landfill next to an abandoned mine pit near the south end of town. The fire was behind the St. Ignatius School on top of the hill next to the Odd Fellows Cemetery. For some time this open mine pit had been used as a garbage dump, but now it was on fire. In a short time the firemen extinguished the flames and covered the burned area with clay. A simple fire was put out and that was that. It was no big deal.

At the time, they did not realize that the fire had spread underground to the coal lying beneath the open pit. Since it was not apparent that there was any impending danger, there wasn't any concerted effort made to deal with the fire in its beginning stages beyond what was done. In fact, it took many years before the residents of Centralia realized how much the seemingly innocent garbage dump fire would affect their lives. The local, state and federal officials did not correctly assess the potential danger early; otherwise, the fire could have been extinguished for only several thousand dollars.

Since the fire was not controlled, it continued to spread underground into old mine shafts underneath the town. Surprisingly, for a number of years the fire did little visible damage. However, over time an increasing amount of physical damage became noticeable at the surface due to subsidence in various places. In addition, both small and large cracks on the ground surface could be observed in many places. The more serious problem was the insidious fire that kept spreading underground, creating obnoxious and poisonous gases that seeped up through cracks in the ground and eventually into the homes causing many people to become sick.

The authorities realized underground fire was being fueled with air from (a) passageways that led to the surface when the mines closed; (b) the Centralia mine tunnel that emptied into Big Mine Run; and (c) bootleg mine operations.

The people of Centralia always seemed to differ on just where the underground fire was located. They were also concerned about which direction the fire was heading and how fast it was moving.

My brother-in-law, Amil Bielarski, had a bootleg coalhole that was located along the Big Mine Run road in Buck's Patch. (I had been down inside his coalhole several times but did not work there.) Amil knew first-hand about burning coal veins down deep underground, because the Centralia fire broke through into his coalhole in 1969. Amil's coalhole slopes down to a depth of 850 feet, however he didn't feel that the Centralia mine fire extended down that far. Sometime later, the fire actually broke through to the surface in several places along the Big Mine Run road near his coalhole in Buck's patch. It was the only place where the Centralia fire surfaced.

Leon Bogdan, Press-Enterprise writer interviewed Amil in 1988 and wrote:

[Amil] was chased out of his bootleg mine operation on Buck Mountain by an approaching underground mine fire in 1969. The entrance to that same coal mine opened in a chasm of sizzling fire [recently], exposing an underground furnace that has burned for more than 25 years and has hundreds of acres of fuel remaining in this rich anthracite coal belt.

It is the easternmost tip of the Centralia mine fire, just over one-mile east of the borough where the government is investing $42 million to evacuate the residents.

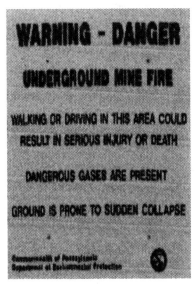

A warning sign posted in Centralia.

For the next two decades, the state and federal governments spent over $5 million in an attempt to extinguish the fire, but without success. The unseen danger, the runaway fire, was taking its toll. The people of Centralia were divided on how to deal with the disaster and the myriad of problems they faced. Sadly, they did not work together and the community suffered from internal conflicts. The town splintered into different groups that fought against each other; therefore, they were unable to come to an agreement on how to deal with the catastrophe they faced. The social conflicts among the people were just as bad as the physical pain and suffering they endured from the fire itself.

A turning point came on February 14, 1981 when Todd Domboski, a twelve-year old boy, felt the ground giving way under him while he was near his grandmother's home. He escaped death by grabbing hold of some tree roots below the ground. His cousin, who was with him, managed to grab hold of his hand and pull Todd out. The hole turned out to be several hundred feet deep and was filled with hot poisonous gases. If Todd had not been rescued right away, he would have fallen down into the ghastly pit to his death. It would have been like falling into a Black Hole in space.

By the early 1980s, the national media was covering and following the mine disaster story. The small village of Centralia, now with a population just under one thousand, was attracting journalists from all over the country. Sadly, help was slow in coming to Centralia. However, many Centralians praised General Dewitt C. Smith, a former commandant of the Army War College in Carlisle, who became a strong supporter for their cause during the 1980s. (I became acquainted with General Smith a number of years earlier when he was the commandant at the Carlisle Barracks. As Dean of the School of Graduate Studies and Research at Shippensburg University, I visited the Army War College often since we had a cooperative master's degree program with them.)

In 1981, Smith became head of the Pennsylvania Emergency Management Agency (FEMA). When he visited Centralia he realized that it was an emergency situation. For several years he fought alone trying to get key officials in the State Department to understand what was going on in Centralia. To this day, those people in Centralia who lived through the calamity applaud his successful efforts in helping a town everybody forgot about.

In 1983 after many attempts to contain the fire, the government decided that nothing more could be done to save the town. They decided to let the fire burn itself out, and so the Centralia had to be sacrificed. The United States Congress authorized $42 million to purchase the properties of the residents. The majority of people accepted the government's offer and one by one their homes were demolished and the families were relocated. Many people in Centralia built new homes in Mt. Carmel, several miles to the West, while others moved as far away as California. Not everyone moved away; a very small number of diehard families stayed on.

In her book titled Slow Burn, Renee Jacobs compiled a number of interviews from people that lived through the terrible disaster. These courageous people shared their thoughts and emotions about what happened. Here are some selected comments from several people:

I sit in my window and watch the snowfall turning to steam I
curse the fire that has burned through my dream.

The damp road, snow falling, steam rising, traffic proceeding
toward the setting sun, an eerie sight they be, here in Centralia
as the nightmare worsens, as the ticking [from the electronic
carbon monoxide monitor] intensifies each evening,

monitoring the air I

breathe

I am poisoned by a silent enemy.

There is no escape from the ticking.

So perched on my windowsill I seethe.

People passing don't see the fire that burns.

Underground--my skin playing a game--that I can't win

I want to leave--I've nowhere to go--the fire burns deeper-

until it scorches my very soul.

MY life is bitter, here on this hellish earth.

When tragic reminders of the happiness I'd planned

The one brown leaf that clings to the tree--

I am it and it is me

We might as well both be damned.

    Catherine Jurgill

All we ever wanted was a chance to get on with our lives.
I don't think that was too much to ask. I just want people to
know how good this feels after all the hurt and bitterness. The
reason the buy-out ceremony was so wonderful was because

we finally got past the quarreling. People hugged me that had not spoken to me in over a year. It was a healing thing.

Mary Gasperetti

I wanted to stay here until I died. But it won't happen that way. And now I know I have to go. I hope I'm just as happy where I go as I was here. I will want to be buried back here. I have a lot up there, a place beside my husband. I don't want to go into a strange cemetery, so I think they'll bring me back.

That's what I want. To come back and be buried beside my husband. Coming all the way home again.

Clara Gallagher

I don't think there is a word in the English language that describes how we feel walking around and seeing those boarded-up houses. When the ones went down over here, it was winter and we closed our curtains as much as we could. But now it's going to happen all through town. No matter where you are, you won't be able to get away from it. They're going to go through, seeing their neighbors' homes, memories, as though the house was once alive and now it is being slowly killed. That's what they'll feel when those houses start coming down. You're going to see it on every corner, every street. The part that gets me--it's all unnecessary. Absolutely unnecessary.

Helen Womer

When I returned to Centralia during the summer of 2001, there were only seven houses remaining in the borough and four in the township—a total of 24 people. The borough homes will probably vanish one by one and before too long there won't be any residents at all living there. As I looked around I could see cracks one and two feet wide in many places including former roadways that were now destroyed beyond repair. Surface rocks in some places were so hot that you could not walk on them with bare feet. The stench from poisonous sulfur oxides continues to rise from the ground. The devastated area has an eerie and primeval look about it, like a microcosm of the earth itself eons and eons ago. It was a good home for the devil himself.

I talked to Helen Womer that summer who has lived on East South Street in Centralia all her life. She and her husband Carl have stayed the course and still live in the borough. She was a very active participant in the entire Centralia mine fire disaster. Helen, who worked at the Pennsylvania National Bank in town, was one of the leaders who was opposed to any plan that involved demolishing the houses of the residents and relocating them. She felt there was a conspiracy against the people of Centralia in order to get to the coal beneath the town. Helen Womer fought for what she thought was right. She wrote:

As long as there is a shred of hope left in me and I have the support of my family and friends, I will work tirelessly against monumental odds toward keeping as much of Centralia intact as is safely possible.

Later that summer I talked with my Aunt Frances about Centralia. She and her husband Nick lived in Centralia for about 20 years. In 1961 (about a year before the infamous garbage dump fire) they moved to Centralia Heights, which is north just adjacent to the borough where she presently lives with her son Nick. Her home is located between Centralia and Aristes, and is one of the four remaining in the township.

She spoke fondly of the good old days in Centralia and reminded me that the town had fine stores, good doctors, many churches and even more barrooms. She also mentioned that church services were still being held in the old St. Mary's Greek Catholic Church, which has been renamed The Assumption of the Blessed Virgin Mary. She had a panoramic view of all Centralia by just walking a short distance from her back yard.

Frances Puketza.
Courtesy of Diane Spokus.

Over the past four decades, she has seen the destruction of Centralia month by month and year after year.

I also spoke with Lamar Mervine, mayor of Centralia and a life-long resident of the town. He mentioned that they have one ambulance and one fire truck even though there are only a total of eleven occupied houses in the borough and township combined. The mayor said, "It's like being in heaven. Neighbors are friendly. No crime. No violence. No nothing." The mayor, Helen Womer and Frances Puketza all agreed that the fire could have been controlled in the beginning for the cost of only one home in Centralia. As it turned out, approximately $50 million dollars have been spent on the Centralia disaster.

Centralia no longer exists on some maps. The town is simply no more. However, there is still a lot of coal beneath what was Centralia. How much coal? No one knows for certain, but some people estimate that it could be as high as five billion tons. Perhaps some time in the future it might be profitable to recover the immense wealth in the coal beds that still lie there.

If you visit Centralia today there isn't any town to see. It's a patchwork of open lots where homes once stood. If you look closely, you also see abandoned broken up asphalt streets with crumbling curbs. However, decaying logs and rusting street signs, which added to the lifeless area years ago are no longer visible. Also young shrubs and trees now mask land that had previously been barren. If you stand at the top of Locust Street (compare the picture of Centralia in the 1960s in this story) and look downtown toward the north, you will not see any evidence that at one time a nice small town existed there. However, St. Mary's Church to the north on the hill still overlooks the little town that was Centralia, but is no more.

According to the State Department of Environmental Protection, the mine fire has claimed approximately 450 underground acres in 40 years. The fire front continues to advance 75 feet each year. Beneath the town the temperature varies from 200 to 1200 degrees Fahrenheit, and poisonous gases continue to flow up through cracks in the ground.

The runaway fire, like a horrible gigantic monster, continues to suck air down through surface cracks and openings to feed itself. If you're standing in the right location, you can hear the hissing sound of the giant fire drawing down air as if it were alive. It will go on burning for hundreds of years.

One story comes to mind that I suppose many people in Centralia have thought about while going through this ordeal. Legend has it that Father Daniel Ignatius McDermott, the first Roman Catholic priest in Centralia, denounced the Molly Maguires from his pulpit in 1869. The angered Mollies, known for getting even with those who oppose them, gave the priest the beating of his life for his comments against them. Father McDermott called his congregation together and told them that from this day forward there would be a curse on the community of Centralia—condemning it to destruction.

Ironically, the anthracite coal, which was the reason for Centralia's birth is now the cause of its death. My last visit was during the summer of 2002. Just before leaving, I turned around and took one last look. I just felt weak. There was no Centralia there. As I got into my car, I thought I heard a long, low mournful siren-like sound. Was it just my imagination?

The countdown continues in Centralia. In March 2005, Lamar Merwine said, "There are only six homes in the borough and three in the Township—a total of only 12 people."

DeKok, David. Unseen Dangers. Philadelphia, PA. The University of Pennsylvania Press,1986.

DeKok, David. "Government Was Slow in Helping Residents." The Patriot News, 27 May, 2002, p.1.

Jacobs, Renne. Slow Burn. Philadelphia, Pa. The University of Pennsylvania Press, 1986.

Kroll-Smith, Stephen J. and Stephen Robert Couch. The Real Disaster is Above Ground. Lexington, KY. Unversity of Kentucky Press, 1990.

Lewis, Jim. "Fire Below Brings Town Long, Slow Death." The Patriot News, 27 May, 2002, p.1.

Postscript

The impact of the Centralia fire on the environment is an ongoing process and will continue as long as the fire burns. So it will not be a simple matter to carry out a comprehensive study of the damage done to the environment due to the fire. An interdisciplinary team of faculty members at Susquehanna University (including students) is currently investigating the effects of the Centralia fire on the surface environment. Their research indicates that in some cases, soil temperatures at the surface can exceed 400 degrees Centigrade (approximately 750 degrees Fahrenheit). And if you walk around the area, you will note that subsidence and venting of hot gases are still common.

While we do not hear much about underground coal fires, they are considered to be a significant contributor to global warming. According to Andrew C. Revkin:

Fires are burning in thousands of underground coal seams from Pennsylvania to Mongolia [in China] releasing toxic gases, adding millions of tons of heat-trapping carbon dioxide to the atmosphere and baking the earth until vegetation shrivels and the land sinks.

In China's huge coalfields alone, hundreds of underground fires are burning as much as 200 million tons of coal each year. Once underground fires get started, it is very difficult to control and stop them. In numerous places in the world, such as India and China, workers continue to mine coal in open-pit areas even as it burns. "In many places, the walls of the open-pit mines glow and hiss like lava flow," said Revkin. In one region in India, coalfields have been burning since 1916. One unbelievable deep fire in Australia is believed to have been burning for 2,000 years.

Revkin, Andrew C. "Underground Fires Menace Land and Clmate." (2002) The New York Times, Internet Article, 15 January.

Tobin-Janzen, Tammy. "Why Science Matters." Excerpt from Susquehanna Today, Spring 2005.

Tragedy and Injustice at the Knox Mine

The Knox Coal Company owned The River Slope Mine at Port Griffith in the northern anthracite region near Pittston, Pennsylvania. For some time the workers at the Rive Slope Mine were concerned that they were conducting their mining operations in a direction to close to the bottom of the Susquehanna River. And it was not unusual that miners had to work in a "wet environment" due to water seepage. Further, miners often remarked that they could hear the rumble of passing railroad trains overhead. Even though mine inspectors stated that there should be 35 feet of coal and rock between the working area and the bottom of the river to provide safe working conditions, the miners still had reservations about their safety. While the miners spoke openly about the dangers of working at River Slope, work went on as usual.

However, on January 22, 1959, a day, which appeared to be just another ordinary workday at River Slope, turned out to be a nightmare. The men working in the mine were sealed underground when the weight of the icy river fractured the rock strata under the river bed and sent water gushing through a huge hole in the roof of the mine tunnel. The mine cave-in allowed over ten billion gallons of water to flood the mine. The disaster that followed is considered to be the most destructive mine flood ever to hit the anthracite region.

Eighty-one miners reported for work at 7:00 a.m. that Thursday. Now just imagine that you're one of those miners working in the mine that day. It's approximately 11:30 that morning when all of a sudden you hear a horrendous noise. Suddenly, the roof of the mine collapses and a river of water comes pouring down on you. That's exactly what happened, the swollen ice-packed river broke through and flooded the River Slope Mine on that fateful day.

If you happened to be standing on top of one of the cliffs overlooking the Susquehanna River, you would have seen a whirlpool of extraordinary size and turbulence in the river where the cave-in occurred. Thousands and thousands of gallons of water along with large chunks of ice swirled down into the mine every minute. The churning water poured down into the maze of passageways throughout the mine.

Whirlpool in the Susquehanna River.
Drawing by Lucas Kalathas.

Assistant foreman Jack Williams and laborers Fred Bohn and Frank Domoracki were close to the point where the river broke through into the mine. When they realized what happened, the three workers ran for their lives and managed to escape by running up the Rive Slope to safety. Upon reaching the surface, they notified Superintendent Robert

Groves that the river had crashed through the mine roof and was flooding the mine. Groves took immediate action and called to the underground stations for everyone to evacuate the mine. Upon hearing Grove's evacuation order, 33 men worked their way to the elevators and were hoisted to safety from the Hoyt and May shafts. The location of these two shafts relative to the River Slope Mine is shown in the aerial view below.

Aerial view of Knox Coal Company's operation.
Courtesy of John J. Dziak.

By early afternoon, a large crowd gathered at the mine site. It was a very cold day and the piercing wind chilled the rescue workers as well as the people standing by. Stories and rumors began to circulate adding further to the uncertainty and anxiety of those present. The agonizing wait by family members for their loved ones was unbearable. The state police were on hand to provide safety and crowd control because of all the activities going on. While 33 miners were saved--family members, relatives and mine officials feared that the remaining 45 workers may have perished.

Meanwhile, the trapped miners ran through dark underground passages to other mineshafts in a race against the rising water. Many of them wandered for hours through water up to their chests. You can only imagine how they felt, but you can never really know.

Rescue workers at Eagle Air Shaft. Courtesy of Bill and Stephen N. Lukasik.

Later that afternoon, Amadeo Pancotti, heroically managed to escape through the Eagle Air Shaft, which was an old abandoned air tunnel. Subsequently one group of workers led by Joe Stella, and another group led by Myron Thomas was also rescued through the Eagle Air Shaft by search teams resulting in saving the lives of 32 additional workers. For comparison purposes, the approximate straight-line distance from the Break-in Site to the Eagle Air Shaft is approximately 1000 feet—see aerial view above.

Joe Stella is rescued from the mine by workers through Eagle Air Shaft. Courtesy of Bill and Stephen N. Lukasik.

In mine disasters, there are always individuals who provide leadership and take risks to try and save the lives of their comrades. The courage and leadership of these men and others is a testimony to the old miners' credo—never leave a "butty" behind.

Lou Randazza is rescued from the mine by workers through Eagle Air Shaft. Courtesy of Bill and Stephen N. Lukasik.

In Robert P. Wolensky's excellent book titled, The Knox Mine Disaster, and his accompanying book, Voices of the Knox Mine Disaster, he describes in detail the leadership and heroism of many workers that played a role in that tragedy.

While everyone was thankful that 69 miners had now been rescued, there was a deepening concern about the 12 that were still missing. There was some hope that perhaps the trapped men may have found a safe haven with sufficient air to keep them alive. However, later that evening a rescue team was forced to return from inside the mine because of the incoming water. Members of the team found it very difficult to face the waiting families when they failed to find the trapped miners. Meanwhile, the icy waters of the flood-swollen Susquehanna River continued to pour into the mine blocking all efforts to reach the remaining 12 trapped miners. The sorrowful families learned that evening that the rescue efforts for their loved ones unfortunately had to be terminated.

By 7:00 O'clock Friday morning, the rising water inside the mine had flooded the River Slope and also blocked the foot of the Eagle airshaft. Methane gas was also reported leaking from the mine. By this time, there was only faint hope that the trapped mines might be found alive. That evening, Friday, January 23, 1959, the headline on the front page of The Pottsville Republican read, "12 Pittston Miners Still Missing; May Be Dead or Trapped."

Shortly after the river gouged a huge hole in the mine and began flooding the interior, mine officials started to develop a plan to plug the breach. Captain Norman Drustrup from the Navy Construction Battalion said, "The Knox cave in at the Knox Coal Company is without precedent as far as Army Engineers are concerned. We never had a case where the bottom fell out of a river."

At first, huge trucks dumped dirt, massive rocks and all types of debris into the pit to stop the river from flowing into the mine. However the entire fill just seemed to wash away.

Then all types of railroad cars, including gondolas, which are fifty feet long and weigh twenty-five tons each, were shoved into the hole. Nothing seemed to plug up the large gap, and so the water continued surging downward. Construction workers realized that it was going to be an exceptionally difficult task to plug the hole. For several days they continued to dump thousands and thousands of cubic yards of more fill into the breach. In addition, 200 more coal cars and over fifty huge gondola cars valued at over $1 million were dumped into the massive hole. After two and one-half days of an unbelievable effort by construction workers, the flow of water into the maze of tunnels was slowly reduced and the whirlpool gradually disappeared. The huge hole in the river was beginning to get sealed off. However, after a week of working around the clock, the temporary patch still did not stop the water flow into the mine completely.

It was estimated that over ten billion of gallons of water flooded into the Rive Slope Mine. Once underground, the water flooded all the interconnecting passageways for miles. The Philadelphia Inquirer reported that in one particular shaft (about a mile away) the surging water had risen approximately 325 feet in a 530-foot shaft. And U.S. Geological Survey instruments indicated that the water in the River Slope reached a height of about 400 feet on January 25. The U.S. Bureau of Mines directed that a total of eleven mines in the area were to be evacuated and closed due to the devastating flooding conditions.

After the cave-in was plugged as well as it could be at this stage of the operation, the Herculean task of pumping out the water from the mines got underway. It was late in January when the initial pumping began. About a week later, more pumps were required to increase the discharge rate. Draining the mine turned out to be a take longer than they had planned. On February 6, the Department of Mines announced that it would take a minimum of three more weeks of continuous pumping before any underground search could begin. The die was cast—it was clear that the 12 miners would never be found alive.

More powerful pumps were now brought in and installed. By early March, water was being pumped out of the mine at the rate of 142,000 gallons per minute. Finally, the water in the mine was now lowered to the point where workers could begin to permanently seal the breach inside the mine. However, it wasn't until early June that the mine was made safe enough for the search team to enter the mine. Sadly, none of the twelve missing miners were ever found. Their bodies are entombed in the depths of the mine forever.

Robert P. Wolensky wrote:

In early spring 1959, construction crews began work on a permanent seal. They diverted the river and built an earthen cofferdam around the hole. They drained the dam to expose the river bottom and then drilled several boreholes into the mine through which they poured 1,200 cubic yards of concrete and 26,000 cubic yards of sand. The federal and state governments allocated nearly $5 million for the project.

In the months following the disaster, the matter of blame and responsibility became a hot issue. Four post-disaster investigations led to the indictments and trials of over 20 individuals and four coal companies. The charges cited were violating labor and mining laws; tax evasions; bank frauds; bribery and conspiracy. While a number of individuals were found guilty of various irregularities and irregularities, it was generally felt that all the penalties handed out were relatively light. Even though it was shown that the mining procedures carried out beneath the Susquehanna River were illegal, no individual or company was found criminally negligent in the death of the 12 miners at the end of all the investigations. Tragically, the 12 miners left behind 42 family members.

As mentioned in the beginning of the article, mine inspectors stated that there should be 35 feet of coal and rock between the area where the men worked and the river bottom to provide adequate safety for the miners. However, at the point where the river smashed through, inspectors determined that the cover (rock and coal) was as little as 19 inches and in some cases only a few feet thick.

The U. S. Bureau of Mines concluded that:

[The] cause of the inrush of water was the removal of the natural support (coal) in the immediate vein beneath the river where the rock was insufficient to support the river. The contributory cause was the swollen ice-laden river.

The Knox Mine disaster dealt a crippling blow to deep mining in the middle portion of the Wyoming Basin. However, some deep mining still continued for several decades in the northern region near Scranton. Also, some deep mining continued as well in the southern area near Wilkes-Barre. Robert Wolensky pointed out that, "One estimate placed the direct and indirect job loss at 7500 and the payroll deprivation at thirty-two million dollars. Total anthracite production in 1959 dropped by 94,000 tons."

The Pennsylvania legislature introduced a number of bills to improve the safety of mine workers following the tragedy at the Knox Mine. Sadly, steps are always taken after a mine disaster to remedy unsafe working conditions that should have been addressed earlier. It was greed that led to tragedy at the Knox Mine—and injustice followed.

George M. Leader, former governor of Pennsylvania, summarized it well by citing the Knox Mine disaster as an example of what went wrong with the anthracite region. He said:

There is something about the extractive industries that, somehow, exploitation seems to be the only word that applies. They don't seem to care about the hospitals or the churches or the community buildings or even the infrastructure unless it directly affects them. They just never did anything to help the community. They just got in and they took their money and they did absolutely as little as they could to protect the workers from dust, from cave-ins, from anything. They just did the minimum. That's what it was all about. Get in. Get out! Get their money and get out.

In January 1999, a State Historical Marker was placed near the disaster site in commemoration of its fortieth anniversary.

Knox Mine Disaster Plaque. Courtesy of Robert P. Wolensky.

"Hope Fades for Men in Tunnel Trap."The Philadelphia Inquirer, 23 January,1959, p.1.

"Upstate Flood Peril closes 11 More Mines."The Philadelphia Inquirer, 24 January,1959, p.1.

Wolensky, Robert P. et al (1999). The Knox Mine Disaster. Commonwealth of Pennsylvania, Pennsylvania Historical Museum Commission.

Wolensky, Robert P. et al 2005). Voices of the Knox Mine Disaster. Commonwealth of Pennsylvania. Pennsylvania Historical and Museum Commission.

The Avondale Mine Disaster

If you picked up a copy of the New York Times on Tuesday, September 7, 1869, you would have seen the following headline on the front page.

Headline, New York Times, September 7, 1869.

This tragedy occurred at the Avondale colliery located on the banks of the Susquehanna River near Plymouth in the northern anthracite region of Pennsylvania. The coal miners at the Avondale Mine had been on strike for a long time and they were eager to go back to work. More than one hundred men and boys went to work the morning of September 6, 1869, with renewed energy hoping to make up for the lost time due to the strike. After only several hours on the job, a catastrophic mine fire caused the disaster with the greatest loss of life in the history of the anthracite region.

The Avondale Colliery disaster--ruins of the coal breaker.
Sketched by Theo. R. Davis.

It was a Monday, an early fall day when the miners left their homes and went to work like any other day—or so it seemed. About mid-morning, a fire believed to have been caused by a ventilating furnace inside the mine ignited woodwork at the bottom of the shaft. The fire quickly spread upward through the shaft engulfing the breaker and spreading to the engine house.

Alexander Weir, the engineer, barely had time to give the alarm and make a few safety changes (to prevent a boiler explosion) before escaping with his life. The fire continued to spread quickly to other nearby structures at the top of the shaft. The workers who saw the flames and smoke shooting from the mineshaft (like a giant flame thrower) realized that the fire prevented anyone from escaping from the mine since that was the only way out.

The news spread quickly and thousands of people rushed to the scene of the disaster. Women, children and relatives of the trapped workers surrounded the mine on every side. Friends and others, including coal miners from other coal companies also came in hopes of somehow assisting with the rescue of the imperiled miners.

The Avondale Colliery disaster—street view in Avondale.
Sketched by Theo. R. Davis.

Calls to fire companies for help were sent out to all nearby towns and cities. Fire departments throughout the entire neighborhood responded quickly. When the fire engines arrived, they poured water over the burning structures, but the fire just raged on. Since the fire could not be contained for some time, part of the burning structures and some machinery fell into the shaft clogging the entrance to the mine. There was no way immediately to provide fresh air to the trapped mine workers, since the only way to supply air was through the main opening that was filled with debris from the fire. By mid-afternoon the fire appeared to be under control, but there was no way that those on the surface could communicate with the miners inside.

It wasn't until early evening that the fire was sufficiently extinguished and it was possible to make any attempt to descend down the shaft. At first a lamp and dog were sent down in a basket to check for black damp which is made up of carbon dioxide and nitrogen. Black damp is deadly because there is no oxygen to breathe and suffocation follows quickly. When the basket was hauled up, rescue workers were glad to see that the dog was still alive. However, there are contradictory reports as to whether the lamp was still burning. The fact that the dog was still alive, however, was sufficient evidence for the rescue teams to get ready to descend the shaft.

The rescue workers assumed that the trapped miners learned of the fire in the shaft relatively soon after it started and immediately realized that their only means of escape was cut off. They thought that many of the trapped mine workers would have proceeded to move quickly away from the fire and through the east gangway, which was over 1,000 feet long. As they rushed away from the fire, they closed gangway doors behind them in an attempt to keep the limited amount of fresh air in the mine from being contaminated with the poisonous gases just behind. When they retreated to the farthest point, they closed the last set of gangway doors—that was the end of their retreat. At this point, they would have to use anything available (including their own clothing) to fill in the cracks and openings in an attempt to block the poisonous gases. The trapped workers would have realized that they only has a limited amount of air available and that their survival depended not only on how well they could seal up the doors and build a barricade blocking out the foul air, but on how soon help would arrive.

Rescue workers are lowered down into the mine. Sketched by Theo. R. Davis.

A 6:30 p.m., Charles Vartue volunteered to go down the shaft to make an initial investigation. When he returned, he reported that he was only able to go half–way down the shaft because the debris was blocking his descent. Two men were now sent down and after clearing out the obstructions they reached the bottom of the shaft. They advanced about 70 yards into a gangway and found several dead mules. They came across a closed door and began to pound on it, but did not get any response. At the same time, obnoxious sulfur oxide fumes were pouring through cracks in the woodwork on the door, so they decided to return to the shaft where they were hauled to the surface.

Bringing out the exhausted miners.
Sketched by Theo. R. Davis.

Two more volunteers, Thomas W. Williams and David Jones, went down to continue the rescue work. The workers on top had not heard anything from Williams and Jones for some time, so several men went down to search for them. Tragically, the rescue workers found both Williams and Jones dead; they had suffocated from poisonous gases they encountered. It was past midnight by the time both bodies were recovered. Since the rescue attempts were not only difficult but dangerous, it was decided to make arrangements to pump air down into the shaft to improve the quality of air so rescue workers could work more quickly and efficiently.

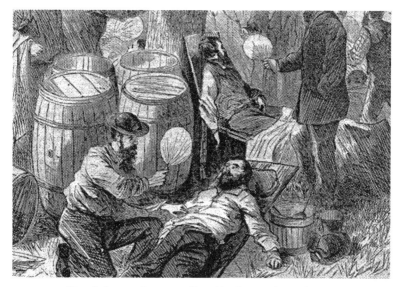

Reviving miners after their explorations.
Sketched by Theo. R. Davis.

By seven o'clock Tuesday morning, the fan and engine arrived and by 9:15 a.m. air was being pumped down an attempt to purge the mine of poisonous gases. Several other search attempts were made to reach the miners, but the poisonous gases continued to prevent the rescue teams from making much progress. By this time, hope of finding the trapped workers alive was fading. About 3:30 p.m. a search party reported that the ventilating furnace located about 130 feet from the shaft was still burning inside the mine. Several rescue teams used water hoses in an attempt to put out the furnace fire; however, it wasn't until midnight that the fire was finally extinguished.

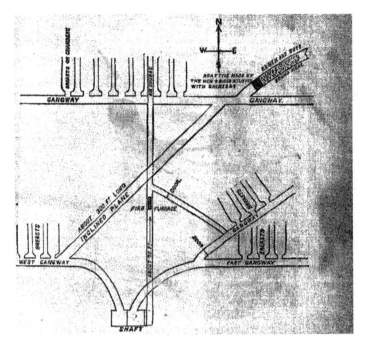

Plan of interior of the Steuben Mine, Avondale.
Harper's Weekly, September 1869.

About 3:00 a. m. on Wednesday morning, a rescue team began working its way through the east gangway and discovered the first dead bodies. As the rescue workers continued to move eastward through the gangway (which was 1200 feet long), they kept opening doors that were apparently closed by the miners as they fled to safety. The rescue team followed a passageway that led them to the eastside of the inclined plane. They followed the inclined plane northeast until they came across the last door blocking their progress; It was about 6:30 a.m. After forcing the doors open, they proceeded to tear down the barricade, which the trapped miners had erected. Several members of the rescue team who worked their way forward, shoved their lights ahead and saw a terrible sight. They found all 67 miners dead, lying behind the embankment they put up in an attempt to block out the deadly vapors. It was a horrible sight.

The heap of bodies found behind the barricade the miners built. Sketched by Theo. R. Davis.

Even the toughest miner would have been appalled at the scene.

Many of the dead miners appeared to quietly drop off to sleep, and probably did. Others were lying on the ground with their faces buried in the coal dust. Were they trying in vain to find just a bit of fresh air to survive? Fathers and sons were found holding each other's hand—finding comfort in their closeness. Still others seemed to be in a kneeling position, perhaps praying at the end. Small groups were found huddled together as though they were talking about their desperate situation—we can only wonder what they were saying. Did they leave messages with each other for their loved ones to be delivered in case either survived? Still others were found alone, as if they wanted to deal with their impending death by themselves.

In some cases entombed miners in the past left written messages describing their ordeal hoping to provide information that might be helpful in future disasters. However, no note of any kind was ever found indicating what went on in those final hours. However, the miners' lunch pails and water canteens were found full and many felt that death may have come rather quickly.

Rescue teams also found mine workers at various places in the mine apparently stricken down suddenly by the poisonous gases while they were working. Other bodies were found in chambers and gangways showing that they too had been overcome suddenly. In some cases, individual bodies were found here and there; in other instances, small groups of miners were found huddled close to each other. It was a difficult task to search out all the small places in the mine to be sure they had recovered all the dead miners.

Late Wednesday night a fierce thunderstorm hit the area and lightning lit up the sky as the recovery process continued through the night. Families still surrounded the mine and waited (not to hear that a loved one was safe)--it was too late for that. They just wanted to know that their family members had been recovered and identified. The strong storm continued and the recovery task went on. It was a strikingly unsettling scene. It was a bizarre night.

The heartrending job of recovering the bodies and identifying them as they were brought to the surface took some time. The rescue workers used a tunnel that was driven into the side of a hill near the Avondale Colliery many years before the accident for the recovery process. The miners who dug the tunnel failed to find coal, so the tunnel was abandoned. The tunnel ran into the side of the Avondale shaft about 40 feet below the head of the shaft at the surface.

Bringing bodies out of the tunnel. Sketched by Theo. R. Davis

When the rescue workers who entered the tunnel reached the opening in the shaft, they were then lowered to the bottom of the shaft on a platform carriage. After the rescue workers placed the bodies of the dead miners on the platform carriage, they were lifted up to the tunnel opening. From here the bodies were taken through the tunnel and then to the surface. It was through this tunnel opening that all of the bodies were subsequently brought to the surface. Unfortunately, the trapped miners were not in a position to use the abandoned tunnel when the fire broke out.

Bringing out the dead. Sketched by Theo. R. Davis.

At noon on Thursday, a recovery team went down and made an extensive exploration of the mine and reported that they did not find any more bodies. However, about 1:30 p. m. two more bodies were found—and they were the last. The dreadful catastrophe took the lives of 108 mine workers (including five boys), along with two rescue volunteers, making the total dead at 110.

There were jealousies between the Irish and Welsh miners at the Avondale Mine, and clearly the two groups did not get along with each other. Not surprisingly, rumors began to circulate that the fire in the shaft was deliberately set. Did the union loyalists set the fire intentionally to stop work at the colliery? Did the underground furnace ignite the fire that traveled up through the shaft?

An investigation of the cause of the disaster got underway quickly. At the inquest, over 24 witnesses were heard and cross-examined. Approximately half of the witnesses felt the ventilating furnace was the cause of the fire, while the remaining witnesses supported the arson theory. After all the witnesses were examined, the eight person jury retired and returned the following verdict concerning the dead mine workers.

[T]he cause of their death was the exhaustion of atmospheric air or a prevalence of sulphuric and carbonic acid gases in the said Avondale mines, caused by the burning of the head-house and breaker at said mine on the 6th day of September, 1869, thereby destroying the air-courses leading from the mine through the shaft; that the fire originated from the furnace in the mines taking effect on the wooden brettice [boarding used in supporting the roofs and walls of coal mines] in the up cast air-course leading from the bottom of the shaft to the lead house. The jury regard the present system of mining in a large number of mines now working by shafts as insecure and unsafe to the miners, and would strongly recommend, in all cases where practicable, two places for ingress and egress and a more perfect ventilation; thereby rendering a greater security to the life of the miners under any similar accident.

No individuals or the coal company was directly blamed for the disaster. However, many new safety programs were eventually incorporated at collieries that improved the working conditions of the coal miners.

For 135 years the cause of the fire still remains unresolved. In the early part of 2005, Joe Keating and Bob Wolensky suggested that the abandoned tunnel (which was used to remove the dead miners) had also been used as a means of entry to the shaft to deliberately set fire to the mine. They wrote, "We have speculated, using circumstantial evidence, how labor-management unrest could have provided a context for the arson integral to a fire set from the tunnel."

There is a third possibility that some have suggested may have been the cause of the fire. A stable boss was lowered to the bottom of the shaft with a load of hay for the mules about the time the fire started. It is not entirely clear whether he discovered the fire or that he arrived at the bottom of the shaft shortly before the fire got started.

Did the stableman, who perished in the fire, discover the blaze when he got there? Or did the stable man accidentally set the hay on fire with his kerosene lamp?

Did the ventilating furnace somehow set the hay on fire? Was the hay a contributing factor in the fire?

Was it arson, with the fire being initiated by those using the abandoned tunnel? If it was arson, could it be that the fire was not meant to completely destroy the beaker and kill all those men at the same time—but labor's way of showing that it could not be ignored. No one knows for sure—it will remain a mystery forever.

A Pennsylvania Historical Marker near the scene of the disaster.
Courtesy of Robert P. Wolensky.

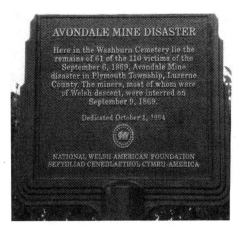

The following memorial was also dedicated
in honor of the dead miners.

Corrigary, James J. (no date) Internet report titled, "The Great Disaster at the Avondale Colliery." U.S. Department of Labor, Mine Safety and Health Administration, 43 pages.

Hall, Patrick J. (no date). Internet page from "The Coal Mines" by Andrew Roy, State Inspector of Mines of Ohio, 1876, pp.134-137.

"Terrible Fire in Pennsylvania Coal Mine." The New York Times, 7 September, 1869, p.1.

"The Avondale Disaster." (All drawings in this story were sketched by Theo. R. Davis.) Harper's Weekly, Volume X111, No. 665, 25 September, 1869, p. 609, 616-617.

"The Mining Calamity." The New York Times, 8 September, 1869, p.1.

"The Great Calamity." The New York Times, 9 September, 1869, p.1.

"The Great Calamity." The News York Times, 10 September, 1869, p.1.

"The Great Calamity." The New York Times, 11 September, 1869, p.1.

"The Great Calamity." The New York Times, 12 September,1869, p.1.

"The Avondale Calamity. Adjourned Session of the Inquest—Further Important Testimony." The New York Times, 15 September, 1869. p. 8.

About the Author

Harry M. Bobonich was born in Big Mine Run, Pennsylvania and graduated from Butler Township High School as valedictorian of his class. He spent three years in the U.S. Army as a deep-sea diver. He is married to Gloria J. Cole from Mt. Carmel, Pennsylvania and they have two sons—Chris and Greg. He earned a bachelor's degree from Susquehanna University, a master's degree from Bucknell University and a Ph.D. Degree in chemistry from Syracuse University. Bobonich has taught at Pennsylvania State University, Shippensburg University and Wilson College. He retired from Shippensburg University as Dean of the Graduate School and Research. Harry enjoys playing chess, reading and keeping up with proper nutrition. He has authored a number of articles on the history of the coal region. His first book is titled, "Seeing Around Corners: How Creative People Think." This is his second book.

CPSIA information can be obtained
at www.ICGtesting.com
Printed in the USA
LVHW112212240219
608616LV00001B/169/P